Grazia Deledda's
Eternal Adolescents

Grazia Deledda's Eternal Adolescents

The Pathology of Arrested Maturation

Janice M. Kozma

Madison • Teaneck
Fairleigh Dickinson University Press
London: Associated University Presses

Associated University Presses
440 Forsgate Drive
Cranbury, NJ 08512

Associated University Presses
16 Barter Street
London WC1A 2AH, England

Associated University Presses
P.O. Box 338, Port Credit
Mississauga, Ontario
Canada L5G 4L8

The paper used in this publication meets the requirements of the American National Standard for Permanence of Paper for Printed Library Materials Z39.48-1984.

Library of Congress Cataloging-in-Publication Data

Kozma, Janice M.
    Grazia Deledda's eternal adolescents : the pathology of arrested maturation / Janice M. Kozma.
        p.   cm.
    Includes bibliographical references and index.
    ISBN 0-8386-3935-6 (alk. paper)
    1. Deledda, Grazia, 1871–1936—Characters—Men.   2. Deledda, Grazia, 1871–1936—Characters—Women.   3. Man-woman relationships in literature.   4. Maturation (Psychology) in literature.   I. Title.
PQ4811.E6 Z749   2002
853′.8—dc21   2001040885

Contents

Preface

Sono nata in Sardegna. La mia famiglia è composta di gente
savia, ma anche di violenti e di artisti comprensivi. Aveva
autorità e aveva anche biblioteca. Ma quando cominciai a
scrivere a sedici anni, fui contrariata dai miei. Il filosofo
ammonisce: "Se il pupillo scrive versi, correggilo e mandalo
per la strada dei monti; se lo trovi nella poesia per la seconda
volta, puniscilo ancora; se fa per la terza volta, lascialo in pace,
perchè è un poeta."

Grazia Deledda

[I was born in Sardinia. My family is composed of wise people,
but also of some violent individuals and of understanding artists. We had authority and we also had a library. But when I
began to write at sixteen, I was opposed by my family. The
philosopher warns: "If the student writes poetry, correct him
and send him out for a walk in the mountains; if you catch
him writing poetry a second time, punish him again; if he does
it a third time, leave him alone because he's a poet."][1]

THERE WAS NO REASON FOR GRAZIA DELEDDA TO HAVE WON THE
Nobel Prize for Literature in 1926. She was born female in a patronistic culture which in the late nineteenth century allowed her
no choices save housewifery, spinsterhood, or the convent. Her
parents and extended family were vehemently against her writing, as was her native Sardinian town of Nuoro. She was uneducated, untraveled, literarily untrained, and unsophisticated to
the ways of the publishing world. Yet within the span of fifty
years, she published thirty-five novels, three hundred fifty short
stories in eighteen volumes, thirty novellas and numerous fables,
sketches, newspaper articles, and folkloristic studies for magazines and scholarly journals. At the height of her distinguished
career, her work was translated into over fifteen foreign languages. She enjoyed a worldwide reputation; her novels sold in
the millions and were widely reviewed internationally.

Who was this tiny, humble, self-effacing, bashful, yet headstrong autodidact who only purchased her first fur coat at age
fifty-five, and even at that, "just to keep warm" in a Stockholm

December where she was to accept the ultimate literary accolade from King Gustav V of Sweden? It was unthinkable for Grazia Deledda to have succeeded even as a minor, regional writer. The odds of her achieving such astounding honors were against her from the day of her birth.[2]

Deledda was considered "just" a woman's novelist; she was and is still regarded by many as a hack writer of romance novels. Yet her prose continues to fascinate an educated readership. For she is much more than an Italian "Barbara Cartland." Deledda was endowed with an agile mind; she was an innate student of human nature and a brilliant, sophisticated (albeit untrained) psychologist who anticipated by one hundred years what was yet to come in clinical research.[3] She depicted a composite adult-adolescent character, the sum of all her male protagonists, who would only be described fully and accurately a century later by professional psychologists. And all this from a self-taught woman who was ostracized by her own people and told by one literary critic to stay home and "tend to her carnations."[4]

Numerous studies have appeared on Grazia Deledda; most critics dwell on trying (unsuccessfully) to pigeonhole her work into one literary -ism or another. Yet, there is an important dimension to Deledda's writing that has largely gone unexplored. In this study I examine an aspect of her writing that cuts across every novel she wrote (as well as many of her short stories)—that of her interest in male protagonists who behave as little boys, in men whose adolescent comportment can only be described as puerile. It is in this context that I discuss Deledda's male protagonists as examples of a psychological syndrome which for the purposes of this study I call "arrested maturation."[5] In using this term I do not mean characters who later undergo the traditional changes associated with the *bildungsroman*. I refer here to male protagonists whose adult, definitive personality is typified by the symptoms of arrested maturation described in the chapter entitled, "The Syndrome of Arrested Maturation."

Deledda identified a seemingly universal pathology and explored it thoroughly. She saw it in her brothers, in her father, in the men she knew as a youth and in the man she eventually married; and she imbued her fictive male characters with it, while not at all disculpating her female characters from partial responsibility for a volatile co-dependency of male/female relationships. She may have been handicapped by geographical, social, professional, and educational constraints, but consciously or not, Deledda was right on the mark psychologically and in a very contemporary way.

The phenomenon of male immaturity is not new in Italian literature;[6] Deledda is, however, the only author who really sounds the depths of the syndrome, who is interested in exploring all the facets of its manifestations, who treats it consistently and who uses it as a *leitmotiv* in most of her works. Clinical psychologist Daniel Kiley suspects the syndrome "has occurred in isolated cases for a long time; only in the past twenty or twenty-five years, however, have the pressures of modern life exacerbated the causative factors, resulting in a dramatic increase in the frequency of the problem."[7] But Kiley never read Deledda and never made the acquaintance of the likes of Elias Portolu! Throughout her complete works, Grazia Deledda presents to her readership such a consistent spectrum of male characters who collectively exhibit the symptoms of arrested maturation that if her protagonists were to congeal into a composite man, together they really would constitute that elusive "classic case."[8]

In the chapter entitled "Manifestations of the Syndrome," I take up the female characters who interact socially and intimately with those men, since Deledda's women also exhibit many of the characteristics commonly associated with psychological codependence. I aim to show that a century ago Grazia Deledda superimposed a psycho/social template upon the relationships of her fictional characters; the result is that arrested maturation advances the plot of her stories in ways that would be improbable otherwise. Deledda's literary strategy subverts conventional expectations in surprising ways; for, in some cases, the effect of her psychologically perspicacious characterizations is a role reversal where eventually men take on feminine traits while women masculinize, and for the first time appropriate a measure of sovereignty over their lives.

One of the overarching principles which guides Deledda's conception of male/female relationships is her preternatural feminist vision. This is one of the many ironies of her career. For, she was clearly a *de facto* feminist. From her biography we know that rather than being a declared adherent to the vigorous women's movement of her times, she was not one to take to the streets. She denied being a feminist. The reasons for her reticence are probably both genetic and cultural. She was notoriously shy and prefered to keep her counsel. She was not raised to make public issue of her private opinions. Deledda's only acknowledgement of women's issues was her guest attendance at the First Feminist

Congress in Rome in 1908; but beyond that one cameo appearance, she kept to herself. Clearly she preferred to make her statements through her prose. Without any schooling, she had a feminist vision which was uncanny, given her lack of contact with contemporary ideas. Her inchoate insights maneuvered her into a feminist position, even if throughout her life she was reluctant to acknowledge that she was plainly in step with her times.

It is tempting to think that Deledda was severely limited by having for models only the men she knew in her circumscribed purview of the spectrum of humanity, or that what she described is typical cultural behavior unique to Sardinia, or that her male characters' behavior is what is expected in a patronistic society which is also widely characterized by *mammismo* (mother fixations). Yet these otherwise valid notions do not explain why the modern description of arrested maturation is almost exactly the same as Deledda's more complete one, despite the radically different cultures and times from which the contemporary assessment emerges.

While it is undoubtedly true that individual subcultures superimpose some kind of unique form onto the expectations of adolescent development, no available literature or documentation exists which suggests that the expectations of Sardinian culture are substantially different from those of the rest of Western European culture. Adolescents are expected to make progression toward adulthood by assuming increasing familial and economic responsibilities and by preparing for gainful employment in commonly accepted ways. These classical notions of what it means to grow up are mirrored in Freud's analogy of adolescent development as the flow of a stream which at puberty gathers the various aspects of pregenital sexuality into a great river of more mature adult behavior.[9]

Psychologist Katherine Dalsimer humorously points out that "it is much easier to specify when adolescence begins than when it ends" (6). And psychologist Peter Blos reminds us that the eminent scholar Erik Erikson's definition of adolescence is a "psychological moratorium" (406). These experts may very well have read Grazia Deledda's novels. For Dalsimer has also noted that:

psychoanalytic theory can enrich the reading of a text by highlighting, with its insights, particular developments in the narrative. Literary texts, in turn, deepen our understanding of psychological processes. Both psychoanalysis and literature attend to actual situations of human life; both register a kind of truth only insofar as they do justice to living moments or phases in the experience of any individual. The force of great fiction or great drama lies not only in the power of its language, but in the power of its insight into particular situations, which language delivers and which the reader, with a shock of personal recognition, acknowledges to be just. Psychoanalysis, too, yields insights of great power, but, emphasizing the *common* matters in human existence, it tends to remove them from the sharp particularity of the language of literature, and treats them instead in a scientific voice. Theoretical formulations often give little hint of the richness of observation in which they are rooted. Works of literature invite us to restore this connection (2).

Doubtless Grazia Deledda has fixed upon something timeless and universal. Diachronically and synchronically she too invites us along on her journey to explore the nature of male/female relationships, perhaps to "restore that connection" across the fault line of psychological, cultural, and temporal borders.

In a private letter to her editor, Epaminonda Provaglio, dated 15 January 1892, Grazia Deledda described herself as a person "who sees men clearly as they are."[10] Deledda translated that ability into her prose with trenchantly accurate characterizations. In *Cosima* she averred that she relied on the facts and characters she knew from reality, and she was an astute observer of human types and behaviors.[11] Writing about literature vis-à-vis psychology, Deledda tells us that a novel "reflects life through the refraction of art, especially with a writer who evokes veristic rules and methods of writing." (Sarale 112). This was her goal—to use her art to bend and splice the details of reality in order to make sense of what she saw.

To appreciate fully what a remarkable voyage Grazia Deledda took from the then backwater village of Nuoro to the writer's pinnacle of Stockholm, it is helpful to understand something of the history, culture, and traditions of her native island and to appreciate the details of her life and experiences which fashioned the contours of her career. I begin, therefore, with the Sardinia of her times, with a biographical sketch of the writer, and with an overview of her professional fortunes and misfortunes. For all relate inextricably to any critical consideration of her *opera omnia*.

Acknowledgments

I AM GRATEFUL TO THE ENTIRE STAFF OF THE ISTITUTO SUPERIORE Regionale Etnografico of Nuoro, Sardinia, for their assistance (especially Ms. Franca Rosa Contu for her kindness and help). I acknowldege in particular the director, Dr. Paolo Piquereddu, for his gracious support of my archival work in Nuoro. I also want to thank the editors of *Annali d'italianistica*; modified material in this study originally appeared in volume 15 (1997): 1–12. I am indebted to The University of Kansas for granting me a sabbatical leave to work on this project. My gratitude as well goes to the Joyce and Elizabeth Hall Center for the Humanities of The University of Kansas for providing me with the funds to travel to Nuoro, Sardinia, to complete the archival research for this study; in particular I am especially beholden to the former director of the Hall Center (and my friend), Professor Roberta Johnson, for her invaluable assistance in discussing this project with me at length and in providing me with her keen, personal insights into the various manifestations of arrested maturation; her editorial advice has been invaluable. I thank Gabriella Materassi for her assistance with certain lexical items which, without her generous help, would have been for me untranslatable. I want to express my sincere gratitude to Adriana Ghergo and to Liliana Giardina, Simona Giardina, and Emiliano Giardina for the gift of their assistance and advice during my archival work in Rome. My thanks go to my friends: Connie Crocker Wantdke for her kindness and time in locating for me two invaluable postage stamps commemorating Grazia Deledda's life, Ann Ruth Roth Williams for her personal helpfulness and her sharp editorial eye, and Bonnie Augustine for her skills in critical reading and her enthusiasm for my research. I wish to acknowledge the helpfulness of Ron and Dianne Strong whose preliminary reading of my manuscript was extremely useful and perceptive. I especially want to thank my good friend, Joan Kraus Brunfeldt, M.D., both for her thoughtfulness in procuring for me valuable research materials on D. H. Lawrence, which I might have otherwise overlooked, and for her

13

professional advice and inestimable help with various issues concerning archaic medical terminology and matters of Sardinian health care. Finally my deepest expressions of gratitude go to my mother, Maria Pedica-Kozma, for her interest in my work (and in Grazia Deledda's prose), for her own particular Italian insights and for her encouragement with this project.

Grazia Deledda's
Eternal Adolescents

1

Introduction

Sardinia in the Mid-to-Late 1800s

DURING THE MID-TO-LATE 1800s, WITH THE CONTINUING PROCESS OF unification, all of Italy was undergoing a predictable series of sweeping sociological and economic changes.[1] Despite steady progress toward industrialization and the comfortable growth of the middle class, the members of the Italian working class and the farmers of the entire peninsula were barely able to eke out a dignified, sustainable existence. Their living conditions were not only substandard; by any measure, they were simply deplorable. Compared to the rest of Europe, poverty, illiteracy, and the poorest of health care constituted the norm for the majority of Italians from the Alps to the toe of the boot. And if this was the case on the *continente* (as the Italian peninsula was and still is referred to by the Sardinians), one can only imagine the conditions in Sardinia.

Sometimes called by its ancient name, *Ichnusa* (Greek for "footprint," which the first explorers saw in its shape), the second largest island in the Mediterranean had been plundered of its most valuable natural resources since even before the Roman Empire. For as far back as the height of the Etruscan civilization (circa 700 B.C.), Sardinia was the place to ravage, especially for copper. Economically exploited fully by Vandals and Goths, and then abandoned by the ancient Romans as a barren penal colony, subsequently invaded by a variety of despoilers from North Africa and the Middle East, Sardinia later fell under the colonial domination of Spain. Dating to 1492, when the island came under the rule of Ferdinand and Isabella, its wealthiest merchants and landowners were Spanish; and almost all profits from the land went back to the decamped Iberian landlords. Very little capital was ever reinvested in the island; Sardinia was a cash cow for absentee rulers.

Piedmont took possession of Sardinia in 1720, but little changed. The island remained equally depressed both sociologically and economically. The only difference was that profits from Sardinia's natural resources now went to the Sabaudi (the ruling House of Savoy), rather than to the Spanish. Still no capital improvements had taken place to ameliorate human existence in a land where famine, malaria, and various incurable diseases characterized the living conditions. Not even the medieval, feudal system of the Spanish barons had changed. While there was a small and comparatively wealthy upper class, the vast majority of Sardinians lived primitive lives.

By the end of the 1700s, after centuries of colonization and foreign domination, and of social and humanitarian neglect, there was little civic vitality left in the Sardinians. There was no cultural life even vaguely resembling that of the rest of Europe; there were no newspapers printed on the island; there were few imported books to read (for that minority who could read at all); sporadic news from the mainland arrived months after events had already occurred. The island remained an unproductive outpost whose own dispirited inhabitants had little inclination to force change from within. The concepts of liberty and equality did not yet exist in Sardinia despite the American and French Revolutions. The feudal upper class remained arch-conservative, against any social progress, revolutionary or minimal, thus ensuring adherence to the status quo at all levels of society.

By the mid-to-late 1800s, Sardinia was in a state of economic, physical, ecological, and social devastation. Taxes imposed by the mainland were as high as economic equity was low. Compared to the rest of Italy, the Sardinians were living in horrifying poverty: for the large majority of the population, housing consisted of little more than one-room dirt huts with sod roofs, shared inside and out with what precious and few animals were owned by the destitute inhabitants. There was little running water. Except for the already established feudal barons, landownership was all but impossible even for the most resourceful and ambitious of the poor.[2]

Nevertheless, land did eventually undergo privatization, albeit heavily favoring the rich; and the medieval system came to an end, incredibly only about fifty years before Grazia Deledda's birth in 1871. Additional economic reforms were instituted after 1847, when Sardinia joined the peninsula's other regions officially to become part of newly unified Italy; but there was no instant solution to the serious challenges the island faced. Perhaps the most damaging problem was banditry, a subject dear to

Deledda's heart and which she utilized in not a few of her depictions of the juvenile, male character.

Entire villages lived in fear of bandits who would attack at will, stealing pigs, sheep, cattle, women, and whatever else was not secured; the bandits would then repair to the mountains into brutally savage areas where it was all but impossible to be captured. The situation got so out of hand in some remote places that the pillagers sometimes even forced their victim/farmers to abandon their own land; the criminal element invariably escaped with impunity to a high, barbarous terrain filled with caves and rugged crags where no one dared to follow. (Deledda's own largely inaccessible region, named appropriately *Barbagia*, is still notorious in Sardinia as the area where banditry was/is most prolific.)[3]

Given Sardinia's political history, understandably there were serious misgivings about constituted authority among the general, law-abiding people.[4] Ironically, however, this attitude favored banditry even more, since its very victims practiced a local version of Sicilian *omertà* when interrogated by authorities, particularly when those authorities were from the mainland.[5] Protected passively by the very countrymen whom they victimized, armed bands of delinquents knew they were free to roam the land unmolested. Much like the Jesse James phenomenon, to be an outlaw was a highly romantic thing to do for many (to wit, Deledda, herself, comes close to glorifying the bandit Simone Sole in one of her best novels, *Marianna Sirca*).[6] Often banditry was the glamorous career choice of many a young Sardinian boy; in some sectors it was admired and secretly encouraged as a form of extreme protest among the disenfranchised.[7] This in part helps to explain the phenomenon which gave Deledda such rich material for many of her fictional characters.

Equally debilitating to the morale of the Sardinians was the problem of usury which was widespread on the island, sometimes averaging 800 percent interest rates in the more remote places. Deledda makes frequent mention of this problem in her novels, and rightly so; for usury devastated the poor; and the problems of the socially marginalized were among the predominant themes of her early novels.[8] The destitute often found themselves so deep in debt that for some the only escape was outside the law—banditry; thus one problem fed the other in a closed circle of despair.

Health care in Sardinia was nonexistent at the time of Grazia Deledda's birth and well into her adulthood.[9] In fact, the subject of physical affliction, serious disease, dying, and death provided her with many *leitmotivs* throughout her prose for medical delivery on the island was the least efficient in all of politically unified Italy.[10] Malaria was the first and most pressing problem because of the numerous undrained swamps and areas of untreated, standing water.[11] Second was trachoma, a contagious viral inflammation of the conjunctiva of the eyelids.[12] Trachoma was widespread and especially tragic when contracted by infants; it caused chronic, severe swelling of the eyelids and often led to early blindness. (Hints of this disease appear throughout Deledda's prose, especially in *Cenere* [Ashes] where the adolescent protagonist's eyes are a subject of constant concern to his doting stepmother.) Tuberculosis was the third most devastating disease with no cure (and it, too, is the downfall of many a Deleddan character). Yet, with these grave problems of public health, in 1886, of the 364 incorporated cities and towns in Sardinia, only seventy-one even had a pharmacy. Hygienic practices were lamentable; indoor plumbing was a rarity. Even as late as 1925, of Sardinia's 364 cities, 260 had no running water from acqueducts; 357 were without a sewage system.

At the time of Deledda's birth, illiteracy in Sardinia was the highest in Italy; and Italy's own rate of illiteracy was among the highest in Western Europe. The ability to read at all (not to mention the luxury of reading literature), was the domain of a very small minority of the educated Sardinian elite.[13] For poor families who barely carved an existence from the earth, educating a female was a simple waste of time; and squandering a male child's youth in school, when he could be working in the fields or shepherding in the hills, was an indulgence few could afford. In a land where shepherds and their sons camped in the mountains for months on end, it was plainly impractical and economically improvident for a child to be at school. (Deledda makes excellent narrative use of this problem, especially in *Cenere* where getting an education is one of the driving forces of the novel.)

Mario Massaiu points out that to exacerbate the above problems, the "continent" also had the bad habit of transferring all of its worst civil servants to Sardinia. Italy's most problematic soldiers and its most troublesome bureaucrats could not be fired; so they were sent (read: banished) to the island that, dating back to the Roman Empire, was considered a sort of unofficial penal colony. The result was a Sardinia run by incompetents, petty crooks, and unscrupulous administrators who were not tolerated elsewhere (Massaiu 101). This added to the problems that Sardinia already had, not only because the ineptitude of outsiders made their problems even worse, but because it increased the hapless Sardinians's diffidence and suspicion of anything from beyond the shores of Ichnusa.

The island could not even count on its own human resources; emigration from Sardinia to anywhere else ravaged the populace of its more capable and ambitious citizens, leaving the less adventuresome to deal with the overwhelming societal problems that Sardinia faced (Massaiu 105). The only people who arrived willingly on the island were those industrialists who exploited the natural resources: the mines (abused especially by the Tuscans), the coal deposits, the lumber, the cork, the peat, all to be taken at cheap labor costs. Like the ancient Romans and the Spanish barons after them, these temporary immigrants raped with impunity what was left of the countryside. Their most egregious iniquity was to leave Sardinia without trees, thus permanently changing its ecology from a once lush and fertile land to a dry, barren, desert-like landscape where the only viable activity left was shepherding. (Even today Sardinia has been described glibly as "home to 3.8 million sheep and 1.6 million people.")[14] Shepherding, however, is the backdrop for several of Deledda's best novels (*Elias Portolu*, for example). The inherent solitude of a life in the hills lent itself well to her introspective, lonely characters.

Hardly for humanitarian or social reasons, but mostly because of the exigencies of economic exploitation, by 1883 there was a railroad system in place; by 1882 there were regular boats to Civitavecchia and Terranova. By 1907 there were telephones from Cagliari to Sassari; the telegraph was becoming more widespread, and by the turn of the century the island was becoming less and less isolated from the mainland (Sanna 231–55). Slowly progress was being made, at least as regards the civic infrastructure. The Sardinian people, however, remained among the poorest of Western Europe.[15]

One hundred years later, in the heady days of the Costa Smeralda's tourist boom when littoral Sardinia has become the European vacationers' summer playground, it is impossible to fathom existing, even living—much less thriving—intellectually under the intolerable conditions of a century ago. But Grazia Deledda did just that. Well into her adulthood she remained isolated from the bustling, stimulating world of the continent.[16] Besides there being little "culture" in Sardinia (at least as defined by the mainland), being female, Deledda was rarely allowed to leave the family's house unescorted by an adult or an older brother. So even if there had been a lively cultural life in Nuoro, she would never have been permitted to experience it or be a part of it.

When D. H. Lawrence called Sardinia "one of the most remote and savage parts of Europe," he did not romanticize nor did he exaggerate.[17] For these were the uncultivated conditions under which Grazia Deledda toiled intellectually and professionally when there was no plausible, external motivation for her to have done so. What was it about this astonishing woman that allowed her to endure, to overcome and to flourish against all odds? Indeed, she had few advantages as a writer, save one: the Sardinian people and the imaginative tales they recounted were a gifted story teller's dream come true. They offered essentially no variables in a quasi-impenetrable, sociological Petri dish.[18] And Grazia Deledda took full literary advantage as she coaxed her island to yield its secrets to us.

GRAZIA DELEDDA: HER LIFE

Ho vissuto coi venti, coi boschi, con le montagne, ho guardato per giorni, mesi ed anni il lento svolgersi delle nuvole sul cielo sardo, ho mille e mille volte appoggiato la testa ai tronchi degli alberi, alle pietre, alle rocce, per ascoltare la voce delle foglie, ciò che dicevano gli uccelli, ciò che raccontava l'acqua corrente: ho visto l'alba, il tramonto, il sorgere della luna nell'immensa solitudine delle montagne; ho ascoltato i canti e le musiche tradizionali e le fiabe e i discorsi del popolo, e così si è formata la mia arte, come una canzone od un motivo che sgorga spontaneo dalle labbra di un poeta primitivo.

Grazia Deledda[19]

[I have lived with the winds, with the woods, with the mountains; I have looked for days, months and years at the slow development of the clouds in the Sardinian sky; thousands and thousands of times I have leaned my head against the trunks of trees, stones, and rocks to listen to the voice of the leaves, to what the birds were saying, to what the running water had to tell: I have seen the dawn, the sunset, the rising of the moon in the immense solitude of the mountains; I have listened to the songs and the traditional music and the fables and the conversations of the people, and in this way my art evolved, like a song or a tune that emerges spontaneously from the lips of a primitive poet.]

Grazia Deledda had already published her first literary pieces as a fifteen-year-old, even before she had ever seen the sea, which in 1886 was less than a day's trip from her island home in Sardinia.[20] By local custom for girls, she completed only three years of elementary school. She had never been out of her hometown, Nuoro, save for trips to local religious festivals. Until she married at twenty-nine and moved to Rome, she had never even heard orchestrated music; her only experience was the sound of an occasional single instrument: a church organ, a guitar, an accordion.

Grazia Deledda had no belletristic training; during her formative years as a young writer, she had no meaningful contact with the literary circles of mainland Italy; and there were none in Nuoro. Her intellectual life consisted of reading popular women's magazines and listening to the ordinary, everyday manifestations of the Sardinian oral tradition: hearing her father, an amateur poet, recite his lyrical improvisations, and paying attention to the stories and folklore tales spun by the endless stream of overnight visitors to her childhood home.[21]

Her first short story written for adults, "Sangue sardo" [Sardinian Blood], was published in 1888 when she was but seventeen.[22] She wrote for nearly fifty more years without pause, without lengthy or unusual interruptions, writer's blocks, or barren periods of inactivity. An indomitably stubborn spirit, she labored with method and with a self-discipline that would be the envy of any professional writer; and within that half-century she produced more than just a few internationally acclaimed novels.[23] In her day alone Deledda's work was translated into all of the major foreign languages; several novels went into as many as twelve editions.[24] In 1926 she was awarded the Nobel Prize for Literature.[25] She was the second Italian and only the second woman ever to receive the prize in literature.[26]

The importance of that event to Italian literature is manifest. By the end of the 1700s Mary Wollstonecroft was a household name not only in England but on the Continent as well; the Brontë sisters were also well-known throughout Europe; George Eliot and Jane Austen enjoyed a wide and enthusiastic readership. In France the shocking George Sand was at the pinnacle of her career by the mid 1800s. As late as the turn of the last century, however, Italy still had no comparable female luminaries who had yet achieved broad European recognition. To be sure, Carolina Invernizio, la Marchesa Colombi, Neera, and la Contessa Anna Roti were well known nationally and were impressive best sellers; but at the same time, they were "romance" writers and as such had garnered no international attention. Matilde Serao was a public figure in certain Italian intellectual spheres, but she was just a literary and journalistic footnote abroad.

Grazia Deledda was the only "serious" Italian woman writer of her day with a truly worldwide reputation. Deledda's books sold in the millions; they were widely reviewed internationally. (The French knew her as "Italy's George Sand." Turkey even put her on a postage stamp.[27]) She had an enormous following; but in 1936, just ten years after receiving the Nobel Prize, the sad news of her passing was reported around the globe. Almost immediately she became the subject of hundreds of encomiastic obituaries from major international newspapers and magazines, including even a newspaper in Mongolia. Lionized by royalty,[28] other European literary figures,[29] and at least one Fascist dictator, she was sincerely mourned worldwide by her readership.[30]

The factors that colluded to germinate such success were informed by the social and cultural humus that molded her character. In his formal remarks introducing Grazia Deledda to the Swedish Academy conferring the Nobel Prize, Professor Henrik Schück (member of the Swedish Literary Academy and President of the University of Uppsala) read the last of his prepared lines in Italian.

> L'Accademia ha aggiudicato il Premio a Grazia Deledda per la sua potenza di scrittrice, sostenuta da un alto ideale, che ritrae in forme plastiche la vita quale è nella sua appartata isola natale e che con profondità e con calore tratta i problemi di grande interesse umano." (Sarale 89)

> [The Academy has awarded the prize to Grazia Deledda for her power as a writer, upheld by a high ideal, who vividly depicts life as it is in her isolated native island and who deals with problems of great human interest with depth and warmth.]

By Swedish law the Nobel Prize for Literature does not make aesthetic judgments. Instead it recognizes works "which allow humanity to discover particular peoples and destinies which were previously undiscovered." Then what was it about this woman that allowed her to push upon the world stage the vicissitudes, loves, tragedies, traditions, customs, and morals of a long-ignored and forgotten people whose destinies "were previously undiscovered"?

Grazia Deledda was born in Nuoro on 27 September 1871.[31] She was the fourth of seven children, with three younger sisters, two older brothers and an older sister. Her father, Giovanni Antonio Deledda, was a relatively well-to-do landowner who also was a respected notary and property manager. Until some serious commercial reversals toward the end of his life, he ran a lucrative business as an exporter of coal, timber, and potash to the mainland. A diplomatic and tactful gentleman in his business affairs, he was appointed by the government as a lay judge to resolve minor disputes among the populace and to maintain a version of small-claims court conducted in his home. This para-judicial system was a normal part of the contemporary Sardinian social fabric; but more important for the young Grazia Deledda, it gave her the opportunity to come into contact with a wide spectrum of people, since one of the few sources of entertainment in Nuoro was storytelling.[32] And storytelling was the main evening's activity for Sardinians and their houseguests. Recounting tales was a serious form of adult amusement.

There were few hotels in Sardinia for lack of tourism and commerce; by cultural tradition born of necessity, it was considered insulting not to stay overnight in an acquaintance's house. Refusal would imply unwillingness to reciprocate. In her autobiography entitled from her middle name, *Cosima*, Deledda talks about servants, townspeople, middle-class folks, relatives, her father's friends, and business associates, who came from all parts of Sardinia and who told stories by the hearth at night before retiring as guests of the Deledda family.[33] In tandem with this famous Sardinian tradition of offering overnight hospitality to everyone who entered, her father's respected social position meant that during almost every evening of her young life, Grazia Deledda heard the stories told by dinner guests of her home. Sometimes based on actual, contemporary events, these tales enlivened the entire evening for the Dededda family. Most often the racconteur captivated his rapt audience with stimulating details of rural Sardinian life, both from within and outside the law. The future writer absorbed the lore and made it her own; for what she heard held a powerful ascendancy over her. She was captivated by the voices of the common folk of Sardinia, especially by the behavior patterns of the men and women who populated the stories she heard.

From all indications, Deledda's mother, Francesca Cambosu, was an emotionally distant and retiring homebody who seems to have suffered from frequent bouts of severe depression. Then known as *melancholia*, from all biographical information this genetic disorder most probably was inherited by the oldest of the Deledda sons, Santus (Giovanni Santo), who eventually became an alcoholic (not unusual for those suffering from what is now known to be a chemical imbalance which can cause depression, cyclothymia, and bi-polar syndrome [manic depression]).[34]

As a youth Santus showed great academic potential. He was the hope of the family. Serious about his studies, he showed early signs of having a promising (and lucrative) career in medicine.[35] What with his father's business reversals and the ever-dwindling fortunes of the Deledda family, Santus's success was not just a matter of pride.[36] It was one of economic survival for the family. Unfortunately, on one of his summer vacations, Santus suffered a painful accident to his hand; to dull his constant pain, he began to self-medicate with large doses of cognac. Santus became quickly addicted to alcohol; and before the end of his studies, he unexpectedly returned home from Cagliari already a hopeless sot. Mistaken for a downtrodden vagabond, he appeared unannounced in a heap on the family's doorstep, unrecognizable from a drunken binge.

Deledda's wrenching descriptions in *Cosima* of Santus's embarrassing failures to behave with probity also point to possibly inherited manic depression. His bizarre comportment included squandering much of the Deledda patrimony in wild spending sprees. Eventually Santus became so mentally unbalanced that regularly he was seeing monsters under the bed and suffering from delerium tremens. He never led a productive life; he rendered no service to his family or to the community. When able to get out of bed at all, he spent his days loitering at the family olive press with Nuoro's human detritus.

In inverse proportion to the high expectations of him, his spectacular and very public failure at the University of Cagliari made the family the laughingstock of Nuoro.[37] Santus's possibly inherited mental disorders may have been devastating to the Deledda family, yet backhandedly, they provided Grazia with a rich model for many of her male characters. In a twisted way, it was he who helped his literarily ambitious sister garner an education beyond her sheltered imagination.

Observing Santus and his then-inexplicably bizarre behavior, Grazia observed at the same time his juvenile friends and acquaintances who also led lives of wasted opportunity dissipated in childish pursuits. A passage from *Cosima* recounts her days at the Deledda olive press where sadly she absorbed everything she witnessed:

From her observation post she saw . . . the scene and the characters of the olive press; she heard the tales they spun there, the songs of the drunk, the childish giggles of the man who killed his brother; and her heart broke and she bowed her humbled head in seeing Santus, her brother born to accomplish great things (695–96).

Deledda's other adult-adolescent paradigm was her second older brother, Andrea, who in his own way was equally problematic for the family. Two years Santus's junior but five years older than Grazia, Andrea was the classic petulant brat. When once told that he should not eat cheese for breakfast lest his teacher be offended by the acrid odor on his breath, he snapped back, "And who's he? I'm a rich shepherd, but he's a starving beggar, a flea-ridden drunk" (*Cosima* 699). Not the studious type, Andrea was as gregarious as Santus was morosely introverted. Andrea shunned his studies in favor of keeping the company both of the local jeunesse dorée and more frequently the local prostitutes. Andrea's over-indulgence in gambling and alcohol and his penchant for troublemaking and public hooliganism got him arrested more than once—he was jailed for chicken thievery; he was imprisoned for being part of a counterfeiting operation.

After the death of the Deledda patriarch in 1892, the worst possible catastrophe befell the once-proud Deledda family: Andrea took over the household finances (*Cosima* 738). Andrea's previous relationship with his emotionally cold and psychologically distant father may have contributed to his problems in growing up. He never did emerge from his juvenile phase, even after his father's death left him with serious familial responsibilities. Andrea managed to squander the family's once considerable wealth in a very short time, leaving his mother and siblings with little of Giovanni Antonio Deledda's patrimony.[38] Andrea, however, accepted no accountability for his actions, a trait that later would provide his younger sister with a blueprint for her conception of male behavior. After the death of Giovanni Antonio, Andrea spent the rest of his lifetime in destructive, adolescent pursuits; his own hooliganism, profligacy, and alcoholism eventually brought the Deledda family to its knees in the face of public opprobrium, dishonor, and bankruptcy.

Toward the end of *Cosima* we learn that both Santus and Andrea were in such dire physical and social straits that, aware of their reputation, they themselves agreed to leave the Deledda home to live in a nearby cottage (detached from the main house) so that the girls in the family would not have to be daily witnesses to their debauched lives. Yet despite the total undoing of her sons, their mother remained faithful to the art of coddling them: "She thought of them as little boys lost in the woods and sought them out regularly" (*Cosima* 750). Francesca Deledda's indulgence toward her sons also made an impression on the budding author who doubtless observed with astuteness female cause and male effect.[39]

Despite his problems with delinquency and with the law, Andrea was a kind and considerate brother to Grazia. He protected her from the public and familial opprobrium of her writing career. (Being a writer was looked upon as a greater scandal than having a chicken thief and an alcoholic for brothers.) Andrea procured for his sister private lessons in the Italian language, so that she could write for a larger audience; he took her on horseback to the small villages and country festivals and to the family grazing lands; it was he who took her to the sea for the first time. It was he who made sure that all the illustrated magazines arrived by mail, so that she could keep up with mainland "culture."

Andrea may have been a disaster of a son and citizen; but he offered an even better paradigm than Santus for Deledda's future protagonists. Andrea's shortcomings were much more varied and colorful than Santus's simple alcoholism and depression. Certainly between the two of them, at their very best the Deledda boys provided their imaginative and talented sister with a motherlode of rich story material for the prose "fiction" that was to come.

Like most girls of her social status, Grazia Deledda attended the traditional three years of elementary school.[40] She then essentially taught herself everything she knew, feeding her voracious reader's appetite with whatever books she could find. She patched together her own literary education by using the library bequeathed to her father by the Bishop of Nuoro, Giovanni Mario de Martis, and the limited library of her uncle, Don Sebastiano, a priest whose haphazard collection was without rhyme or reason. She also devoured the books left behind by her sometime tutor, a professor who absconded from *zia* Paulina's boardinghouse across the street without making his final payment.[41] Perhaps he thought that leaving his library would be payment enough for *zia* Paulina (it was not). It certainly was a windfall, however, for the young Grazia Deledda who systematically appropriated his entire abandoned collection.[42]

Although by age ten, in 1881, Deledda had finished her formal schooling, by her teen years she had managed on her own to read much of contemporary literature (Verga, Capuana, D'Annunzio, Fogazzaro, Scott, Tolstoy, Dostoevsky, Hugo, Balzac, Flaubert, and Zola, with a predilection for the French Naturalists).[43] Her accidental readings, however, had no formal direction and certainly were without broad perspectives with which to place what she was reading in any kind of meaningful literary context.

Knowing his sister's passion for reading and writing, Santus, while still able to function as a medical student at the University of Cagliari, would keep her abreast of the latest European literary trends. He also invited to the Deledda home in Nuoro for an extended summer visit his best friend and fellow-student, Antonio Pau, an adorer/imitator of the immensely popular poet, Gabriele D'Annunzio. Romantically and hopelessly in love with Pau from a circumspect distance, Deledda would eavesdrop on the educated university students; and as a by-product of her crush on the dashing Pau, she enhanced her own literary education by secretly absorbing their discussions of contemporary poetry and literature.

Her two brothers also arranged for her to receive illustrated magazines from the continent in which she discovered the short stories that always appeared in the last pages. From her avid reading of those stories, Deledda hit upon the notion of sending one of her own, "Sangue sardo," to a magazine, along with a biographical sketch of herself and her daily life in Sardinia. When first she tried her hand at writing, she had to create her own narrative orbit.[44] Wisely, she stuck to doing what she knew best—tell a good story and provide realistic, intuitive, psychological underpinnings for the motivations of her characters. To her unqualified shock, her first submitted story was accepted; and that was the beginning of Grazia Deledda, professional writer of fiction. She was seventeen years old. Invited to submit more stories, to her delight she was even paid for what she would have willingly done free of charge.[45]

In the short story, "I primi passi" [The First Steps] from *La vigna sul mare* [The Vinyard on the Sea], there appears a very moving paragraph on Deledda's own feelings upon seeing her name in print for the first time. "It seemed like a dream to me: and my name in print, for the first time gave me the feeling of a hallucination. I stared at it for a long time: the letters got bigger, black, alive, alarming. Was that person really me? No, it was not me, the little, secret, almost mysterious writer: yet that name was the echo of mine, that answered from a far away distance, beyond the mountains, beyond the sea as yet unknown to me: it answered to the cry of my very essence yearning to expand into that immensity. Still today my name in print produces in me a reflection of that first impression" (791–92).

Speaking of herself in the third person in *Cosima*, Deledda describes her need to write as a "physical need."[46] She talks about how much of herself is in her novels.[47] From early childhood Grazia Deledda was psychologically invested in writing to the point where eventually it became an emotional and spiritual lifeline for her.[48] At one point in *Cosima* Deledda confesses how, to further her ambitions, she even filched money from the household accounts by selling an occasional liter of home-produced olive oil to passersby and keeping half of the profits: "metà alla casa, metà alla gloria" [half for the household, half for glory] (764).[49] She needed the olive oil money to pay the postage to send her manuscripts to her publisher. This had to be done in secret, because her writing from the very beginning was the object of vehement contention in the Deledda house. (Evidently, at first her father encouraged her epistolary efforts, that is until he learned she was publishing them. To be sure, he would never have given her the money for stamps.)

Deledda's professional handicaps were not limited to the necessity for oleic subterfuge. Initially she also lacked the tools and sophistication to carry out the career of which she dreamed. Deledda was so sheltered and naïve that she had no idea what galley proofs were. Thinking that her first set constituted the finished product, she ingenuously kept them as her author's copy, although she deemed those long printer's sheets a rather strange way of publishing. Her failure to return them prompted her dismayed and impatient editor to remark in a letter to her that "neanche Carducci" [not even Carducci] kept him waiting so long for corrected proofs! Little did the publisher suspect that he was reprimanding a child who would become the next Italian to win the Nobel Prize for literature after Carducci himself won it in 1906.

Deledda also had no idea that there were such things as proofreading symbols. She corrected all errors within the body of the text in long hand much to the despair of her typographers (who were by no means cryptographers). Orthographic and grammatical errors abounded because Italian was not her native language. She grew up speaking only the local dialect of Logudorese and had to study Italian formally as a foreign language in order even to consider having a viable writing career.

Oblivious to her problems, her entire extended family, but especially her parents, considered it nothing short of scandalous that a young girl (worse yet, their own flesh and blood) would be writing what they considered tawdry, romantic stories and sully-ing the good name of Deledda. Apart from the family's humiliation, they were most worried about their chances to marry off their other daughters to suitable partners. With such opprobrium brought down upon the once proud Deledda family by Grazia's disgraceful writing career (not to mention by the debauched lives of their two older sons), indeed it would have been difficult for the Deleddas to regain their previous social status.[50]

Unbowed by the torrent of local criticism in Nuoro, Deledda continued her work in relative solitude. If it had not been for her writing, this intelligent teenager would have surely perished spiritually.[51] In his introductory remarks to the collection of Grazia Deledda's *Romanzi e novelle* [Novels and Short Stories], Natalino Sapegno points out how isolated she really was. In fact in her youth she had *no* contact with the literary world of her contemporaries.[52] She lived through all the -isms of Italian and European literature from *verismo* to naturalism to the Russian novelists to the idealism of Fogazzaro to esthetism of D'Annunzio to antinaturalism, and later in her life even through modernism. Yet for most of her formative years as a writer, she had no intellectual intercourse with the literary or cultural world.[53] There were no art museums or institutes of art in Nuoro where gifted students could be trained and encouraged.[54]

In arguably one of her most autobiographical novels, *Il paese del vento* [The Land of the Wind], Deledda refers to Nuoro as having "all the traits, warmth, and climate of a village from the Iron Age" (24). She was bombarded by local criticism (from the clergy, from important citizenry, from her own family), and she had to endure it all in obedient silence. She loathed the provincial attitudes of Sardinia. It was her lifelong fantasy to leave Nuoro forever and live in Rome.[55]

When Grazia was in her twenties, with one alcoholic brother in prison, a severely depressed mother, her father and two sisters already deceased, and another brother incapacitated from alcohol and depression, she became the de facto head of the Deledda household. As such she often had to tend personally to the family's financial records at the Deledda's commercial olive press. She welcomed the opportunity, because there she could listen to the stories of a wider variety of individuals than most people meet in a lifetime. There were those clients who came to purchase olive oil or to have their own olives pressed, as well as many of the derelict friends of her alcoholic brother, Santus. There were the town drunks and hangers-on, even a man convicted of fratricide, along with the unemployed, the poor, and society's rejects.[56] None of them had a thing to do, save loiter in the olive pressing area of the Deledda courtyard. In this venue Grazia had much and varied contact with the public, especially with a wide spectrum of men who never matured enough to leave the emotional comfort of their equally adolescent peers. She based many of her future fictional characters on aspects of these social types and individuals.[57]

From these rich and multifarious experiences, it is not surprising that her themes include the grand ones of all literatures: love and hate, faith, envy, greed, pride, motherhood, anger, banditry, guilt, fear of God, and expiation of sin.[58] Her protagonists are mostly the dispossessed: drunks, illicit lovers, dissipates, outlaws, and beggars, in addition to many landowners and their hired help, priests, ex-priests, future-priests, shepherds, farmers, servants, and peasants. Deledda's works are the accumulated record of Sardinian passions, fears, and collective mental states. Clearly, the young Grazia Deledda was not wasting her time while balancing the books at the olive press.

Deledda also gathered story material during her short trips to local religious festivals. Occasionally, her favorite brother, Andrea, would take her on horseback to the nearby small towns where she heard stories told around the fire at night. In her fiction she wrote often about pilgrimages to various rural sanctuaries where again the social life was characterized by storytelling—small towns such as Oliena, Orgosolo, San Francesco, Lula, Mamoiada, Fonni, Dorgali, Orosei, and Desulo, where on many documented occasions the Deledda family would spend the night in the homes of friends or camping outdoors with even more storytelling for entertainment.

By July 1888, Deledda had already published her first short story, "Sangue sardo," in the Roman magazine, *L'Ultima Moda* [The Latest Fashions] edited by Epaminonda Provaglio. Other stories followed; by 1889, Deledda was attracting the attention of her mainland contemporaries in literature.[59] Encouraged by her initial success, she produced a steady stream of stories and novellas; in 1890, the Milanese publisher, Trevisini, issued in one volume her first collection of short stories, *Nell'azzurro* [In the Blue].[60] When the influential novelist and critic, Luigi Capuana, reviewed positively her novel, *La via del male* [The Path to No Good] in 1896, Grazia Deledda's career began in earnest. With the well-connected Capuana's nihil obstat, Deledda began acquiring a faithful readership all over Italy. She was earning money for her work; magazines were actively soliciting her stories. She no longer had to pilfer the olive oil accounts to pay the postage for her manuscripts; but she was still the disgrace of her family and a pariah in Nuoro for bringing such infamy upon her hometown. On a very personal level her own islanders made her existence a living nightmare. In Sardinia public indignation over her writing was nothing short of scathing; and it had little to do with the quality of her work. (Indeed, few could read!) She endured a caustic local virulence unequalled in Nuoro's collective memory. The bitterness carried over to her as a person as well.[61]

Deledda was brutalized by her own people; she was made to feel guilty all her life for the mere act of writing, not for what she wrote. Arnaldo Fratelli reminisces about the inevitable local scandals that ensued whenever she published anything at all and then word got back to town that she was the author; the people in her hometown could not comprehend "how she could write about such things without having done them."[62] Mundula points out that when she published her first short stories she became the target of all the town gossips who foresaw a grim future indeed for the young Grazia Deledda (54). People in Nuoro felt free to malign (and fear) her books as though they had been put on the Vatican's *Index Librorum Prohibitorum* (which they were not). The entire town turned on her; Mundula likens the situation to a burning at the stake (55). He indicates, perhaps not surprisingly, that Nuoro's middle class had "no great love for the young writer" (78). When Grazia Deledda shamefully won the Nobel Prize, she was dismissed by the Nuorese as being "atypical" and thusly disposed of in that offhanded way.[63] It is a bizarre, almost surreal, twist indeed when a town denies its association with a figure of international renown because she dared to win the world's most coveted prize in literature, as though that were an inadmissible thing to do.

The aspersions were most painful coming from her own mother whom Grazia overheard telling a servant that Grazia's "crazy ideas" and "filthy books" would ruin her other daughters' chances to marry well (Sarale 98). When Deledda's mother saw the money she had earned for a reprint in translation of one of her short stories, "she looked at it almost surly; it seemed to her to be the fruit of a mortal sin" (Sapegno 816). Understandably the overheard conversation and her mother's reaction to her earnings drove the headstrong Grazia to intensify her search for a way to escape Nuoro.[64]

Nevertheless, writing made her happier than she had ever been. She was even receiving fan mail. Letters from admirers on the continent were delivered to her home in Nuoro, one of whom was so ardent that he even wanted to name an unexplored region in South America after her. In a letter to Provaglio dated in early September 1892, the young writer confided that her fantasy was to marry someone who would take her to a land of "civility and intelligence."[65] It had always been Deledda's flight of fancy to escape the stultifying atmosphere of Nuoro and move to Rome. The capital was for her a lifelong dream, a haven where she could write free from patronistic control and prejudice; but she knew that Rome for her was a chimera.

After a flood of literary activity (three more novels, a new collection of short stories, and some poetry), on October 22, 1899, the tenacious Grazia Deledda somehow prevailed over the violent and prolonged objection of her family and was allowed to accept an invitation to visit Cagliari. By now a published author of five novels and two short story collections, the twenty-eight-year-old had still never been out of Nuoro on her own; she had never been on a train. As part of the compromise, Andrea was to accompany her on the day's journey to Cagliari, Sardinia's southernmost, large city. The invitation had been extended by an admirer of her work, Maria Manca, editor of a popular magazine, *La Donna Sarda* [The Sardinian Woman]. Deledda was to stay with Manca in her villa on the sea, and, well-chaperoned, partake in the comparatively dazzling city life of Cagliari. This opportunity was for the sheltered Grazia Deledda a dream come true.

In fact, that trip was to change the course of Deledda's life in ways she could never have imagined. It would introduce her to the man who provided yet another, confirming model for her thoughts on arrested maturation and, more importantly, to the man who really *did* take her to Rome, that longed-for land of "civility and intelligence." In Cagliari she met Palmiro Madesani whom she married six weeks later.[66] It was November 1899, and apparently the last time the century turned, matters of the heart were resolved expeditiously:

Durante un gioco di società in casa di Maria Manca, direttrice della rivista "La Donna Sarda," non avendo la Deledda eliminato la parola "perchè" dalla risposta che doveva dare, fu sottoposta alla cosiddetta "penitenza" dalla parte del Madesani. La penitenza consisteva nel dichiarare come avrebbe desiderato il suo futuro sposo e la scrittrice nuorese, senza esitazione rispose "Come lei!" Il giorno seguente ricevette dal Madesani una dichiarazione d'amore e per metterlo alla prova lei rispose che avrebbe accettato di sposarlo solo a patto che il matrimonio avvenisse entro due mesi. E così fu (8).[67]

[During a parlor game in Maria Manca's home, editor of the magazine, *The Sardinian Woman*, Deledda, not having avoided the word "because" from the answer she was expected to give, had to submit to the game's penalty to be administered by Madesani. The penalty consisted of Deledda's describing her ideal future husband; without hesitation, the writer from Nuoro answered, "Like you!" The next day she received from Madesani a declaration of love, and to put him to the test, she answered that she would accept his marriage proposal only if the wedding took place within two months. And so it did.]

Immediately after the wedding in January 1900, Grazia Deledda and Palmiro Madesani moved to Rome where they made their permanent home.[68] The Madesanis had two sons, Sardus and Franz (the Sardinian nickname for Francesco).[69] Once established in Rome and secure in her ability to write professionally, Deledda earned the attention (and sometimes begrudging praise) of such contemporary critics as Emilio Cecchi and Benedetto Croce, while at the same time serving as a target for many others.

At the very beginning of her career, while still a teenager, she was taken both with the style of Romanticism and by the "women's" writing available to her in magazines and in the Italian equivalents of the "dime novel." Some of her early work evinces all the clichès of the literature of the day.[70] This is understandable, given her age and lack of literary sophistication. However, after her discovery of Verga and Capuana, she learned to dampen her romantic bent. What those two authors were for Sicily, she would eventually become for Sardinia. She began to explore the themes and *leitmotivs* of freedom and social equality; and on her own she acquired a social conscience. Her first broadly successful novels, (especially *Dopo il divorzio* [After the Divorce] and *Cenere*), in fact are scathing indictments of the deplorable social situation in Sardinia. Yet she was considered by not a few luminaries as just another formulaic writer of women's "heaving-bodice" stories.[71] Despite the generally negative critical reception, in 1900, *Elias Portolu* was a popular success in all Europe and even caused her name to be first proposed for the Nobel Prize (she was nominated a total of six times).[72]

By any standards, Deledda's most fertile period was from 1903 to 1920, when in Rome she filled in the contours of a career begun in the backwaters of Nuoro when she was just a teenager. She published, among many other works, *L'edera [Ivy]*, (1906), *Colombi e sparvieri [Doves and Hawks]*, (1912), *Canne al vento*

[Reeds in the Wind], (1913), *Marianna Sirca* (1915), *La madre* [The Mother], (1920), and *Cenere* [Ashes] (1904).[73]

Despite her success and fame, she always lived a withdrawn life, working at home in a systematic way without fanfare. She wrote for a few hours in the morning; then she cooked for the family and tended her garden. She *always* wrote in the afternoon from 4:00–6:00 P.M. Her minimum goal was two hours of writing per day producing at least four handwritten pages (Balducci 169). Her sons both remember as children having to be quiet during those two hours so their mother could concentrate. Later in life her son, Franz, wrote a sketch of his late mother where he quoted his brother, Sardus, during those quiet hours, "Speak softly, be quiet, 'cause Mama is writing!" (Viola 58). She used only pen and ink, avoiding the typewriter at all cost. In the late afternoon reluctantly she received the media and others who demanded her time, an activity she detested. She was at her happiest during private family vacations. At first they preferred the beaches of Viareggio, but after that vacation city became too tony for her simple tastes, in 1920 the Deledda-Madesanis built a summer home near Cervia. There the family could have the privacy and seclusion they craved, at least during the summer months. Franz elaborated on her desire for privacy and solitude; "She rarely went out, especially in the last years of her life; the times she had to go out, she got ready as if she had to undertake a long voyage. After dinner she usually retired to her study and read all the papers and magazines that she received. Everything interested her, and the next day she would mark for us kids everything she thought would be useful for our cultural education" (Viola 58).

One invitation Deledda could not refuse came just after receiving the Nobel Prize. However disinclined she may have been, Grazia Deledda agreed to meet with Benito Mussolini. She was asked to an audience in the intimidating *Salone Mappamondo* [World Map Room] of Palazzo Venezia which the Duce used as a ceremonial office in Rome. After her encounter with Mussolini, a highly placed military aide escorted her out of that immense and imposing hall. He politely suggested to her that she might want to write something for the Regime. She answered tersely, "L'arte non ha politica." [Art is not political.] Almost immediately her work was ordered out of all bookstore windows and showcases and was prohibited to all Fascist Party members. Her editor at Treves told Deledda that it was orders from the top; she felt the tangible evidence of those "orders from the top" when her next royalties check arrived—a greatly reduced sum from what she had come to expect before her courageous refusal and subsequent fall from Fascism's grace.[74]

Deledda was barely five feet tall, not at all a commanding figure. She preferred the quiet company of her family to the lush life in Rome (which ironically she had so craved as a starstruck teenager back in Nuoro).[75] Grazia never imposed a systematic orientation on her intellectual life, nor did she ever continue her rudimentary formal education; but by the time of her mature adulthood in Rome, she had acquired a sophisticated knowledge and appreciation of European art and literature. She accomplished this with her insatiable reading and through her friendships with such literary figures as Emilio Cecchi, Antonio Fogazzaro, Matilde Serao, Pietro Pancrazi, Sibilla Aleramo,[76] Ugo Ojetti, Marino Moretti (with whom she shared a lifetime friendship punctuated by a long and rich correspondence), and, tangentially, Luigi Pirandello. Her archives show that she corresponded as well with such contemporary luminaries as Giuseppe Giacosa, Giovanni Verga, Selma Lagerlöf, Ada Negri, Edmondo De Amicis, Lorenzo Viani, Federigo Tozzi, Ruggiero Leoncavallo, and Alfredo Panzini. In general, however, her professional and civic involvement was apolitical.

Deledda was always true to her origins. The attacks she suffered on her own island did not dampen her desire to teach her sons about her homeland and their maternal heritage.[77] Deledda returned occasionally to Sardinia with Sardus and Franz when they were children; but her last trip to her native island was in 1911. She lived for twenty-five more years without ever returning. One can hardly find fault with her reluctance to spend a great deal of time in a place where she clearly was not appreciated, respected, wanted, or even tolerated.

She was so modest and self-effacing that when she was awarded the Nobel Prize her only celebration was with her immediate family.[78] Upon receiving notification of this singular honor, she finally uncorked her prized bottle of wine, a *Nepente* from Oliena. Brought with her from Sardinia, for years she had been saving it for just the right occasion. However, the *gloria*, for which as a girl she purloined the family's olive oil profits, was short-lived; one year later Grazia Deledda was diagnosed with breast cancer. In 1928, she underwent two operations to remove the tumor, but the cancer had already spread. Her villa in Cervia was her hospice where Grazia Deledda died on 15 August 1936 at age sixty-five. She was interred in the same dress she wore to accept the Nobel Prize. A month later *Cosima* was published. In retrospect the autobiographical material in her last book can be considered a matrix for almost all of her fiction, a fountainhead of plot lines and a trove of character material from which to dip. No one even knew she was writing it; the manuscript was found in her desk after her death; it became the gift she left her readers, an invaluable personal grid to overlay upon her life's work in fiction.

In 1947, the Italian government placed in the Villa Borghese (Rome's central park), a bust of Grazia Deledda in a place of distinction on the prestigious Viale dell'Obelisco, a winding pathway of honor which serves as a sort of modern Italian pantheon with busts of important figures of Italian culture and history. Her monument stands near the Pincio just to the side of the historic Casina Valadier. Several years later a memorial chapel was built in Deledda's honor in Nuoro on the site of the original church of the *Madonna del Monte* [Madonna of the Mountain], renamed the *Chiesa della Solitudine* [Church of Solitude]. The church's new name reflected the exact title of her last novel (tellingly about a woman dying of breast cancer).

In 1959, Deledda's remains were flown back to Sardinia for re-interment at that memorial chapel with full state ceremonies. A witness to one aspect of the ceremony recalls that when it was announced that the mortal remains of Grazia Deledda were being taken through the airport to the official government plane bound for Nuoro, spontaneously, as if by tacit agreement, the normally crowded and bustling Roman airport then at Ciampino fell silent to honor one of the nation's grandest figures.[79] Grazia Deledda was to be laid to rest in a free-standing, polished, black granite sarcophagus to the right of the altar inside *la Solitudine* which commands a majestic view of Mount Orthobene, the same view she had as a struggling writer from the window of her childhood room.[80]

Just a sampling of her obituaries from around the world gives an idea of the high esteem in which she was held. The Parisian literary review, *Minerva*, called her "la George Sand italienne" [the Italian George Sand] in its laudatory obituary published on 30 August 1936, just days after her death. Other international papers were equally enthusiastic in recognizing her achievements as a writer. In her own country, however, compliments were more difficult to extract. Yet even the Fascist press had to bow to her celebrity, although many of the state-controlled newspapers could not resist twisting the knife. In an article just days after her death in *L'Avvenire d'Italia* [The Future of Italy] on 30 August

1936, the singularly ungracious Branca Paulucci wrote that "despite her deficiencies," perhaps she was an author worth reading "now that she was dead."[80]

At the Deledda archives in Nuoro are collected hundreds of obituaries from international clipping services forwarded to the Madesani-Deledda family on the event of the writer's death. Encomia from every conceivable country evince the high esteem in which she was held abroad. Cuttings from as far away as Mongolia, items from countries in Africa, South America, the entire English speaking world, all acclaim her as one of their beloved writers.[82] She was a world figure; her name was known to almost everyone who could read; her death was marked in the same public and universal way that occurred with all the great writers of our time: Pirandello, Hemingway, Sartre. Yet, ironically, on her own turf, in her own home town, even today, Grazia Deledda is nowhere in evidence (with the exception of an old train station hotel which bears her name). Arguably Grazia Deledda is Nuoro's most legitimate claim to fame; yet, as of this writing it is nearly impossible to purchase even one photo of the writer, not even on a postcard, although it *is* possible to purchase a photo of her sarcophagus! (One interprets that fact however one chooses.)

Today if one asks a random older woman in Nuoro about Grazia Deledda, chances are excellent of receiving an excoriating response, replete with spitting remarks to the effect that "sa femmina" [that woman] did nothing but bring ill repute to her homeland. Deledda is still considered an embarrassment by those very few still alive who as children had heard rumors of her shabby reputation. Even some middle-aged women still revile her mercilessly for being a disgraceful woman, a common slattern who brought ignominy upon her people. Deledda was revered around the globe, but in her own time and beyond she was/is notorious among some sectors of Nuoro. Deledda's own recollections of this period are especially painful.

> I had published my first works, my first sketches . . . So just imagine my pain, anger, and disillusionment when my first works were met in a terrible way and I earned laughter, censure, malicious gossip, especially from the women. It was a terrible blow for me; I cried and regretted this step I had taken; and confused, discouraged, duped, I decided to pull back and never write again (Scano, *Versi* 18–19).

Antonio Scano sums up Deledda's reaction to the opprobrium she suffered in her hometown by pointing up her lifelong bitterness against her native islanders; and in a newspaper article Silvio Negro is quite express on her understandable mordancy toward her fellow Sardinians.[83] He points out how she had to overcome incredible obstacles to her writing, eventually resorting to working secretly. Negro quotes Deledda on the specifics of her vilification. "The whole town was gossiping about me; it was said that I was on the road to no good (because unfortunately in many towns, and not only in Sardinia, they believe that a woman writer is, shall we say, not too virtuous); they sent me anonymous letters; I was hounded in all sorts of ways. For a long time I wrote on the sly." And Mundula quotes Deledda on her dismay over the lack of encouragement from her fellow Sardinians: "I never receive one word of encouragement from Sardinia" (73). In a pathetic passage from *Cosima*, Deledda describes what normally should be a joyous day for any writer, when her one hundred author's copies arrived of her first novel. "The big package thudded down in the house like an exploding meteor. Her mother was stricken with terror; that evening she circled around it with the frightened suspicion of a dog who sees a strange animal" (101). Her mother's reaction to those evil books was eclipsed only by that of the Deledda's extended family who felt free to add their opinions of her work at every opportunity.

Fratelli writes about the heart-rending fact that Grazia Deledda actually felt shame for her success even in her full maturity when she saw her name on the cover of a book. "For the rest of her life, she was always afraid that her writing was not proper and that she 'was about to be reprimanded.' The relatives judged Grazia a girl without honor who would never be able to get married; she was practically ostracized by her own family. 'Even now,' Deledda once confessed to me, 'when I see my name printed at the end of an article or on the cover of a book, I feel a sense of sorrow. I am afraid that it is not proper, that I am about to be reprimanded' " (*Ricordo* 10). That the emarginated Deledda could have endured such a demoralizing thrashing alone, without a supportive base of friends and without encouragement from any of the traditional sources, especially from her immediate family, is truly a testament to her determination and grit. That she was made to feel guilty for writing is another kind of commentary on the society in which she lived.[84]

Perhaps Deledda was parodying her critics when she wrote an interesting passage in *Sino al confine* [Up to the Border], on the dangers of letting young women read novels (such as her own). Gavina's imperious fiancè, Francesco, laments this bad habit now "of letting married women read just anything." He asks rhetorically if perhaps "a married woman is different from an unmarried one?" He complains that "in big cities women read everything. This really helps the devil do his work." And he cautions Gavina, his fiancée, to "be sure not to follow the example of other women" (112). Deledda seems to delight in tweaking the noses of her critics when she creates a fictional Gavina who does not really love Francesco. Instead she is in love with Priamo, a sensual priest who would *never* prohibit any genre of reading material. Gavina is forced to marry Francesco. Significantly, after her wedding, her mental health deteriorates rapidly; but it is greatly restored by her disobedient reading of every novel in the censorious Francesco's library. The reluctant feminist, Deledda, was signalling her literary critics about the invigorating effects of women's reading and writing.

Deledda probably would not have been bothered by her own necrology, neither negatively nor positively. In 1932, in the face of bitter criticism, she said, "Non guardavo in faccia nessuno" [I took care of myself first].[85] Grazia Deledda was monolithic, truly a self-made woman; she willed herself to be. She was not satisfied just to flourish locally in Nuoro as a "Sardinian" regional writer; she forced her greater success to happen by becoming a national and international figure. Not lacking in self-esteem or ambition, as a young girl she dreamed of glory and celebrity. As she tells us in *Cosima*, at a decisive moment in her young adulthood, "She decided not to wait anymore for something to come to her from the outside, from the turbulent world of men; but everything from within herself, from the mystery of her inner life" (795). In a private letter to the Roman drama critic, Stanis Manca, dated 4 August 1892, she wrote, "In ten years you will hear about me." On 9 August 1892, she wrote him, "I have the constant, tormenting, feverish dream of celebrity." In the same letter she wrote, "But I feel a bold artistic ambition; but I believe one day I will become something."[86] She often prayed to the Lord "heal me from this fever and make me become great!" (Sarale 90).[87] Incredibly, the woman from Nuoro had inserted herself into the same league with Verga, Capuana, Pirandello, and D'Annunzio, despite having to endure the opprobrium which she experienced personally and professionally.[88] Even after her death, she suffered one last affront (and one charitably hopes it was inadvertent).

A spectator at the state ceremony in Nuoro in 1959 to dedicate the church of *La Solitudine* to Deledda's memory and to re-inter her body near the altar recalls that at the moment of being transfered into her final resting place, it was discovered that her casket was too long for the space carved out of the sarcophagus. It was no secret that in life Grazia Deledda was a very tiny woman; she was under five feet tall (to be precise, 1.55 meters). So surely before the public ceremony, someone could have thought to calculate the approximate dimensions of the remains of a smallish woman. But because of this seeming indifference and inattention to detail, Deledda's body was left to wait in a temporary coffin outside the *Chiesa della Solitudine* until the interior sarcophagal space could be enlarged to allow one of Sardinia's greatest writers to rest in dignity. The plan to enlarge the space, however, was never carried out.

A recent discovery, described in "Quel sarcofago ancora vuoto," brings to light the fact that Grazia Deledda's remains have *still* not been laid to rest in the sarcophagus. Her casket was put temporarily under it (but some maintain that it is not even under the sarcophagus, rather still buried unceremoniously and unmarked against an outside wall of the church). A recent pronouncement (forty years later) from the mayor of Nuoro promises, however, that Grazia Deledda's remains will be laid to rest properly "in tempi celeri" [as soon as possible].[89] The cavalier attitude that permitted such shabby treatment of a national hero in her death is unfortunately emblematic of the ruthless way she was treated in life.

THE CRITICAL (MIS-)FORTUNES

Nel numero degli avversari, sul principio, erano anche persone di conto, le quali, mosse da una falsa tenerezza verso l'isola sventurata, si scandalizzavano di tanta rude franchezza, e, accesi da sacro sdegno, fulminavano con la loro arcigna riprovazione la novellatrice, che svelava e anatomizzava, come medico poco pietoso, per uso di estranei, certe magagne, che non era prudente neppure confessare a se stessi.

(Giuseppe Ruju)

[At the beginning, numbered among her adversaries were also people of renown who, moved by a false tenderness toward the unfortunate island, became scandalized by such crude frankness; and urged on by righteous indignation, they fulminated-with their surly criticism against the novelist who, like a cruel doctor, for the use of outsiders, denuded and dissected certain blemishes which were unwise to confess even to oneself.]

One of the great ironies of Grazia Deledda's career was that as much as her work was respected by reviewers abroad, for a variety of reasons she was scorned precisely by Italian literary critics. Despite her world renown, ironically, Deledda was never appreciated in her homeland, not by the mainland literary circles, and even less so by the Sardinians. She was not taken very seriously as a writer; when she was acknowledged at all, she was most often considered a "woman" writer, implicitly not a "real" writer. While at best most were ungraciously begrudging of her merits, many critics in Italy outright panned her work, often with little or no effort to attenuate their contempt.[90] Theirs was more than just negative literary criticism; what they said about her was often tinged with churlishness and real attempts to debase, hurt, and insult her. A great deal of what was written smacks of poorly disguised sexism and in some instances unquestionable misogyny. Much was delivered with a vocabulary of derision that seemed to be inexhaustible.[91]

When the 1926 Nobel Prize announcement was made, almost all the notables in Italian literary criticism (as well as numerous lesser lights) decried the choice. Croce was the leader of the most scandalized that they had given the prize to "a provincial housewife" (Sarale 98). He set the tone for what was to come. He referred to the Nobel committee as "imprudent judges."[92] The Sardinian, Giuseppe Ruju's assessment of her work included the pronouncement that she was "lucky" her books were promoted so well, that she had very "effective rewriters" and advisers who "cleaned up her work both in form and language." He characterized her as having "the boldness and courage of a man." He ended his evaluation with the remark that "her gender served her well" (106).

If Ruju is to be believed, Deledda had a successful career only because of aggressive packaging and effective cosmetic changes to her work, because she wrote like a man, and worse because she took advantage of being a woman. Spittingly backhanded, sexist remarks such as Ruju's were not the exception. Dismissive and derisive treatment of her as a successful professional was not limited to literary critics. Mouthpieces for the Roman Catholic Church habitually delivered stinging broadsides especially for Deledda's depiction of priests. One of the main attackers was Pietro Casu, a well known Sardinian priest who had literary ambitions of his own and who once asked Grazia Deledda to write a preface to a collection of short stories he hoped to publish. In a kind and supportive letter to him, she offered understandable reasons why she had to refuse.[93] His reaction was to write a ripping critique of her work for *Arte e Vita*, a popular Catholic magazine.[94]

Casu may not have known (or cared to mention) that Grazia Deledda had two uncles, Don Ignazio and Don Sebastiano Cambosu, who were priests and that she had much contact with the clergy when numerous clerics visited her father at the Deledda home. In his diatribe Casu completely sidesteps the notion that her keen insights and powers of observation may have reflected what she had seen and experienced directly from life itself when she characterized her fictive clerical protagonists, as well as her adult-adolescent males. Rather than addressing these issues, Casu simply accuses Deledda of having "a perverse spirit" that contaminates her work (Ruju 98). Her depiction of clerics was not Casu's only complaint. He also objected strongly to her descriptions of the average Sardinian.

To prove he was not alone in this judgment, Casu cites the archconservative critic, Luigi Lucatelli, from an article in the magazine, *La Civiltà Cattolica* [Catholic Civilization], where the writer complains that Deledda's characters are "morally reprehensible." He sees her characterizations as a "demolition job" perpetrated on the good people of Sardinia.[95] Casu worried that the "continentals" would judge all Sardinians by those in Deledda's novels. Casu pillories her characters as *animacce tenebrose* [shady souls]. He wishes she had used her talent to depict a pleasant world, a Pollyanna ambience where God's goodness would be reflected. He finds it incomprehensible that she never took a Christian stance against the outrageous behavior of her characters (Ruju 89).[96] It is unclear what Casu really wanted from Deledda (besides that elusive preface to his book of short stories); what is clear is that she could do no right in his estimation.[97] And he was not alone.

On 18 August 1936 (just three days after her death), Giuseppe Molteni, who wrote for a right-wing Catholic newspaper, *L'Italia*, published an essay in which he applauded Casu for having written that "dangerous germs" were breeding in Grazia Deledda's writing.[98] Religious criticism of this nature was common and prolific both during Deledda's life and especially after her death. She felt the animosity deeply.[99] At one point she became so exasperated by the intrusive, relentless, and very open attacks on her morals and spiritual life that she was reduced to defending herself publicly: "I was born for house and family; I am religious; I feel that my art is my duty" (Dore 36).

Deledda was not surprised by the pounding she took from the critics. The personal attacks and public scorn (in the guise of literary criticism) had come so early and so often in her career that by her mature years she had almost become inured to it all. The carping was quick, severe and cruel. One critic suggested:

Let her go home, go home, the little girl who likes to write, to the confines of her father's garden to cultivate her carnations and her honeysuckle; let her go home to knit, to grow up, to wait for a good husband, to prepare herself for a hale future of family love and motherhood.[100]

Gratuitous remarks of this type and the chauvinistic interlinear must have been hard for Deledda to ignore. (In fact, she did not ignore them; instead she dealt with them in her prose where her proto-feminism bubbled to the surface in the subtlest of ways.) Some other critics were less patronistic; some toned down the usual vitriol to which Deledda had become accustomed. "One critic called her writing 'gray and monotonous.' Another said her attempt to be realistic included too many bandits, revenge, and blood' and resulted in a 'mannered Sardinia' " (King x). Alfredo Galletti dismissed her international fame and her Nobel prize as "superior to her real merit."[101] Renato Serra is typical; he was completely negative regarding Grazia Deledda. He found nothing redeeming about her work and found it tedious. He referred to Deledda as "an exasperating mediocrity."[102] The best Arnaldo Bocelli could say was that there is no lack of defects in Grazia Deledda's novels.[103]

Even Capuana, who initially had helped launch Deledda's career, later pointed out her limits and "deficiencies," including the "total lack of interest that her characters inspire."[104] This reevaluation is surprising, given his original enthusiasm for her youthful work. There may have been a "bandwagon" effect in the torrent of negativity that her work underwent. Pietro Pancrazi was one of the few critics to come to her defense. He chastised the Italian critics for "being unfair" to her.[105] Deledda's good friend, Marino Moretti, points out that more recent critics vary on their estimation of her artistic and literary merits, but in general their assessment is "more gentle" than that of her contemporaries.[106] Progressive acceptance of women writers over the years surely contributes to recent, more positive reevaluations. But the misogyny from some of the earlier criticism is undeniable.

Neria De Giovanni empathizes with Grazia Deledda's problems. She points out how difficult it is for a woman to insert some of herself into her own writing. She was not only battling the fact of being a woman vis-à-vis the general expectations of male critics, but worse yet in Deledda's case, she was a prime example of extreme female diversity in a patronistic society.[107] A female writer was a rarity within the context of Sardinian womanhood, where marriage, family, and spinsterhood were the only secular options. De Giovanni defends Deledda's work by pointing out that Italian literary criticism has failed to recognize the female esthetic. She discusses the fact that Deledda refused to adhere to the male models; she stresses that women's writing is different from men's.[108] And herein may reside part of Deledda's problems with the literary critics—a matter of gender and one about which she could do nothing to satisfy their exigencies. Women *are* different from men. Just a cursory look at the well-known arguments of Sandra Gilbert and Susan Gubar or of Julia Kristeva puts to rest the notion that writing across the genders is the same.[109] It is important to remember as well that women's psychological development also traces a very different course.[110] And that process inevitably affects the way women write. Unfortunately, in Grazia Deledda's day literary theory did not touch upon these widely debated, contemporary ideas; furthermore, in Deledda's day female critics were not accepted in the conventional media; consequently there was no one to defend her. In the view of the critics, Deledda's prose style may have been too unlike that of Verga's, for example, which is characterized by a linear development with almost no attention paid to human emotion. On the contrary, Deledda sometimes traces a circular pattern in her emplotments, constantly doubling back to examine and re-examine a protagonist's inner struggle and psychological dilemma. When a character takes one step forward, thus advancing the plot, he may then take three back in order to re-assess his previous decision and agonize over his moral problems. Elias Portolu comes to mind, as does Anania of *Cenere*. While Deledda's narrative strategies eventually do move the plot forward to logical conclusions, the linear itinerary is not as well delineated as in the prose style of some of her male contemporaries. This was clearly off-putting to many of her critics who misinterpreted the weaknesses of her adult adolescent characters as deficiencies of the writer.

It is not within the scope of this study to dwell on the many differences between the genders's styles; suffice it to say that women's writing *can* be rigorously evaluated, but not necessarily with the same measures used to assess the work of their male counterparts. The different sexes use different criteria to judge the written word. In Deledda's case, her discerning psychological insights vis-à-vis the adult-adolescent's arrested maturation and male/female relationships were a radical innovation in the context of the Romantic-then-Veristic, contemporary writing of her times. What she offered the reader was a modern woman's viewpoint, a new way, a profoundly psychological way, of approaching fictive characterizations. And male Italian critics almost unanimously skewered her work.

Once she was secure in Rome, however, Deledda somehow acquired the aesthetic distance and professional confidence to deal with the sarcasm and vilification of her compatriots. But earlier, in a letter to Stanis Manca, Deledda had written that she *thought* she "was bringing honor and giving pleasure to [her] countrymen." She told him about almost being stoned by her own people. They even accused her of having a ghostwriter. Later she learned to live with the slander, insults, ridicule, and criticism and essentially to ignore the personal attacks. Perhaps she had grown to understand (even to appreciate) that the impediments she had hurdled to become a writer had shaped the very stuff of her text.

Giuseppe Petronio accurately calls her work an *impasto* [a blend of styles] (155); this is true in many respects, since she was influenced by various trends. It would be surprising if she had avoided all influences, given the length of her career and the young age at which she began writing. Attilio Momigliano believes that Deledda actively ignores all literary tradition; this is also true; she never engaged in writers's circles or considered herself an adherent to any of the artistic movements through which she lived. Bravely Nicolino Sarale argues that the critics are in error and that not even Croce understood Deledda's art.[111] Ada Testaferri probably comes closest to a balanced and accurate description of Grazia Deledda's *opera omnia* when she observes that of all the various -isms in literature, Deledda belongs to none.[112] Scano agrees that despite critical efforts to pigeonhole Deledda, she was never part of a literary tradition, save the oral tradition of her acquaintances in Nuoro. He considers her "true only to her land and her people."[113]

At various times in literary history Grazia Deledda has been called a Romantic, a Decadent, a Verist, a Realist, a Naturalist; she has been compared to Fogazzaro, Verga, D'Annunzio, Flaubert, Zola, Maupassant, Tolstoy, and Dostoevsky; but most comparisons lie in one-time, random, and isolated examples of discrete textual similarities between one or two authors. For example, at times Deledda will mention another contemporary author in her own prose. In *Fior di Sardegna* [Flower of Sardinia], she expresses her desire to have Victor Hugo's pen just for a moment (218); and D'Annunzio's name occasionally comes up in her early prose in connection with fictional characters who want to emulate the flamboyant poet who was all the rage in her day (see *Cosima*, for example). Thematically there are some fleeting intertextual similarities to Dostoevsky, especially with the subjects of sin and expiation. On the whole, however, Deledda adhered to no particular literary school, nor did she slavishly imitate any one master. Neither was she just a starry-eyed Romantic who wanted to clone the typical nineteenth-century heroes and themes of the "bodice-rippers" she read as an immature teenage writer. If she copied anything, it was some aspects of life as she saw it lived. Hers is a prose born of authentic experience and observation, mixed with an elegant writer's creativity and imagination. She fashioned something original and uniquely her own which defies traditional categorization. Deledda really did not belong to any of the -isms perhaps also because of her extreme geographical and cultural isolation; in that she was truly sui generis.

Quite aside from the extravagantly critical reproof, through the years spanning Grazia Deledda's career, even down to present times, in general most of her more objective critics have expended their efforts in debating which literary tradition Deledda best represents. Few have engaged in the practical criticism characteristic of more recent methodologies which allow us to analyze her prose and to form a Deleddan hermeneutics of the complete works.[114]

One of the many puzzling aspects regarding the critical attention she has received, both negative and positive, is that while otherwise occupied either with traducing Deledda's character or with her placement within the -isms of literary history, the major critics have failed to recognize her as a sophisticated, intuitive psychologist who in many ways was far ahead of her time. To be sure, some reflection has been devoted to her psychological characterizations of certain protagonists. Critics invariably talk about the psychological aspects of her protagonists' obsessions with guilt and expiation of sin, hate and love, desperation, passion and redemption, and mostly about her Dostoevskian similarities. But those who take up this facet of her writing focus on her thematic presentation of moral vacillation, of anguish, penance, remorse and atonement. Little printer's ink has been invested in what an observant and instinctive psychologist she was vis-à-vis the realistic creation of her individual characters.[115] Yet as she grafted her interest in the life of the mind onto the unique Sardinian milieu, Deledda was intensely engaged in expansive psychological definitions of humankind and in contextualizing the inchoate motivations of her protagonists as they function as part of a small, isolated society.

D. H. Lawrence, who was a great admirer of Deledda's prose, detected this aspect of her novels. In his introduction to the translation of *La madre* he applauded her ability to sound the depths of the Sardinian psyche. "She does more than just reproduce the transitory psychological positions of her age. She has real underpinnings and deals with something more fundamental than sophisticated sentimentality . . . what she really does is create the passionate complex of a primitive mass" (18). Also, there are those critics who truly appreciate Deledda's psychological acumen; some have correctly pointed out (albeit in passing) that her men are weak and ineffectual.[116] But no one to date has examined in depth the complex motivations of those men who protagonize her works and how the women in their lives form a psychologically perfect fit with those men. Deledda had an innate grasp of and ability to penetrate human nature vis-à-vis male/female relationships[117]—what Elisabetta Rasy calls the "the terrain of unexplored psychological dynamics."[118] Rasy's is almost the same notion that causes Arnaldo Fratelli to comment on Deledda's ability to identify and describe psychological states. He finds an unequalled "scientific rigor" in her writing.[119]

Deledda forces her reader to deal continually with the evolution of male/female interaction where profound psychological dramas occur mostly with the men of her novels whose motivations are driven by a destructive emotional neediness which ironically makes their women love them even more passionately. Deledda explores complicated pathologies and interdependencies, and one way to examine these issues is with the help of modern clinical psychology which elucidates the very characters and situations created so accurately by Deledda over a century ago.

2

The Syndrome of Arrested Maturation

"Avevo più di cinquant'anni ed ero come Peter Pan che si ac-
cingeva a rientrare in volo dalla finestra per rimettersi a letto."
(*Lieto Fine* Francesca Duranti)[1]

[I was over fifty and I was like Peter Pan who was getting
ready to fly home through the window in order to go to bed.]

THE PATHOLOGY

WHEN CRITICS ARE NOT TRYING TO FIND A PLACE FOR DELEDDA
among nineteenth- and twentieth-century literary movements,
most interpreters of her work center on the Deleddan protagonists' need to expiate their sins and find spiritual redemption.
They are correct; for this major theme is present in most of her
best novels; and the notion comprises a large part of her themat-
ics in general. At the same time, however, much more transpires
in her prose than just the process and resolution of moral dilem-
mas. There is another important dimension to her work, the facet
that examines the failure to grow up and face life accountably,
the psychological flaw typically responsible for those thematic,
moral problems. Just as it did in the lives of her brothers, adolescent (mis)behavior on the part of male adults occurs in all of
Deledda's novels, and in many short stories as well, a *motif* that
the agile reader can count upon to reappear with regularity. And
when it occurs over and over in every single work, it looms large
indeed as an overarching building block of Deledda's prose.

Writing a century ago, Grazia Deledda's inchoate understanding of the syndrome of arrested maturation indeed makes her a
sort of "miner's canary" in Italian literature. She addresses important psychological issues that do not come up again for almost
a century after her first attempts at fiction. Surely her interest in
this matter is the partial result of the fact that while in Sardinia

she was rarely out of the house, neither as a child nor later as a young writer eager to experience what life had to offer. This social deprivation may have honed her powers of observation, along with a braiding of her talent and ambition. What she knew best about human behavior was from firsthand experience learned initially at home where outside visitors, her father's clients, and especially her brothers provided the vivid model.[2] In later life her earliest notions about men were substantiated by marriage and a more well rounded, mature, social experience.

At the very beginning of *Cosima*, Deledda describes her brother Andrea as one who disdains the intellectual life, but prefers to be a shepherd (one suspects much as Marie Antoinette was a shepherdess). As such Deledda re-envisions him on horseback and calls him "an adolescent centaur" (700). It is understandable that Grazia Deledda, sheltered as she was, had her brothers as main models for her male protagonists; in her youth they were among the few men she knew closely and saw behave in everyday situations. So when she presents us with the rich array of juveniles who protagonize her fictive world, it is a certainty that Santus and Andrea Deledda provided the prototype. But her husband, Palmiro Madesani, also reaffirmed her intuitive notions on the maturity of the men she knew best. From the beginning of their whirlwind courtship, she conceived of him as a baby. In a letter to her fiancè, dated 5 December 1899, Deledda writes, "I always feel you close to me; I always see your sweet eyes and your kind smile, the handsome cleft of your chin . . . and I hear your voice and I remember your mouth, fresh and pure like a baby's." She promises that after they are married, "I will devote to you the sweet affection of a mother, sister, friend. You are my dear Palmiro, my beloved baby." On at least two other occasions she likened his mouth to "a baby's," and then referred to him as "my beloved little boy."[3] Later in life she wrote, "My husband is like a boy, still so handsome" (Balducci, 1). In a letter to her son written during her final illness, Grazia Deledda wrote of her husband, "Papa has returned, fresh and sprightly as a small boy" (Balducci 191). Judging at least from the undeniably autobiographical nature of her life's work, one indeed suspects that her husband was just like a boy in many other ways as well, much as were Deledda's two brothers: indulged sons of well-to-do, cold and distant parents, raised without responsibilities or accountability for their actions.

Some of the other men whom she observed in her days at the olive press were even worse than her brothers and husband.

When she parades before us the astounding array of juveniles who protagonize her fictive world, surely it was Santus's friends (and later the wide spectrum of their cohort) who inspired her as well. In another context Massaiu presents a list of examples of the societal misfits from Deledda's prose. He mentions a whole gamut of hapless and unheroic heroes, dispossessed and disenfranchised protagonists from her *fiction*; significantly the last one he mentions is Santus Deledda, who of course is not a fictive protagonist at all but the author's flesh and blood prototype (109).

It is inaccurate to dwell only on the misfits whom Deledda observed. For she also came into daily contact with numerous men from a sweeping cross-section of society. Her father hosted numberless guests in the Deledda home. These respectable, socially upstanding visitors interacted with the entire Deledda family; the young writer had close contact with these individuals as well. There is no doubt that Deledda's novels are in part based on events and people in her life in general.[4] Deledda had an innate grasp of the problem; and her natural expertise was acquired without so much as one course in psychology. Clearly Deledda's intuition and depictions are *dal vivo*, and her men seem to be a faithful reflection of her Sardinian experience.[5]

To be sure, she may have made her occasional observations on the men in her life in a most off-handed way.[6] Nevertheless it becomes difficult to dismiss the perhaps not so nonchalant comments when one remembers that the juvenile traits she mentions time and again in her private correspondence are shared by almost every one of her fictive, male characters.[7]

Known to psychologists sometimes as "borderline adulthood," and more colloquially as the "Peter Pan" syndrome, the mostly incurable problem of arrested maturation predominantly afflicts the adult male who exhibits some, many, or all of the characteristics elucidated throughout this section.[8] As with any syndrome, the ensemble of symptoms has its own dynamic. So that while anyone—man, woman, child, adult—can exhibit individual symptoms (narcissism, for example), when a preponderance of the identified symptoms come together, they conspire to form an altogether different problem. There is rarely a case of arrested maturation where the sufferer exhibits every symptom (although most people think they know one personally). This is true of any syndrome, psychological or biological.[9] One cannot reduce a syndrome to a checklist of traits; yet exhibiting a number of recognized characteristics is strongly indicative of a serious problem. This is true as well with Deledda's protagonists. There is never a victim with all the characteristics. Yet some come very close.[10]

PARENTAL PROBLEMS

Arrested maturation besets grown men who are usually the sons of relative privilege and who, ironically, grow up in loneliness (Kiley, *Peter* 94). Usually the victim is the oldest male in a traditional family. Parented by well-to-do but cold and emotionally detached mothers and often harsh and equally absent and "remote" fathers (like the Deledda parents), early in their teen years these adult-adolescents fail to grow up, to mature and assume adult responsibilities. As boys they feel unloved by parents who typically shower them with money in place of love.

Nancy Leffert and Anne Petersen point out that "authoritarian (or autocratic) parents tend to provide strict discipline (or demandingness) without offering much warmth or conceding psychological autonomy. Indulgent parents express love but little control and practice laissez-faire decision-making. Indifferent parents are deficient in all areas; their offspring have the worst outcomes" (18).[11] The key word among most authorities is "warmth," the lack of which carries serious consequences. For as adults these immature men almost never value themselves or their work. No one ever told them they have intrinsic merit. They almost always lack a strong identity and sense of their own "presence;" they rarely experience feelings of self-worth that come with a warm, nurturing environment rather than a cold and distancing one. The grown man suffering from arrested maturation never learned from his parents' example what it means to love someone else; consequently he does not love himself, believe in himself, or listen to himself. In turn, he never learned to love others, believe in others, or really listen to them, as mature adults are normally expected to do (Kiley, *Peter* 36–39).

Presaging today's research, many of Deledda's men have similar problems with their mothers and fathers. Deledda knew firsthand about distant parents and of the child's perceived lack of their love. Her own well-to-do parents were cool, undemonstrative and clearly not in love with each other in the desirable ways that might otherwise have provided an ambience of warmth, psychological security and reassurance to the children. Theirs was most certainly one of those numerous, epochal, marriages of convenience; the businesslike atmosphere in the Deledda household also underlined the parents' emotional distance from their children. In the case of the patriarch it was not simply a matter of remoteness. Giovanni Antonio Deledda could also be brutally harsh and cruel to his sons (while he mostly ignored his daughters). In a particular instance, one cannot help but sympathize with the troublesome Andrea. As Deledda recounts in *Cosima*, when Andrea was sixteen his father caught him with his hand in the family till. In forcing him to admit to his thievery, the elder Deledda threatened to hang him on the spot. He was not posturing. When the boy still refused to admit to stealing the money, his tyrannical father literally strung a noose on one of the rafters of the family home and screamed, "Ti impiccherò con le mie mani" [I'll hang you with my own hands] (951). The juvenile Andrea confessed.

To judge from their behavior as young adults, Grazia's two older brothers seem emotionally to have suffered the most from the generally frigid aura of the Deledda home.[12] In fact, through the venerable Efix of *Canne al vento*, Deledda voices a partial explanation for this syndrome.

> Il ragazzo a me non sembra cattivo: È stato finora mal guidato; ha perduto i genitori nel peggior tempo per lui, ed è rimasto come un bambino solo nella strada e s'è perduto (124).

> [The boy doesn't seem to me to be bad: up to now he has been raised badly; his parents died at the worst time for him, and he remained like a child alone in the streets, and he got lost.]

Efix hits the mark; for part of the problem is indeed one of a lack of appropriate parenting, and Grazia Deledda writes knowledgeably of those parental problems. One prime example is from *Colombi e sparvieri*, where by page fifty Jorgj has already been sulking in self-indulgence for five chapters. We then learn that he too was unloved, orphaned of his mother's nurturing, and essentially obliged to raise himself.

> Ero un monellaccio, non lo nego, ma nessuno badava a me se non per maltrattarmi. Mi par di rivedermi ancora fanciullo in questa tana che non era squallida come lo è adesso; mi aggiravo sempre in cerca di qualche cosa, sollevando con la testa il coperchio della cassa, arrampicandomi sugli sgabelli per guardare cosa c'era nell'armadio; e rivedo nel vano della porta la tragica figura della mia matrigna, gialla e nera in viso come nei vestiti. . . . Eterna storia di tutti i fanciulli abbandonati a sè stessi! Io provavo dolore, umiliazione, dispetto, e pensavo

solo al modo di poter guadagnare qualche cosa per sottrarmi alle ingiurie della mia nemica. . . . Mio padre rientrava, parlava del fitto della tanca, del contadino che voleva i denari; parlava delle capre, delle vacche, del servo che guardava l'ovile; di tutto fuor che di me (50).

[I was a street urchin. I don't deny it; but no one ever paid attention to me, except to mistreat me. I can still see myself as a boy in this lair which wasn't so filthy as it is now. I was always rummaging around in search of something, lifting the cover of the chest with my head, climbing up on the stools to look at what was in the wardrobe; and I can still see in the doorway the tragic figure of my stepmother, yellow and black both in her face and in her clothing. . . . The eternal story of all children left to fend for themselves. I felt pain, humiliation, spite, and I only thought about the way in which I could earn some money to get myself out from under the abuses of my enemy. . . . My father used to come home and talk about the rent for the grazing grounds, about the farmer who wanted his money; he spoke about the goats and the cows and about the worker who watched over the sheep—about everything but me.]

Through Jorgj Deledda explores two of the main components of parental nonfeasance: abandoning the child to loneliness and establishing a distance and remoteness rather than a close bond. In his childhood Jorgj suffered more than most of Deledda's characters. He lived in filth with a nasty stepmother and essentially raised himself without knowing how. Jorgj is an exceptional example of the results of extreme child neglect; most other protagonists are the victims of more subtle parental abuse. In the novel whose title bears his name, Elias Portolu's father, for example, is a forceful, autocratic, intimidating blowhard. His sons are the greatest; he has the most money of anyone; he is the bravest and strongest of all the men he knows; he brandishes his knife with ease and regularity; he knows the price of everything and the value of nothing. In some ways (as with Deledda's brother, Andrea), Elias's puerile behavior is not surprising when one considers his brutish father. This big talker's lack of love for his son is evident in the humiliating way he berates the sensitive Elias. He accuses him of not being a man; he likens him to a "blob of unripened cheese;" he reminds him how weak he is in the presence of the first "air-headed woman" who comes along.[13]

When Elias is at his most miserable, his father ratchets up the torment. Again he questions his manhood and compares him to a "twig of straw," a "hunk of cow's milk cheese."[14] Obtusely insensitive to Elias's illness, the father continues with the advice to

either get better or to die because he does not want weaklings in
his presence; he wants "to see lions, eagles and you are a lizard"
(83). Elias's father constantly derides him for being a *femminuccia* [a little woman], for not being strong and masculine. He has
a decided predilection for cheese metaphors as well.

> Un uomo di caccio fresco sei diventato tu, Elias figlio mio. Eccolo che
> diventa pallido come una femminuccia per ogni piccola cosa. Uomini
> bisogna essere, uomini, leoni; non commuoversi, non cambiar viso,
> non piangere. Cosa è un uomo che piange? È un corno (66).

> [Elias, my son, you've become a man made of unripened cheese. You
> become as pale as a little woman over nothing. A man!! You need to
> be a man, a lion; never get emotional, don't ever change expression,
> never cry. What's a man who cries? He's a cuckold!]

The elder Portolu surely epitomizes the requisite "harsh and
remote" father of Kiley's description of the syndrome. His constant belittling of Elias ensures a son who will never love or believe in himself.[15] As such Elias becomes an adult who cannot love
and trust others. At a later point in the novel, there are hints that
Elias might be slowly growing up, breaking away from his father,
becoming his own man. Crying from desperation, he is still trying
to please his father. Elias remembers that his father always ad-
monished him that only "vile men cry" and that "Sardinians
don't cry;" but then he gives in to his emotions "because it feels
so good." By contradicting his father's folk wisdom, Elias is forging his own truths; for an instant he is his own person. Unfortunately for his well-being, he does not engage in these self-edifying
activities often enough.

When Elias vacillates between resuming his affair with his
brother's wife, Maddalena, or continuing on his path in the religious life, the fear of his father's predictable reaction (if he knew
the truth) is enough to petrify him. He fears his father would
murder him, that he would "squash [him] under his foot like a
spider" (122). Elias's lack of self-confidence is directly traceable
to his overpowering father; for clearly someone taught Elias to
consider himself nothing more than a lowly insect.

In *Cenere*, as a young adult Anania Sr.—the irresponsible
father—established the juvenile male model for his namesake,
Anania Jr. As a youth he impregnated Olì, a woman other than
his wife; and then he abandoned her and his child (Anania Jr.).
He is an undependable, capricious dreamer who is forever search-

ing for buried treasure. Anania Sr. at first refuses to take responsibility for his son when Anania Jr. comes to live with his father
and his father's spouse. If it were not for his saintly wife who insists they take in his abandoned, illegitimate child, Anania Jr.
would be left completely to his own devices.[16] The father then
mistreats him, humiliates him in public, and never shows him a
a jot of affection. Like Elias's father with his emotional abuse,
Anania Sr. helps to create in Anania Jr. the typical adult-adolescent son who finds it difficult to love others because he has been
offered no reason to love himself. When this psychological situation occurs, there often ensues a complex, snowball effect whereupon the victim rarely emerges as a sentient, mature human
being. He in turn provides that flawed model for his sons and the
vicious circle remains unbroken.

NARCISSISM

It is widely agreed among modern psychologists that the syndrome of arrested maturation revolves around the concept of narcissism. The narcissistic personality disorder, as described by the
Diagnostic and Statistical Manual of Mental Disorders, applies to
one who has a grandiose sense of self-importance which typically
calls back to a need to belong. The victim needs admiration from
friends; he needs to "fit" with others. Erik Erikson recalls
Freud's original notion that the sources "of human self-esteem
are the residue of childish narcissism, i.e. the child's natural self-
love.[17] But if a healthy residue of infantile narcissism is to sur-
vive, the maternal environment must create and sustain it with a
love which assures the child that it is good to be alive in the social
coordinates in which he happens to find himself."[18] On the contrary, the result of an upbringing based on parental distancing
and perceived lack of love is that the victim not only engages in
almost complete narcissism beyond adolescence, but is forever
ambivalent toward his mother; he wants to pull free from her in
an adult way, but boyishly he feels guilty; tension with his mother
causes swings between sarcasm toward her and random, unpredictable acts of tenderness. He is equally estranged from his
father whom ironically he idolizes. He has learned that he can
never earn his father's love and approval, and this leads to problems with authority figures in his adulthood (Kiley, *Peter* 93).
    Clearly the linchpin of all modern research on arrested matura-
tion is narcissism; and if they are anything, above all Deledda's

protagonists are narcissistic. Self-centered, arrogant and filled with their own importance, most of her primary male figures doubtless could edify the "me generation of the late twentieth century." Bellia, for example, a young man from one of Deledda's later novels, *Il dio dei viventi* [The God of the Living], more than exemplifies his fellow Deleddan predecessors.

> Bellia è un giovane animale, fondamentalmente egoista: uno di quegli esseri che, per aver sempre avuto tutto e per sapere che tutto possono avere, poca o nessuna pietà riescono a concepire per gli altri, per gli infelici, per coloro che non hanno nulla. Idolatrato dai genitori, ricco erede, privo di problemi e di scrupoli (133–34).

> [Bellia is a fundamentally egotistical young buck: one of those people who, having always had everything handed to them and knowing that they can have everything, succeed in having little or no empathy for others, for the unfortunate, for those who have nothing. Idolized by his parents, he is a wealthy heir, devoid of both problems and scruples.]

Deledda creates a young man raised by well-to-do parents with all the advantages of a life of privilege, save one—the feeling of being loved. This lack of affection translates into his own inability to love himself and others; and it ushers in for him all of the attendant problems of narcissism, especially the need to focus only on himself.

In yet an earlier (and much better) novel, *Elias Portolu*, Deledda presents the unforgettably exasperating protagonist who must have the best of both worlds. Elias would like for his ex-lover, Maddalena, not to remarry but to remain his brother's widow so that he, Elias (now a priest), can help to raise the son he incestuously fathered with her while his brother was still alive. To deprive Maddalena's new suitor, Jacu Farre, of the opportunity of raising Elias's baby, Elias actually hopes "for the death of [his] own son" (170). Unable to empathize with anyone including his own terminally ill baby, for Elias this tragic situation is only about himself. His son's death promises to liberate him from his obsessive jealousy. His narcissism will have left in its wake one deceased baby and a devastated widow bereft of her only child; but for Elias the payoff is his own mental health and well-being. In the end, only that matters and only that will satisfy him.

The son dies, and Elias finds peace. The last paragraph of the novel is a testimony to his self-centrality; Elias is elated because now no one can take away his baby, "no one could ever come between them" (172). Astonishingly, for Elias the expendable boy is better dead, as long as Elias's motivations for jealousy have died with him. Along with his freedom from jealousy, he feels settling over him "un velo di pace, quasi di gioia" [a veil of peace, almost of joy] (172). Even at the conclusion of the novel, in his psychological immaturity Elias still fails to recognize the moral consequences of his actions, except as they relate to his personal needs.

In the eyes of his mentor and confidant, *zio* Martinu, Elias is a self-indulgent, poor excuse of a man.[19] He convinces *zio* Martinu to accompany him to the confessional where he intends to make peace with God; but on the way to see the priest, Elias vacillates between stopping to tryst with his lover, Maddalena, or going straight to the church. An incredulous *zio* Martinu can only question rhetorically "what kind of a man" Elias is (127). Elias returns from his confession with a (temporary) zeal to reform and a renewed determination to forget Maddalena. He tells *zio* Martinu that he has decided definitively to be a priest. He is emotionally invigorated; and in his usual self-indulgence, he does not even stop to thank *zio* Martinu for dedicating his entire day to taking Elias to see the priest. As though they were two distant acquaintances who had just met by chance, Elias flippantly indicates that he might see *zio* Martinu around, and then saunters off to indulge himself even further. *Zio* Martinu is pessimistic about Elias's plan to function effectively as a man of the cloth.[20] And his skepticism is fully warranted. For Elias never does lose his exaggerated sense of self-importance.

Hand in glove with the concept of narcissism, it is symptomatic of arrested maturation to want to be the center of attention.[21] The immature man demands (and gets) everyone's focus. Everything must revolve around him; all issues are about him. This symptom was not lost on Deledda. In *Colombi e sparvieri*, when the physician who comes to treat him also pays some polite attention to Marianna, the bedridden protagonist, Jorgj, becomes jealous. "Gli pareva che quei due si dimenticassero di lui" [It seemed to him that those two were forgetting all about him] (164).[22] Deledda subtly alludes to Jorgj's immature craving for attention; she conceives of a boyish individual who in his self-absorption really believes that he is the epicenter of other people's lives.

PEER ORIENTED

Kiley explains that these emotionally immature men, motivated by a sense of self-preservation, learn quickly as boys to be peer-oriented, to turn from their absent parents to search for love instead among their friends. L. Joseph Stone and Joseph Church believe that the normal "adolescent is still very much dependent upon other people to tell him what he is and where he stands" (84).[23] Following that notion, Petersen writes that in "youths with weak family ties, there is much more risk for negative peer influence" (20). Yet despite that risk of delinquency, the pursuit of other people's acceptance is the only way to achieve a sense of self-acceptance. Existing in a kind of perpetual, emotional embargo, the victim craves love, a scarce commodity for him throughout his childhood. He can never get enough and spends most of his efforts looking for it. That practice continues into adulthood. The victims of this syndrome turn to coeval friendship (typically in the form of "nights out with the boys") for the love and secure identity that eluded them as children. They are unduly influenced (almost driven) by friends' decisions, opinions, and desires—not by their own convictions, of which usually they have few, not having had in their childhood an adult model by which to mature. The normal adult has a strong identity which obviates the necessity for external definition from friends; this is not so for men of prolonged adolescence.[24]

For Deledda's men, this state lasts forever; whereas for a normal adolescent headed for a well-adjusted adulthood, there comes a time to put aside emotional dependence upon friends and parents and become one's own person. Characteristically the victim of arrested maturation wants only to be accepted by the gang. He much prefers his male friends to female company; from same-sex acquaintances he seeks the affection and approval that his parents never gave him; he thinks he can find in his external relationships the close family love that he never had as a youth. Many of Deledda's men follow this pattern, and her women suffer from the results of the symdrome.

In *Marianna Sirca* Deledda creates a romantic bandit, Simone Sole, the dashing, illicit lover of Marianna; but Marianna wants him to give up his life of crime so that they can marry. She delivers an ultimatum: he must function as a law-abiding citizen or their relationship is over. Typical of one suffering from truncated development, when the threat registers on him, Simone thinks only of the reaction of his male hero and role model, Bantine

Fera, the celebrated bandit of the notorious Barbagia region. Simone is more concerned with what Bantine will think than with Marianna's warning. Fiercely attached to his friends, Simone wants only to be one of the "boys." He seeks the approval he never had at home; he needs peer acceptance more than he needs her. Notably, he will always go against his woman's wishes to please his male friends (who rarely live up to anyone's mature definition of *real* friendship). When he thinks of Bantine's reaction, he cannot make a commitment to Marianna.[25]

Bantine Fera had already scorned Simone for being too lovesick to join his fearsome band of robbers. Ever the adolescent, Simone does not want to risk the further contempt of his peers for being a sissy; his only grip on an identity of his own is in the acceptance of his idol's wishes. A third party talks to Marianna about Simone:

Per fingere anche a sè stesso che è forte, ha tirato fuori la solita scusa: che non sapeva cosa si faceva, ch'era ammaliato, che tu lo avevi ammaliato, ma che ora vuol essere forte, libero, generoso. Perchè Bantine Fera ha abbandonato una donna . . . anche lui ti abbandona. E ti ama, Marianna! . . . Ma egli vuole imitare Bantine Fera; ed egli esagera; per imitarlo, gli corre davanti come il cane corre davanti al cavallo (848).

[To pretend even to himself that he is strong, he dredged up the usual excuses: that he didn't know what was going on, that he was bewitched, that you [Marianna] had entranced him, but that now he wants to be strong, free, generous. Because Bantine had abandoned a woman . . . he too is leaving you. He loves you, Marianna! . . . But he wants to imitate Bantine Fera; and he goes to extremes; to imitate him he precedes him like a dog trots ahead of a horse.]

Simone will do anything to be one of the boys, to be part of the group, to be recognized as "one of them." He wants their approbation, yet he also wants to wait for a final answer from Marianna. To do that he must delay joining the bandits; he needs an excuse, so he childishly resorts to playing sick (849). He tries not to think about Marianna, because Bantine once said that it was a sign of weakness (849). At a certain point in the novel Simone and Costantino, his best friend and fellow bandit, crouch side by side by the fire in their hideout (a cave which lacks only a "No Girls Allowed" sign scrawled on the door), "piccoli e trepidi come uccellini nel nido" [small and trembling like little birds in their nest] (766).This is where Simone feels most comfortable, in a hideaway with one of the gang, basking in peer approval.

Peer-oriented men are often promisers who cannot deliver on their pledges. Usually they take on obligations to women, but then have to renege on their commitments to please their male friends. Consequently, their relationships with women deteriorate. In *Marianna Sirca* Simone eventually promises to do what Marianna asked (to give himself up, to take his punishment, and then to marry her); but instead he causes her to be vilified and ridiculed by everyone; he abandons her without explanation. He does it all to please his presumed friend, Bantine. Costantino reproaches him:

> Solo perchè un prepotente malfattore ti ha detto che è vergogna amare una donna e rimanere con lei; sì, sì, l'hai abbandonata senza dirle niente, perchè è da molto che tu l'hai abbandonata, col pensiero, e lei credeva d'essere ancora con te e invece era sola e tu correvi a fare il male col tuo compagno . . . e neppure hai avuto il coraggio di andare a dirle la verità" (852).

> [Just because a bullying delinquent told you it is shameful to love a woman and stay with her. Yes, yes, you abandoned her without explanation long ago in your mind, and she believed you were still together, but instead she was alone and you ran off to commit crimes with your pal . . . and you didn't even have the courage to go and tell her the truth.]

Simone knows Costantino is right but he is filled with hate toward everyone. So the ever-juvenile Simone hits Costantino with a live coal to silence him; he then goes off on his own to sulk in an adolescent rage.

Wastrels

As adults, men afflicted with arrested maturation are typically spendthrifts. From the negative example of the parental model, they learned young to purchase the attention and (they think) love of their friends with lavish gifts, with wanton spending sprees, and with acts of largesse and extravagance. For these individuals the pursuit of others' acceptance is the only means to self-acceptance, the only way to procure an identity. Consequently they are easily led by their peers. They will spend prodigious amounts of money to maintain what they believe is a friendship.

They have a desperate need to belong. But their longings for peer approval transfer to adulthood and often lead to financial mayhem, as they engage in an impetuous and prodigal lifestyle of pure self-indulgence. Their only satisfaction is the pseudo-love of their purchased friendships. For this reason, they need to party; participation in group activities becomes for them a public validation of their sense of belonging.

Along the same lines, they are addicted to the instant pleasure of their impulsive whims. Gerard Fountain discusses "the adolescent's need for immediate gratification." He points out that the typical adolescent "has not yet learned to postpone" and has an "inability to tolerate frustration" (for example in being defeated in a game). Fountain observes that the normal adolescent, upon becoming a normal adult, "can appraise with accuracy his own behavior and that of others and can begin to live as if he is a member of the world and not merely of a small corner of it" (209).[26] This is not so for the adult of truncated development. And neither is it so for Deledda's men. For along with their moral, civic, and social irresponsibility, often Deledda's protagonists are wastrels, spendthrifts, and gamblers (almost always with other people's money). Mario Miccinesi describes some of Deledda's men and their adolescent need to spend money without regard to the consequences.

> He is addicted to vice which consists generally of drinking, spending large amounts of money gambling or on women, above all on holidays, in a relaxed atmosphere that further weakens his ability to resist the temptation to be imprudent, to let himself go, to always choose the easiest and least onerous path. In Deledda's male characters there is often a kind of propensity toward self-destruction, almost as though it had an obscure fascination for them which is almost impossible to resist. There is self-abandonment to the bitter pleasure of ruin and at the same time the desperate desire to derive enjoyment from all aspects of life when there is nothing left to assure his salvation (52).

In an early work, *Il tesoro* [The Treasure], Cosimo is an ineffectual, undependable figure who is a precursor of the major examples of exaggerated behavior in Deledda's later novels. He is a gambler, a drinker, and a spendthrift who finds himself in serious financial trouble. Rather than commit suicide (one of the options he considers), he claims a three thousand *lire* bounty to pay off his debts, considered a pusillanimous and unscrupulous act even for a desperate man. He realizes that he is a weakling and he despairs of it.[27] To his credit, however, with all his faults Cosimo does take a momentary, moral stock of his misdeeds. Not every Deleddan character does that. Consider, for example, Paulu of *L'edera*. He is a spendthrift like no other, a peer-oriented promiser who cannot deliver and who lacks any sense of decency or responsibility. Sarale describes him.

> There is an air of decadence, of destruction, that hovers over all of them, and in the face of which no one seems to have the will to react. Paulu is an addict absolutely incapable of keeping himself from spending money, especially when he is with his friends. He constantly makes promises that never get kept; he lacks the minimum sense of responsibility, not only toward the older people, but even toward a hydrocephalic daughter of his whom he had with his late wife, Kallina, dead for some time now (64).

If Paulu is one of the prototypes, his literary "first cousin" appears in *La danza della collana* [The Dance of the Necklace], where the *Conte* [Count] spends his family money with no regard to his family obligations. As his girlfriend, Maria, describes him, he is just a "rich kid" who has nothing to do but "spend his parents' money" while he waits for "a high paying sinecure" (139). But Giacinto of *Canne al vento* goes the *Conte* one better. A braggart and a blusterer, he gambles his aunts's money away; and when he bleeds them almost dry, by forging their name on a promisory note, he then borrows money from a notorious usurer at the unconscionable interest rate of 1000 percent. Typically he lavishes gifts on everyone he meets with high interest money; to others he makes promises he will never keep.

SELF-ENTITLED: PROMISERS AND CHARMERS

Narcissism has an array of collateral effects; the peer orientation, prodigious spending, and dissipation discussed here are but a few of them.[28] Another important manifestation is a sense of self-entitlement. "The narcissist needs others to admire him; he needs others to provide ideals and values he did not integrate into his childhood; and he needs others to act as chums, to create a sense that he fits into the community. Everyone has these needs; the issue is how they are satisfied, whether through substantial relationships or superficial ones. Narcissists do best if they are charming—which is why they often make fine politicians."[29] Narcissism brings with it a sort of side effect which is an exaggerated sense of having something "coming to him." The victim truly believes himself to be special and deserving of favorable treatment. He is usually one who takes full advantage of others. He is arrogant. Dalsimer points out that normally during adolescence the childhood ties to parents are in the process of being relinquished, "but new bonds have not yet been consolidated." There ensues "a period of transition in which an enlarged self-preoccupation must substitute—temporarily and partially—for relations with others." Normally "the propensity of young persons to magnify themselves ordinarily subsides in time, as the withdrawal into the self yeilds to the establishment of new ties outside the family" (Dalsimer 7–8). With the boy who fails to mature, however, the self-magnification never does subside. It continues to flourish into adulthood where it can and usually does lead to a kind of narcissistic despair.

In many cases Deledda's men feel automatically entitled to all the world has to offer, and as such they take advantage of others without a trace of empathy. They use the device of a promise or a commitment coupled with a certain fey, endearing quality which they have learned to use effectively, especially with women. Not just a few of Deledda's men are promisers and charmers who manipulate women with impunity, and their relationships with their wives and girlfriends deteriorate accordingly. In *L'edera* Paulu is an unemployed, heavy drinker who time after time promises to change, not to drink anymore, and to find a job. But Annessa knows that his promises are worthless and that he will never willingly seek gainful employment (133). Naturally he never does change; he never stops drinking; he never gets a job. And in the end, Annessa is right to be wary of his promises; he never keeps them.

In *Canne al vento* Giacinto too makes promises that he will not want to keep, including that of marrying Grixenda. When his mentor, Efix, tells him he must marry her to save the family fortune, Giacinto protests at length against being held to his word. Marianna Sirca, on the other hand, knows better than to really believe Simone when he promises to return to her. She is aware that he has never kept his word. Eventually she becomes exasperated by what she considers his empty promises. Indeed, his friend Costantino Moro comes secretly to tell Marianna Sirca that the fugitive Simone cannot fulfill his promise. She knew it all along.

So many of Deledda's men are irresistably appealing and personable; and so many of their women find them boyishly cute. The symbiotic nature of their mutual attraction is the source of their eventual problems. Consider once again Giacinto of *Canne al vento*. Even his archenemy, *zia* Noemi, is seduced by his magic; his charisma can (and does) get him through all of his delinquent behavior; and he knows it. When she looks at this captivating, enchanting good-for-nothing, all the bad things he has done disappear in her mind "per lasciar posto all'immagine di lui buono, pentito, appassionato" . [to give way to the image of him as good, repentant, passionate] (144). *Zia* Noemi has been a hard nut for Giacinto to crack, but even she is as duped and conned as everyone else by this seductive ne'er-do-well's ability to endear himself. Giacinto is such an operator that women fall all over themselves in a spirited competition to nurture and mother him. When they gather at the flour mill where eventually he is forced to work, they look at him with "a mother's eyes" (198). In *La madre*, when Paulo can no longer stand to listen to Agnese's correct reasoning, he kisses her to stop the flow of her unbearable words (112). He deflects her logical arguments by using his allure and his sexual wiles; he manipulates her knowing how much she craves him physically, how she finds him so appealing, and how easily she can be seduced by his personal charisma.

IRRESPONSIBILITY

In *The Wendy Dilemma* Kiley observes that the narcissist cannot feel empathy or give love. "Exploitation of others for personal gain characterizes the narcissist's pattern of living" (199). He thinks only of himself; he lacks any affective emotional connection with others; he never puts himself into someone else's place. Leffert and Petersen discuss how in normal adolescence one "learns to form meaningful relationships with others" (8). The parent–child rapport is crucial to this capacity; unfortunately in the case of the adolescent-adult, the parent–child paradigm typically is nonexistent. At times the victim is in emotional paralysis from his inability to express love, joy, disappointment, or sadness. He is so self-centered that he is unable to share his feelings. He is socially impotent; he cannot make true friends.

The main cause of their failure to come of age is fear of manhood and its responsibilities. As an antidote to their despair, as adults these men long for their carefree school days. In their adulthood they remain the insouciant boys of their pre-teens, like walking time capsules of their youthful selves. Anecdotal evidence shows that in some cases even the physical characteristics of adolescence, such as teenage acne, can erupt in full adulthood during an adult-adolescent's fit of pique; thus the mental and physical aspects of the syndrome actually sometimes dovetail, evincing tangible evidence of the seriousness of this problem.

Dalsimer reminds us that "Adolescence is a period of widened possibilities and of experimentation with alternatives, before the individual narrows the range of what is possible by making those commitments which will define adulthood" (5). Grazia Deledda's characters rarely do that on their own. While they engage in a great deal of experimentation, they never come out of that adolescence where they continually test *inappropriate* "alternatives." They never focus on their possibilities; they never make those necessary commitments which will define their adulthood. To a large extent Deledda's men have no self-accountability; they are undependable. As Mario Miccinesi has said of Paulu in *L'edera*, he is lacking in that "minimum sense of responsibility" (49). Paulu is reliably unreliable. Even at the very end of the novel, old and decrepit, he remains unchanged. "Durante tutti quegli anni aveva sempre continuato a vivere di ozio, di imbrogli, di vizi" [During all those years he had always continued to live in idleness, by swindling people, by vices] (221). Even after an entire life of misadventures, Paulu never does grow up. He never experiences an adult existence.

Elias Portolu is no different. Toward the climactic resolution of this gripping story (after his brother has died leaving Maddalena widowed and Elias's baby ostensibly "orphaned"), in his self-absorption Elias somehow overlooks the fact that he is now responsible for his child. He fails to recognize that Maddalena comprises only half of the morally guilty duo.[30] He never realizes that his spiritual fight with the devil may not be the only problem in this world, and that he owes it to Maddalena to care for her and for their son. Instead he decides it is better for his own mental health not to get too close to them emotionally, "altrimenti mi perdo ancora, e adesso più che mai" [otherwise I'll be even more lost, and now more than ever] (153). As those of other novels, this protagonist just wants to leave and abdicate his responsibilities.[31]

Much like his narrative twin Elias, Paulo of *La madre* has trouble facing his awful destiny as an adult. Instead he sits forlornly on the church steps, waiting for someone to come to help him (123). This is a grown man who is pastor of a church—a pillar of the community; yet, he crouches on the steps like a hapless, little boy. In *Canne al vento* Giacinto's outrageous conduct has brought about the eviction of his three elderly maiden aunts from their ancestral land and family home, along with a possible jail sentence for himself. When confronted with the consequences of his egregious behavior, Giacinto simply shrugs that he never *meant* to cause any trouble. The faithful servant, Efix, bluntly and impatiently tells him to get a job. Giacinto's astonished reaction is that he really expected to be bailed out once again. Like Paulo of *La madre* making himself small on the church steps, Giacinto too is waiting for someone to come and help him (98). (Years previously when he was living on the "continent," Giacinto had been rescued financially by the very kind and generous person whom he "repaid" by then stealing a larger sum of money from him.) Unaccustomed to living up to his responsibilities, he borrows yet another fifty *lire* to leave town, but on his way out he gambles it away in a card game!

In the short story, "La porta aperta" [The Open Door], from the collection, *Chiaroscuro* [Light and Shade], Simone Barca attributes all of his transgressions to the fact that his mother died (an imaginative twist on a man's sins being a woman's fault). He then emumerates for his father-confessor his many crimes and inevitably concludes that he will have to serve time in jail. But even while the priest ponders Simone's spiritual pennance, Simone is busy hoping that the priest will help him pay off a promissory note, thus getting him out of yet another jam of his own making.

When a man like Simone Barca remains a child forever, often those around him grow accustomed to treating him like a child, never really expecting him to leave the realm of adolescent irresponsibility. Ironically this both absolves him of obligations toward others, and it casts his relatives, friends, lovers, and acquaintances in the eternal role of protector and abetting caregiver. It is not the best solution; it is the worst, but it is the easiest way out for those who must live with the sufferer of arrested emotional development. It surely never accrues to the benefit of those around him who are left to pick up the pieces of his disasters and clean up his messes after he has absconded.[32] But this is precisely what happens to the women who choose their company.

DISAPPEARANCES

Adult-adolescents are experts at the cut-and-run: they usually vanish when trouble arises. Running away from serious problems often appears hand in glove with the character flaw of categorically denying responsibility. Mature adults know that eventually the piper must be paid, that solutions are not found in the act of disappearance; but Deledda's protagonists never learn that principle of life. They evince little ability to deal constructively with reality. For example, in *Canne al vento* Giacinto is the wastrel nephew who comes to town with the one goal of depleting his three maiden aunts' assets. After forging one of their names on a promissory note for the enormous sum of 2600 *lire*, Giacinto vanishes. His jilted fiancée, Grixenda, is desperate; his aunts are driven to the verge of bankruptcy; but as usual, when things get out of hand, he evanesces.[33]

In *Le colpe altrui* [The Faults of Others], Mikali wants to run away to America to be a cowboy, where (according to his understanding of America), men are free and without any restrictions. He wants his wife's blessing and permission to leave; she tells him that she cannot condone his decision to depart, that he has responsibilities; and she reminds him that he is the *paterfamilias* now. This mature reasoning confuses him; eventually she has to shake him up to get him to come to his senses.

A unique variation on vanishing appears in *Il segreto dell'uomo solitario* [The Secret of the Solitary Man], where Cristiano almost literally buries his head in the sand when he does not want to see Sarina. She is coming toward him as he lies on the beach; so he thrusts his face into the sand and squeezes his eyes shut "as children do to hide themselves" (470). And he is not alone. In *Canne al vento* when Efix sees someone he knows, but to whom he does not want to talk, he does much the same thing, shutting his eyes "like little boys when they want to hide" (218). In *La Chiesa della Solitudine* [The Church of Solitude], Maria tells Aroldo that she has had breast cancer and now has a disfiguring scar. He too holds his face like "a little boy who wanted to hide."[34]

In *La madre* Paulo entertains the idea of escaping from his small town parish to avoid being caught in the lurid sex scandal of his own making. He is under great pressure; for his lover, Agnese, intends to expose him publicly during Mass by walking to the front of the church and telling the entire congregation that they are lovers.

È bene svegliare mia madre, avvertirla, possibilmente partire assieme . . . che ella mi riporti una seconda volta con sè, come da bambino, e che io possa ricominciare una nuova vita (119–20).

[It is well to wake up Mother, to tell her, maybe to depart together . . . Oh, I wish that she would take me away again, like when I was a little boy, and that I could begin a new life.]

Deledda deploys every plausible, juvenile machination in her arsenal to depict a Paulo who has to face saying Mass under his lover's blackmailing stare from the back of the church. He thinks that he still might have time to avoid ignominy. He could pretend to be sick and not say Mass (121). When that childish solution seems impractical, Paulo measures out mentally the number of footsteps Agnese will have to take in order to put her threat into action. He concludes that when he sees her get up to accuse him, he will have time to escape (121). Paulo wants to pull the covers over his head, as though his physical absence from the breathtaking scene will make the whole sordid mess disappear (just as he, himself, would like to do).

THE MASTER OF ALIBI

The victim of arrested maturation is undependable; he is nowhere to be found when needed most. And when he is caught, he engages in endless "blame-a-thons" to mask his own shortcomings. "It's not my fault," is the mantra he recites as a first reaction in the face of trouble. In the minds of most of Deledda's typical men their problems are the responsibility of someone else or attributable to some external event. Above all Deledda's men are deniers; they are *never* to blame. They point fingers in all directions; patterns form in the choice of their scapegoats: women, demons, parents, and bad company are among the most prevalent. The passive Elias Portolu, for example, finds himself drawn inexorably to Maddalena "come una farfalla intorno alla fiamma" [like a moth to a flame] (104). He has no control over himself. He says he is is *ammaliato* [bewitched]; something external is the problem. He concludes irresponsibly that *il demonio* [the devil] is the one who tempts him (105). He blames his troubles on destiny.[35] He engages in all manner of adolescent rationalization to explain away what he thinks is beyond his control. In his mind Elias is dragged along by other forces; he is not directly accountable for his own behavior. He blames being "led into temptation" by parties, wine, and fun.[36]

There are many potential solutions to Elias's problems, but self-discipline is never an option for him. Whatever goes wrong is *never* the fault of the Deleddan male. In *La madre* as well, Paulo's failure is also someone else's responsibility.

Se avessi continuato a studiare sarei diventato qualche cosa, ma già mio padre, mia madre, i miei nonni, tutti, tutti hanno commesso un

grave errore cacciandomi in seminario. Ti ripeto sono rimasto un
bambino; tutto in me si è fermato nel meglio del suo sviluppo; sono
come quei frutti che si seccano prima di maturare (98).

[If I had continued with my studies, I could have made something of
myself, but—yes—my father, my mother, my grandparents, everyone, everyone made a serious mistake sticking me in the seminary. I
repeat to you, I remained a baby; everything in me stopped at the
prime of my maturation; I am like one of those fruits that dry up before they ripen.]

In his favor, Paulo does show a great deal of uncharacteristic
self-awareness in this instance; at least he acknowledges the
problem. He is immature; but few of his Deleddan fictive peers
share the rare insight of recognizing it. What is even more interesting is the way in which Deledda describes the problem. The
fruit simile is an effective one which is consonant with the lin-
guistically folksy, vernacular way in which she tells the story; but
underpinning the stylistic device is a sophisticated diagnosis of
Paulo's problems.

Elias Portolu shares maturity problems with Paulo. Speaking
of the predicament that landed him in prison, Elias swears that
he is, "innocente. I cattivi compagni mi avevano traviato, ed è
perchè praticavo con male compagnìe che sono stato travolto in
quella disgrazia" [innocent. Bad friends led me astray, and it is
because I hung around with bad company that I was caught up in
that mess] (21). Elias allows for no possibility that he, himself,
might bear some of the accountability for his own behavior.[37] It is
all his friends' fault; it is all the prison's fault. It never occurs to
Elias that he made clear choices which led to negative results,
that the blame should be placed within, not without.[38]

In the short story "La porta aperta," Simone Barca confesses
himself to a priest; he attributes his sins to the fact that as soon
as his mother died, he fell under the influence of others. "I cattivi
compagni mi hanno assediato come le mosche un granellino
d'uva" [Bad friends jumped all over me like flies on a grape]
(584). He enumerates his crimes for his confessor and again
blames it on his bad friends (585). Simone is a true fictive brother
and kindred spirit of Elias and Paulo; cut from the same Deleddan cloth, the men point fingers at every possible opportunity.
They even use many of the same excuses (bad companions is a
favorite).

Elias Portolu falls for Maddalena, but he puts the onus on her for their love affair because in his perception she looks at him "in a certain way," and will not leave him alone (44). Later when she continues to see him, he is near despair. With no one left to blame for his own lack of maturity, he turns against Maddalena, herself.

> È lei la tentazione. È lei che mi ha perduto: perchè è venuta? Perchè mi ha tentato? Non pensa a Dio, alla vita eterna, quella donna? (133).

> [She is the temptation. She is the one who led me astray. Why did she come? Why did she tempt me. Doesn't that woman think about God, about the eternal life?]

After blaming a woman, cursing the devil is the next most popular activity with Deledda's men.[39] In the short story, "Le tredici uova" [The Thirteen Eggs] from the collection, *Romanzi e novelle*, Mareddu cannot come to terms with his own unfounded suspicions of his wife's infidelity. He blames his torment on Old Scratch. He is solely responsible for his groundless thoughts, but delegates that responsibility to an external force. Like Mareddu, as soon as Elias Portolu lets down his mental guard, his old demon pounces again (57). When Elias confesses his sin of incest to his mentor, *zio* Martinu, he blames the whole predicament on fate and the devil.[40] Elias even asks *zio* Martinu to tie him up physically to prevent him from returning to Maddalena and from escaping to go do the devil's work. *Zio* Martinu correctly diagnoses the problem and tries to force Elias to grow up.[41] He explains that the devil is Elias, himself.[42] But Elias is having nothing to do with *zio* Martinu's advice.

The next day Elias learns that his brother has a fatal infection; his first, gleeful thought is that if his brother dies, he can finally marry his lover/sister-in-law, Maddalena. He momentarily repents of that notion, but is tormented nevertheless.

> Ah, qual mostro lo assaliva? Perchè, appena egli si dimenticava un istante, quel mostro gli susurrava parole di gioia gli dava desideri colpevoli, mostrandogli di continuo l'immagine del fratello morto, sepolto? (150).

> [Oh what kind of a monster was assaulting him? Why, as soon as he dropped his guard, did that monster whisper words of joy, give him sinful desires, showing him constantly the image of his brother, dead and buried?]

In this instance the reliable scapegoat of a devil has transformed itself into a monster; but heedless of *zio* Martinu's advice,

Elias fails again to recognize that the demon resides within. With his own brand of schoolyard reasoning, Elias assures himself that Maddalena looked at him first (31). She may very well have "started it" with a sidelong glance; she may have been the temptress; but at his deceased brother's wake Elias cannot help but notice that the newly widowed Maddalena looks awfully seductive *in lutto* [dressed in mourning clothes].

La madre's Paulo, too, is ever the passive one, while Agnese is the ensnarer. For Paulo the woman makes all the moves and is the aggressor who will eventually land him in trouble with her inebriating charm.[43] Emotional drunkenness caused it to happen. Paulo even blames his own mother. It is all her fault; she made him become a priest (although as a grown man he had a choice in the matter).[44] Later in the novel he goes back in thought to his amorous dilemma. He concludes that the devil ensnared him.[45] But no matter who or what is to blame, always the responsibility is external to the Deleddan protagonist.

Devils and demons notwithstanding, women constitute the most common targets in Deledda's arcade of blame-finding. Elias and Paulo are not alone. In *Sino al confine*, despite his having finished his seminary studies and his being about to take Holy Orders (à la Elias and Paulo), Priamo declares his love for Gavina, but that illicit love is all her fault.[46] He kisses her and tells her that if she does not receive him at 11:00 PM, he will kill himself at her doorstep! She receives him and tells him that he must go through with his final vows in the priesthood. He answers, "Mi hanno condotto fino al punto in cui sono, come un puledro che si doma" [They have led me up to this point like a colt to be broken] (92). He informs her that only she can save him (one wonders why he does not choose to save himself.) Then he accuses *her* of having destroyed him.[47] Once again the relationship between the man and woman gets tested because of the man's juvenile comportment and the woman's willingness to endure his behavior. Similarly in *Il segreto dell'uomo solitario*, Cristiano tells Sarina why his life has turned out to be such a mess.

Ed io, piano piano, mi lasciavo prendere nella rete che mi tendeva la mamma: piano piano mi lasciai condurre da lei, quasi per mano, come da bambino mi conduceva nei giardini dove c'era il sole e la gioia al gioco: piano piano mi trovavo legato. Solo una madre può fare questi miracoli . . . può creare a questo figlio i più gravi mali del mondo (564).

[And very slowly I allowed myself to be caught in the net that my mother held. Very slowly I let her lead me, almost by the hand, as when I was a little boy she would take me to the gardens where there was sunshine and the fun of playing games. Very slowly I found myself tied. Only a mother can perform these miracles . . . can create for her son the worst sickness in the world.]

It was his mother's fault. She tied him to her. He sees himself as the passive partner, even grammatically using a passive tone in his description of the scene. He is the one acted upon; he is not the master of his life but its victim.

With *Le colpe altrui*, Deledda gives us a novel whose convenient (for this study) title could be translated as "The Fault(s) of Others." Its protagonist, Mikali, hears that his brother has been killed. He is distraught, but he is quick to decide that the death is in no way his responsibility. Immediately he finds a woman to blame.[48] He points his finger at Vittoria. Mikali reproaches her for their love affair; he accuses her of having bewitched him and given him a potion to drink (202). Deledda's men never own up. They never listen to themselves and to the absurdity of some of their accusations. In *Colombi e sparvieri* the protagonist feels persecuted (with no apparent reason). He likens himself to Jesus Christ nailed on a cross by the truly blameworthy (155). Marianna Sirca makes Simone think long and hard about fulfilling her ultimatum, to confess his sins and pay the price. Simone, however, does not think he will go to jail for long because in his mind everything he has done is someone else's fault (799). In *Nel deserto* [In the Desert], Piero describes himself to Lia, "con tutti i miei difetti, i miei errori, le mie debolezze . . . E so che son diventato così perchè altri lo hanno voluto, non per colpa mia" [with all my defects, my errors, my weaknesses . . . And I know I am like this because of others, not because it's my fault.] (233). Furthermore, he characterizes his present state as being all his wife's fault; "E m'ha preso e ha devastato la mia anima" [and she took me and she destroyed my soul] (233).[49]

It is not helpful to these irresponsible boys that some have family members who second their denials, thus encouraging their refusal to accept blame. Early in *Elias Portolu* the enabling Portolu family agrees that his bad companions are at fault (19). In *La madre* Paulo's mother is firmly convinced that his paramour is at fault for their illicit love affair. She sees the problem as external: "che era portato via da qualcuno, contro la sua volontà, come uno che viene trascinato riluttante al ballo" [he was led astray by someone, against his will, like a reluctant man who is dragged to a dance] (92). She is not alone in enabling him to place blame elsewhere; in *Sino al confine* Gavina has a serious talk with her alcoholic brother. She reassures him that if he is a failure, it is not his fault (203).

In the short story, "Chiaroscuro" from the collection *Chiaroscuro*, the main character is an adult-adolescent braggart who refuses to go to work or take responsibility for his actions (rape and theft). His father threatens to disinherit him if he ever sets foot in his hometown again; his ex-fiancée's boyfriend threatens to kill him if he ever returns. Yet, his mother writes him the following letter.

> Se tu continui a vivere lontano di qui, vedrai che non ti calunnieranno più. Penseremo a cercarti una moglie seria e benestante, quando tu avrai messo giudizio; con questa speranza ti saluto e alla fine della settimana ti manderò la solita mesata. 'Tua madre' (560).

> [If you continue to live far away from here, you'll see that they won't slander you anymore. We will take care to find you a good and rich wife when you acquire some judgment. With this hope, I'll sign off and at the end of the week I'll send you your usual allowance. Your Mother.]

Like Deledda's own mother who coddled the self-destructive Santus well into his dissipated adulthood, this mother helps her juvenile son to avoid all responsibility for his crimes. She even finds a way out for him to the detriment of his future bride.

Destiny, God, the devil, women, fate, bad friends, enemies, wives, parents, distant relatives, magic potions, monsters—they are all to blame, enabling families notwithstanding. But it is never, ever the Deleddan protagonist whose feet are held to the fire. Ironically in almost all cases, any impartial, objective evaluation of guilt would place the responsibility precisely where it belongs—on the shoulders of those very protagonists who refuse to be held accountable for anything.

JUVENILE BEHAVIOR

Deledda's characters engage in all manner of juvenile behavior indicative of the adult-adolescent syndrome. Their actions sometimes border on the unbelievably childish; indeed, one struggles to keep in mind that these are meant to represent physically grown adults. In *La madre* the priest-protagonist, Paulo, incarnates the paradigm. He indulges in the childish superstition of setting arbitrary conditions upon fate (such as convincing oneself that if a bird chirps by noon, all will be well, or if a red Ferrari passes, one will win the lottery). In Paulo's case, he decides that if the night goes by, he will be all right (83). The passage of eight hours has no value to the plot or tangential relationship to the solution to his problems; nevertheless Paulo places his hopes in an arbitrarily selected, external event; in doing so, he sets up a smoke screen for himself which obviates delving into the causes of his problem. Significantly he does not search for the solutions that most adults know lie within.

At one point in *La madre*, the young priest's lover, Agnese, points out to Paulo his childish reasoning. She reminds him that he is only terminating their relationship because his mother found out about their affair, and that he would continue their dalliance if he had not been exposed. In psychological denial, he disagrees and maintains instead that he has had "an illumination" from above. The one mature adult in the relationship, Agnese answers him.

> Adesso è troppo tardi. Perchè Dio non ti ha illuminato prima? Sono forse venuta io, nella tua casa? Sei venuto tu, nella mia, e mi hai preso come una bambina al gioco. E adesso, come devo fare? (110).

> [Now it's too late. Why didn't God illuminate you earlier? It wasn't I who sought you out. You are the one who came to me, and you acted as if you were playing a kid's game with me. So now what am I supposed to do?]

Paulo deflects her rational argument (because he probably knows she is right), and begins instead to engage in the adolescent game of "what-if-I-died-boy-would-they-be-sorry." He predicts that he will drop dead, his heart will break and in that way everything will come to an end (126). Paulo's salvation from public humiliation comes only as a result of his mother's boundless and unconditional love for her son, not because of anything he does to redirect his irresponsible trajectory through life.

In *Il segreto dell'uomo solitario*, Cristiano is the adult protagonist who still likes reading stormy night, romantic novels.[50] When the love of his life, Sarina, fails to seek him out, he indulges himself in a session of self-pity.

> Ecco che da giorni e giorni ella non lo vedeva, e non si curava neppure di mandare a prender notizie di lui. Poteva essere malato, poteva mo-

rire: nessuno se ne dava pensiero. Un desiderio puerile di ammalarsi davvero, di morire abbandonato lo prese (480).

["Now she hasn't seen me for days and days, and she doesn't even care to send for news of me. I could be sick; I could die; nobody even cares." He was taken by a juvenile desire to get sick for real, to die alone and abandoned.]

Engaging in the "what-if-I-died" syndrome, Cristiano closely resembles not just Paulo of *La madre*, but as well Luca, the protagonist of *Il vecchio e i fanciulli* [The Old Man and the Children]. Luca obsesses over Francesca and plays the child's game of imagining the ramifications of his own romantically tragic death.

Sì, sì, me ne andrò, lontano nei campi della morte, e quando cadrò ferito, col mio sangue scriverò il tuo nome sulla pietra. Così qualcuno te lo verrà a dire: e tu mi aspetterai, allora, come io ti ho aspettato adesso; mi aspetterai per tutta la vita, e solo dopo la morte c'incontreremo. Amen (716).

[Yes, yes. I'll go far away into the killing fields, and when I fall wounded, with my blood I'll write your name on the stone. Then someone will come to tell you, and you'll wait for me then as I have waited for you now. You'll wait for me all your life, and only after death will we meet again. Amen.]

The comforting notion that someone might dedicate her entire life to his memory is what links Luca to his fellow, emotionally uncentered sufferers, such as Anania Jr. of *Cenere* who also fantacizes his own death.[51] To his credit, however, he catches himself and becomes ashamed (231). Every now and then Deledda hints that some kind of maturation process is possible.[52] On occasion her men do have flickers of self-realization (but rarely, if ever, are those elucidations the behavior-altering kind).

There are many additional examples of juvenile behavior; some border on the extreme. The more contemptible instances show how the male protagonist fails to cultivate in himself an ability to sublimate. He always seems to be filled with hostile impulses but cannot redirect them toward more constructive behavior. In *Il vecchio della montagna* [The Old Man of the Mountain], for example, at the very beginning of the story, Melchiorre Carta is being teased by the local laborers when they find that his girlfriend has broken their engagement. To get revenge on his tormentors, out of pure juvenile spite, Melchiorre urges his horse to

drink in the fountain reserved only for humans. He is glad that
he has ruined the water for those *signori* [big shots] who poisoned
his soul. For good measure he even throws three handfuls of mud
into their trough of drinking water. Like Melchiorre, Elias Portolu also works out his adolescent rages in less than mature ways.
He is angry with everyone, above all with himself. He feels a need
to hurt someone (106). In *Il vecchio e i fanciulli* Luca is jealous
when his friend tells him that someone else might ask for his girlfriend's hand; this physically grown man actually has the urge to
stick out his tongue.[53] In *Le colpe altrui* Mikali fantasizes engaging in vindictive vandalism.[54] Later this destructive juvenile day-
dream is really played out when Mikali kills the town doctor's
horse. The doctor was showing too much interest in Vittoria; so
instead of limiting himself merely to dream of childish pranks, as
a man Mikali now plays them out in vindictive anger. These are
but a few examples of the most immature behavior of these men;
but in general Deledda does not depict extremes when the norm
is sufficiently convincing.

Isaac Kugelmass tells us that emotional control is one of the
signs of a maturing adolescent. On the contrary, "emotional an-
archy" is not. A lack of social values (self-discipline, responsibility, personal initiative) will impede his progress. Inability to
adapt socially hinders him (167), as does a lack of respect for the
paradigms of society (171).[55] This is because the adolescent fears
adulthood and its attendant duties. In general the male adult-adolescents never deliver on their commitments or live up to their
undertakings, personal or professional. As a chronologically mature individual, the adult-adolescent pretends to be grown up in
public, but at home behaves like a small child.

THE IRRESOLUTE

Most of the men who protagonize Deledda's more important
novels (*La madre, Elias Portolu, L'edera, Marianna Sirca*) are especially submissive and irresolute. Miccinesi sums up this characterization when he discusses Paulu of *L'edera* and then compares
him to Elias.[56]

In creating her characters the author tends to give us in the male
characters a very different image from that of the female characters.
Like Elias, Paulu is a weakling, even though in a different way. The
man is almost always lacking in the strength necessary to face life

with dignity, and in general his actions are the kind that lead to ruin and desperation, not only for himself, but as well for those who are near him and who love him. If perchance he saves himself, it is always to the detriment of others (51).

If Miccinesi's Paulu accurately represents Deledda's weak-willed protagonists, Elias, indeed, is the prototype. As Miccinesi describes him, Elias Portolu is a sissy who cannot conjure up the power to face life (42–43). Miccinesi deems Elias genetically weak: he refers to his having *costituzionale irresolutezza* [bodily indecision], and *intrinseca debolezza* [intrinsic weakness]). Whatever the origins of Elias Portolu's indecisiveness, languor, passivity, and inability to grow up, be they genetic or social, he is incapable of overcoming his problem; yet he does not lack sound, mature advice. His chosen father-figure (significantly not his own father), is the mountain man, *zio* Martinu.[57] This mature, spiritual adviser tells Elias that he should "face situations that confront him, without running away" (43). Elias always listens to *zio* Martinu and then predictably resolves to do better; but inevitably he reverts to his former, wishy-washy self. He remains irresolute throughout the novel.

Exacerbating Elias Portolu's fundamental problem of being spineless is that he knows it. At the very beginning of his story, when he returns to Sardinia from serving his prison sentence, he conducts a self-assessment. "Come sono debole! Non sono più un uomo, io: non sarò più buono a nulla" [How weak I am! I'm not a man any more; I'll never again be good for anything] (24). He arrives at this conclusion on his own; he blames his passivity on prison. Elias is desperate; he thinks back on his misspent youth and his first impulse is to blame the prison system for making him weak.[58] Elias does not realize that one really cannot be *made* spiritually and emotionally weak. One's resolve can be weakened by stressful circumstances, but typically only an intrinsically domitable individual can be "tamed" by others; yet this is how Elias conceives of himself. The alert reader knows it is not *prison* that has weakened him; for his mother remarked at the very beginning of the novel that Elias was *always* the weak son, the different one, long before he was jailed. Elias Portolu knows that he has no moral courage. When *zio* Martinu advises him to confess to his mother that he has been consorting with Maddalena, his brother's wife, he again refuses on the grounds that he is weak. His excuse is that this is "something bigger than me" (79). His self-definition conveniently relieves him of the burden of taking action; it allows him to abdicate all responsibility for his present situation. In his exasperation, *zio* Martinu concludes that Elias is considerably less than a reliable man. He reprimands Elias with his most severe and fatherly tone.

> Come dice tuo padre, tu non sei un uomo, sei un fanciullo, una canna che si piega al primo urto di vento. Ecco perchè sei innamorato di una donna che non puoi possedere, che non hai voluto possedere, ecco che vuoi diventare un cattivo sacerdote, mentre potresti essere un uomo abile al bene. Aquile, bisogna essere, non tordi, Elias: ha ragione tuo padre (98).

> [As your father says, you're not a man, you're a boy, a reed that bends with the first gust of wind. That's why you fell in love with a woman whom you cannot possess, whom you didn't want to possess; now you want to be a bad priest, whereas you could be a worthwhile man. We have to be eagles! not thrushes, Elias: your father is right.][59]

Despite his older friend's advice to the contrary, Elias takes his first priestly vows. Following up on his previous animal metaphors, *zio* Martinu derides him again when Elias confesses his fear of being near Maddalena; he accuses him of being a scared rabbit, a cat, a hen, a lizard (126)—all metaphors for weakness, or femininity or baseness of character. Yet, Elias is not shaken into resolving his problems.

Two years pass. Ironically, as prison did, the seminary has given Elias an adolescent's ashen pallor (144). He returns to his hometown as a priest (but one who also happens to have fathered his brother's "son"). He knows that he could succumb to Maddalena's charms again with the slightest temptation. He still dreams about her. He has not found peace. The prospect of a secret life with Maddalena as his lover is still too strong and enticing; the emotionally feeble Elias has not been transformed at all by his vocation.

> Ed Elias fu vinto; la vita lo riafferrò tutto: ed egli cadde inginocchiato alla finestra, sotto la luna, e pianse come un bambino colto da un supremo delirio di disperazione (148).

> [And Elias was conquered; life grabbed hold of him completely; and he fell on his knees at the window under the moon, and he cried like a baby overtaken by a supreme delirium of desperation.]

Deep in prayer he asks God for help acknowledging his own weakness but typically makes his troubles God's fault; he asks

God why he "made [him] so weak."[60] He agonizes and tries to make the spiritual agony disappear, but does not succeed.[61] He attributes his weakness to a passing *pazzia* [craziness] and blames it all on the way he was born with no acknowledgement of his power to change his thoughts and actions. Sarale correctly observes that "Elias blames "destiny," the evil sphinx who torments men, fate. But in reality he is the victim of his weak will and yet at the end, he accepts pain with patience as expiation for his sin" (59). What Sarale fails to mention is that the "pain" of his son's death also relieves Elias of his jealousy of the boy's future relationship with Maddalena's new suitor, Farre. Elias is happy to lose his son because that means Farre cannot raise him either.

Miccinesi deems Elias a weakling who cannot face reality. "But at the same time there is in him a quality that redeems him; it is his patient acceptance of pain, his offering up of himself to suffering" (45). Like Sarale, Miccinesi correctly characterizes Elias's moral weakness; it is difficult to agree with the latter, however, that Elias ultimately redeems himself. For even at the very end of the novel with the death of his son, Elias remains so self-absorbed that he is still incapable of comprehending the meaning of love. Suffering from primary narcissism, Elias tries to experience love but just cannot grasp his reflection at the bottom of that mythological pool. Failing to love himself, the *sine qua non* of external relationships, he will never know what it is to cathect with another.[62] He may achieve peace for the moment; but what will he do when he realizes (if ever) that his son's death is not *about* Elias Portolu, that a human life has been lost, that the death of a child should not be welcomed as a liberating event, that something is seriously wrong with a man who can only find peace in the loss of his own son.[63]

Indeed Elias may be the most exasperating of Deledda's cowardly men, but Elias can take consolation in belonging to a vast brotherhood.[64] Miccinesi accurately describes the young wastrel of *Canne al vento*; he sees Giacinto also as a weak man, much like Elias and Paulu are weak, but unlike the latter two, he detects in Giacinto "a fundamental capacity to recover which was absent in the other Deleddan characters. He takes to drink; he abuses the good name of his aunts to get credit and he takes them to the brink of financial ruin; yet you cannot deny that there is in him a certain capacity to recover, to fight for his own salvation" (70). Generally Miccinesi provides a flawless description of Giacinto. But he is wrong on a crucial point: the problem with Giacinto is that his own (debatable) recovery exacts a tremendous price, as he causes everything and everyone around him to collapse in the wake of his petty, self-indulgent life of dissipation. Giacinto may have a "certain capacity to recover," in Miccinesi's words, but his own personal restoration involves an astounding amount of inconsideration for the lives of others.

3

Reflection and Self-Reflection

"Si può dire che l'opera sua ha anche un'importanza scientifica come valore documentario per lo psicologo futuro e il sociologo, che potranno ricorrere ai suoi romanzi, come a fonti ineccepibili, col ritorno alle origini per la ricostruzione storiografica folkloristica di un'epoca già tramontata . . ." (Scano 22)

[One could say that her work also has scientific importance for its value as a document to future psychologists and sociologists, who will be able to refer to her novels as exceptional sources, given her return to our origins, for historic and folkloristic reconstructions of a bygone era.]

GRAZIA DELEDDA'S NOVELS ALMOST ALWAYS DEAL WITH JUVENILE men breaking moral laws and social taboos, and flouting constituted authority through personally motivated actions which fly in the face of socially constructed, civic expectations. Taken together as an ensemble, her complete works offer a collective description of the quasi-psychosis of Deledda's individual protagonists who often learn too late the inexorable quality of punishment, be it social, spiritual, or auto-induced by consuming remorse. Deledda takes up the same human frailties that are the subject of so many contemporary studies in adolescent psychology; furthermore she adds to the modern clinical mix her own thematic interest in the blindness of fate and destiny and in the randomness of larger, historical or public events which inevitably convene to bring down her characters. Grazia Deledda's male characters present a paradigm, a sort of prototype when considered together as a "collective protagonist."

The exemplary adult-adolescent exhibits certain predictable characteristics; today's research tells us this is so; but a century ago somehow Grazia Deledda already knew that. Hers, however, had to have been an instinctive (rather than received) wisdom, corroborated only by direct observation.[1] She was completely on

83

her own with her analyses and conclusions; for in her day, there was no research on her perceptive notions. Even if there had been relevant studies during that era, she could not have known of them, particularly in her youthful, and most productive, writing years, especially given the limits of a third-grade education. What is certain is that she knew exactly what she wanted to do psychologically with the men (and women) in her novels.

ADOLESCENTS AS BABIES

In consonance with the modern definition of arrested maturation, Deledda expands the concept by describing most of her men with terminology more appropriate for babies than for adults. A passage from *Il segreto dell'uomo solitario* indicates how Deledda embeds these concepts into our consciousness via her *seemingly* random prose allusions to adolescence and to the puerile traits of her protagonists. Cristiano is thinking about his future, "sognando di nuovo come da adolescente la sua vita avvenire" [dreaming again about his future, as he did when he was an adolescent] (575). Deledda's reference to adolescence appears to be unnecessary to the movement of the story at this point. To the plot reader, it is simply "there." The protagonist continues thinking and he ponders his plans to reform; " 'Ed io lavorerò, anima mia,' egli pensava come un adolescente, 'lavorerò tanto da poterti esaudire in ogni tuo desiderio' " ['And I'll get a job, for the life of me,' he thought like an adolescent, 'I'll work really hard to be able to fulfill all your desires'] (576). Again at first glance—an "unnecessary" reference to adolescence (and this is not an isolated example; there are dozens woven throughout her prose).

At times she carries the notion to implausible extremes where even the aged Efix, the faithful old servant of *Canne al vento*, is "tiny and thin as an adolescent" (34). When technically the men do not thematically merit the mention of adolescent characteristics or behavior in their fictive roles (such as in the case of Efix), Grazia Deledda still manages liberally to dust her novels with references to their juvenile traits. In *La danza della collana* one of the very first things we learn about Giovanni is that he has regained his "adolescent agility" (44)—on the surface, an irrelevant fact. References to the phenomenon of truncated maturation also cut across all genres. In Deledda's collection of short stories, *Chiaroscuro*, in the short story of the same title, Caralu is like "an Arab adolescent" (555). In the short story

"Lasciare o prendere" [Take It or Leave It], the protagonist returns to his hometown, and "feels like a kid again" (654). Later she refers to the above male protagonist's *sogni adolescenti* [adolescent dreams] (656). In "La volpe" [The Fox], an old man thinks of *cose puerili* [juvenile things] (662) for no ostensible reason even vaguely connected to the story. Even though it is logical that a dying old man's thoughts would turn to the past, on another level, one would think that it is not necessary to the story to include that particular touch unless there is perhaps another *leitmotival* reason (which, of course, there is).[2] There is not one novel of her thirty-five where Deledda fails to exhibit in one way or another this narrative engrossment. Mentions of juvenile behavior are so common throughout her works that one justifiably comes to expect them; and she does not disappoint. Predictably, when all of the "random" examples are considered together, their "randomness" disappears, affirming the close reader's suspicion that something deliberate is afoot. Once one realizes that the pattern is being established, it is logical to think about Deledda's motivations, to wonder in what ways do Deledda's adolescent-like characters fully exemplify the psychological pattern.

Most of the cases in which Grazia Deledda makes concerted and frequent mention of adolescence are thematically pertinent, but many others have no initially apparent literary purpose other than to present time and again the mere *fact* of adolescence in association with her adult males. All of Deledda's immature men, however, in one way or another fall into the descriptive category of being little boys, infants, or babies.[3] Deledda uses similes and metaphors to depict men as big babies in their own estimation, in the eyes of the women with whom they deal, in the judgment of other more mature men, and in the assessment of the narrator who sometimes is patently a direct reflection of Deledda's own personal experience. In Deledda's *opera omnia*, the male characters view themselves as little boys, babies, infants and/or young children about twenty-five different times. This is approximately as often as their women see them as babies—about thirty times. But other, non-juvenile men in her stories do not have that same perspicacity. They describe the immature males as infants and babies about half the number of times as women do, in about fifteen instances. This is understandable when one considers the child-rearing role of the women in the Sardinian culture of those days. Clearly Deledda's women are quicker to identify the trait; perhaps as well, they *want* to see their men as babies, as a component of a psycho-emotional need of their own. In addition, when women see men as babies, often it is with tenderness. When men conceive of other men as babies, it is to find fault. The third person narrator is the one voice that declares that men are "big babies" in the greatest number of occurrences and in the broadest spectrum of venues and circumstances. There are about 110 different instances of such "neutral," omniscient description—twice as often as the combination of other men, other women and even the male victims themselves. Furthermore Deledda presents the ways of being a *bambino* in surprising variety. Deledda did not leave this feature of her writing to chance. Clearly at some ratiocinative level she meant very earnestly to imbricate this theme consistently into her prose style.

ADULT-ADOLESCENTS VIEW THEMSELVES

At first glance a man's viewing himself as a baby might indicate a glimmer of self-awareness. For example, if the man thought there might be a problem with his being "a baby" and subsequently decided to rectify that situation, then there would be some hope for a change in his behavior. In most Deleddan instances, however, the man seems to think his juvenile comportment is perfectly acceptable. In most cases the Deleddan man conceives of himself as a baby or as a little boy in metaphorically generic ways—ways that convey only the idea of immaturity and juvenile behavior without other, loaded connotations. There are many instances of this kind of self-assessment. For example, in *Anime oneste* [Honest Souls], as he is running away from a problem, Sebastiano wonders if he might be acting like a baby.[4] But his wondering does not lead to corrective action; it stops there. In a similar exercise of seeming self-awareness, the protagonist of *Nel deserto* tells his girlfriend about his sheltered upbringing and admits that at twenty-five he was "still a baby" (233). He too draws no useful conclusions from this observation. In *Marianna Sirca* Simone confesses why he disappeared without notice long ago when he was still Marianna's family's servant: because he still thought like a child.[5] What he does not realize is that he *still* thinks like a child. By now these and other examples have become tired clichès or "dead" metaphors. In any other writer's context the triteness of the metaphors and similies would allow the reader to dismiss them as a bit of local color to flesh out the character study or as a component of everyday speech patterns. But when applying the psychological overlay of arrested maturation upon Deledda's works, being a *bambino* tells much about that man's way of seeing himself; contextually and intertextually *bambino* means more than just *bambino*.

There are other instances where the Deleddan man views himself not only as a generic baby, but as a weak and powerless child at the same time. In *L'edera*, for example, Paulu is vaguely aware of his weakness and his own ultimate responsibility for his troubles. He confesses to a friend:

> Io sono un bambino, e capisco che la mia debolezza e la mia impotenza furono causa dei nostri guai: e più che questi guai mi accora appunto il vedermi così, sempre debole, sempre fanciullo (98).

> [I'm a baby, and I understand that my weakness and my inability to act were the cause of our troubles; and more than these problems, it grieves me precisely to see myself like this, always so weak, always a little boy.]

A reasonable response to Paulu's confession would be to ask him if he has any plans to reassess his behavior. Rather than only to self-describe, could he not also self-analyze and put into action some corrective measures to solve his problems? One suspects, however, that the question would be rhetorical.

Another young man concerned not only about his little boy status but his own weakness is Anania of *Cenere*. Anania looks back on his idyllic school days. "Come ero bambino!" pensò amaramente. "E dicevo di essere uomo!" ["What a baby I was!" he thought bitterly, "and I said I was a man!"] (200). He knows he must grow up and face his responsibilities to his mother. He plans to take care of her and vows to pay his debts, "e sarò un uomo. Un uomo!" [and I'll be a man. A man!] (200). Anania needs to convince himself that this will actually transpire, that he will be a man, his acknowledged weakness notwithstanding.[6]

Deledda takes the concept of male characters seeing themselves as generic babies or as weak and helpless little boys a step farther when some male characters connect their boyishness directly to their mothers in so far as their mothers still behave maternally toward them in their adulthood. In a kind of symbiosis, the two adults relate to each other still as mother and baby boy; they see each other only within the parameters of that relationship, not as separate, mature individuals. In *Dopo il divorzio* [After the Divorce], for example, Costantino is a prisoner who daydreams that he is curled up in a baby's cradle and the cradle rocks him while his wife makes sure he does not fall out. Costantino psychologically shifts the nurturing duties of his mother to his wife as he acts out the role of the helpless baby in a fetal position. As well, in *La madre* Paulo thinks back to his first entry as a young pastor into a new parish when his mother came with him, tending to Paulo "like a baby taking his first steps" (83). Paulo craves her maternal protection in this big moment in his life. At the conclusion of the novel, his mother is still looking after him, much to her own peril; for she literally dies doing so.[7]

Yet the man-as-baby played against a father-figure appears only once in Deledda's writing. In *Canne al vento* Giacinto tells Efix how rough life has been on him, how he tried to kill himself upon first escaping to Nuoro, and how his landlord was such a help—he "put him to bed like a baby" (192). This is the only adult-adolescent to earn the sympathy of another man. In the overwhelming majority of instances, women, not men, are the baby's protectors, as in *Nel deserto* where the protagonist declares that if Lia leaves him,

> io non so cosa farò . . . Sarò un uomo perduto . . . sarò come quei bambini lì . . . se tu li lasciassi soli, qui, davanti al mare . . . Che farebbero? Si perderebbero, cadrebbero nel mare . . . Così io, Lia, se tu mi lasci adesso . . . (282).

> [I don't know what I'll do. I'll be a lost man. I'll be like those babies over there. If you left them alone, here on the shore . . . what would they do? They'd get lost; they'd fall into the water. Like me, Lia, if you leave me now.]

Most of the men in Deledda's prose see themselves as babies with references that usually imply no more than generality. In a number of instances, however, they see themselves not just as babies without additional connotations. They conceive of themselves as helpless infants in relation to their women being stronger, protective, and nurturing in the face of their own weakness and ineptitude. Some of these situations reflect intimidating women, further implying the oftentimes negative ascendancy that women have over men in this ironically patronistic society (see chapter 5, "Manifestations of the Syndrome: Relationships"). In only one instance (*Canne al vento*) does a man see himself as a baby in relation to another man—a benevolent mentor who is specifically *not* like his own father (cruel and harsh, or dead and otherwise out of the picture completely). Clearly the presence of women plays a looming part in how Deledda's men conceive of themselves; and this combines well with the way those protective women in turn see their men.

WOMEN EVALUATE THEIR MEN

Nel rileggere quel che ho scritto ieri mi viene fatto di domandarmi se io non abbia incominciato a cambiare carattere dal giorno in cui mio marito, scherzosamente, ha preso a chiamarmi "mammà." Mi piacque tanto, sul principio, perché cosí mi pareva d'essere io la sola persona adulta, in casa, la sola che già sapesse tutto della vita. Ciò accresceva quel senso di responsabilità che ho sempre avuto, fin dall'infanzia. Mi piacque anche perché in tal modo riuscivo a giustificare l'impeto di tenerezza sempre suscitato in me dal fare di Michele che è rimasto candido, ingenuo, anche ora che ha quasi cinquant'anni. Quando mi chiama "mammà" io gli rispondo con un piglio tra severo e tenero, lo stesso che usavo con Riccardo quando era bambino.

(de Céspedes 11)[8]

[In rereading what I wrote yesterday, it occurs to me to ask if my personality has not begun to change since the day in which my husband began to call me "mama." At first I liked it a lot because I seemed to be the only adult in the house, the only person who already knew everything about life. It increased that feeling of responsibility that I have always had since childhood. I also liked it because in that way I was able to justify my tendency to be tender toward Michele's behavior which has remained pure and ingenuous even now that he's almost fifty. When he calls me "mama," I answer with a demeanor somewhere between severe and tender, the same one I used with Riccardo when he was a baby.]

Alba de Céspedes presents us with a fictional text written within a different sociological and personal context during radically different times. Yet in this passage, her later, more mature reaction to being called "mamma" by her own husband is curiously reminiscent of some of Deledda's female characters who also combine disdain with a sort of indulgence of superiority toward their men. The strong and forceful women who relate to Deledda's afflicted men exhibit a much greater variety of ways to see their men as juveniles than the men do themselves.[9] They have much more creative fantasy, much more imagination. One of the most prevalent manners in which women evaluate men as little boys is with disdain and disparagement. Only secondarily do they see the men as needful of maternal coddling and safekeeping. In other words, if one can judge solely from how men get assessed by both sexes (in their own minds respectively), it could be said that men mostly want nurturing, and that women think less of them for doing so. Nevertheless, women are more than willing to provide their men with protection and cossetting. In fact a number of women derive their identity precisely by insulating and caring for their male "babies."

Vis-à-vis the men who in their eyes are just little boys, women manifest their protective side in a number of ways. In some cases they see their men in need of refuge and safety from wicked people who do bad things to them. For example in *Colombi e sparvieri*, Marianna observes her man as a helpless and threatened little boy (153). In *Colombi e sparvieri* Columba sees a man as a poor orphaned and paralytic baby (173). In *La danza della collana* a man needs the woman's guidance and strength, at least as Maria describes him needing a firm hand (presumably hers).[10] There is little room for doubt that the women have a side to them that cannot resist mothering and protecting their grown men. This obtains despite their often expressed disgust for their sons', lovers', and husbands' juvenile behavior.

Indeed Deledda's women often deprecate men who need them. In *Canne al vento*, after the mature spinster, Donna Noemi, decides to marry the elderly Don Predu (for convenience since her delinquent nephew, Giacinto, bankrupted her), he visits every day to discuss the wedding and is always in a frisky, randy, jokey mood. At one point, distinctly annoyed and disgusted with his juvenile silliness, she angrily brushes him off and retorts testily that he is "behaving like a child" (251). In *Cenere* Margherita is angry that her fiancé would leave her to care for his miserable mother and accuses him too of being "a child" (226). She tells him to grow up and "be a man" (226). In *Sino al confine* Gavina has a heart-to-heart talk with her alcoholic brother.

Io vorrei vederti tranquillo; sei sempre irritato, diffidente, pauroso: sei ancora come un bambino, che accadrà di te, se nostra madre viene a mancare? Io non lo so! Diventerai come un bambino orfano, abbandonato da tutti (203).

[I'd like to see you serene; you're always angry, diffident, fearful; you're still like a baby; what will happen to you if mother dies? I really don't know! You'll become like an orphaned baby, abandoned by everyone.][11]

In the first case above, a marriage of convenience to a big baby makes Noemi extremely peevish; in the second instance, competition with Anania's mother enrages Margherita; in the example above, her dipsomaniacal brother's immaturity makes Gavina rip into him. In other cases women's opinion of men is not simply limited to exasperated observations of their brattiness and implied need to grow up as in these archetypical situations.[12] At times the women threaten physical punishment of the kind that frustrated mothers sometimes administer to their children. For example, in *Nostalgie* [Nostalgia], when Regina gets into a heated argument with her husband, Antonio, first she tells him, "tu parli come un bambino" [you're talking like a little boy] (219); then, beside herself with anger over his extramarital affair, she threatens battery. "Fanciullo stupido, essere debole e vile . . . io tornerò a casa, ora, e ti prenderò a schiaffi, come si fa coi bambini cattivi" [You stupid baby, weak and vile creature . . . I'll go back home now, and I'll slap you up as one does with bad little boys] (219).

Equal in number to the instances where women disparage their men are other, not necessarily negative but more general, cases where women see men as their helpless babies. One representation is a woman who views a man as an unhappy little boy. In *Colombi e sparvieri* Columba wants to help Jorgj but remembers that "l'uomo infelice è come un bambino" [an unhappy man is like a baby] (154). Another way for women to envision the man is as a weak and sometimes moribund baby.[13] Yet another variation is seeing him as a profligate son who needs forgiveness. Marianna Sirca thinks of Simone as the reckless son "who squanders his riches" (825). And to complete the simile, even Simone's father seems to Marianna to be "the father of the prodigal son" (825). Significantly the unhappy baby, the weakling, the dying child are all in need of a mother's protection and nurturing.

Yet, women very often imagine their childlike men in benign terms, in ways that please them. When Simone eventually shows up for Christmas dinner after a long time apart, he steps back to look at Marianna Sirca and laughs. She appreciates his boyish ways.[14] He brings her a suckling pig as a gift.[15] She feels a tenderness for him "come per il dono di un fanciullo: dono piccolo ma sincero" [as one would have for the gift of a little boy: a small but sincere gift] (794). In *La via del male* Maria considers her partner "un fanciullo, non un uomo" [a boy not a man] (283); and she is well aware that she has the ascendancy over him in matters of love. Maria is convinced he is innocent of accusations. "Egli era sempre il fanciullo d'una volta" [He was still the little boy of the past] (370).[16] Implicit in her statement is his inculpability. She is the protector. And when a sympathetic neighbor comforts Elias Portolu's mother with these tender words: "Annedda mia, gli uomini sono tutti così [My dear Annedda, all men are like that] (19), one cannot help thinking that her words are uttered with an indulgent, supercilious, all-knowing smile. Generic "little boys" abound in the minds of men's wives, lovers, and mothers; men just seem to be "that way" for Deledda's women.[17]

There are dozens of other examples exactly like these. As discussed in "Manifestations of the Syndrome," the women cannot help themselves; the men know it, and in turn they act out their part in an endless dance of role playing and fulfilled expectations. It is a "given" with Deledda's women that men are little boys, be they weak and helpless, endearing, or naughty. Women say that they do not like their men acting like babies; a man's crying irks them immeasurably; and they look with disdain upon a juvenile man's emotional dependence upon his parents. But Deledda's women seem not to want men to behave differently. For Deledda's women it is their lot to nurture, protect, and provide for men's comfort. They prefer it that way despite their protestations to the contrary.

Men(tors) Assess Men(tees)

The few truly mature men of Deledda's prose have no forbearance for the childish behavior of the many adult-adolescent men; they see through the posturing; they quickly recognize the symptoms of irresponsibility. Much like the strong women, the male mentors and truly adult, older figures cast a variety of aspersions upon these little-boy figures; but only rarely do male mentors indulge them or even describe them generically without judgment (as most women do, and above all as do the narrators themselves). The mature men are much less forgiving and patient. For example, in *Dopo il divorzio* while Costantino is in prison one of his companions scolds him for "being like a child." When he returns to Sardinia, even the drunken town doctor has the wits to tell Costantino to quit standing there "stupidly like a child." A whole spectrum of other men considers him nothing but "a little boy only pretending to behave" in order to get what he wants.

Efix is an exception to the typically surly, male mentor; but Efix carries a burden of guilt which colors his behavior toward Giacinto. We learn late in *Canne al vento* that long ago, and in self-defense, Efix had killed the three sisters' father when he discovered the father's pattern of abuse toward a fourth sister (Giacinto's mother). Because Efix secretly loved her, he helped her escape from the abusive situation. To expiate what Efix considers murder, he has spent his life as the faithful servant to the remaining three sisters, effectively taking the place of their father whom he killed. It follows that in his self-redemptive efforts, he would extend himself to accommodate Giacinto's outrageous behavior. Giacinto is the son of the woman Efix loved. This explains why at a certain point in the novel, Giacinto arrives and Efix smiles at him "come ad un bambino" [as one would at a baby] (82). For Efix, Giacinto has a *curiosità infantile* [a childlike curiosity] (87) which delights Efix. The saintly, old servant offers him the wine gourd "come la madre offre il seno al bambino che si lamenta" [as a mother offers her breast to a crying baby] (90). But Efix is not representative or illustrative of the usual male reception given the adult "little boys" and their unacceptable behavior. Don Predu, in fact, considers Giacinto a boldfaced prevaricator who, having convinced himself he is telling the truth, lies "come i bambini" [as little boys do] (117). Most of the mature men in Deledda's prose are like Don Predu. [18] They will not put up with misbehavior. The patience of mature men is not that of women. There is no coddling of the adolescent figure by his mature male counterparts.

The Omniscient Narrator Assesses Men

In general the omniscient narrator is not as negatively opinionated as the mature male characters, nor as biased toward little-boy men as the women characters. For the most part the Deleddan narrators' references to men-as-babies are generic; often they are comprised of dead metaphors and similes. But the narrator is by far the most fixated on the very concept of men as little boys. There are over ninety different examples in addition to the ones just in this section. Deledda's variety of characterizing strategies to depict immature men as babies is quite remarkable. Deledda's men engage in all manner of infantile comportment, attitudes and positions, especially vis-à-vis the women who nurture, abet, and encourage their behavior. The extreme is when in *Canne al vento* even after the old man Efix is dead, *zia* Esther cares for his corpse "come quello d'un bambino" [like that of a baby] (261).

There are over twenty-five instances just of generic babies, where a character is "come un bambino" [like a baby], or he acts "come da bambino" [as a little boy would]. In addition to those neutral images, there are men as infants and little boys who are crying, sobbing, dreaming, happy, sad, distracted, guilty, questioning, desperate, beaten, enormous, ingenuous, fearful, calm, satisfied, and shocked. There are men who are like babies listening to fairy tales, men as little boys who have found the solution to a problem, men like kids who play coin-flip, men as babies who are about to cry and babies who are about to laugh. There is a man who is a little boy at his first confession, one with his new clothes, one alone in the dark, and another just learning to walk. One man is described as a baby who refuses to take his medicine; another is a little boy who runs away for fear of punishment.

On balance there are just as many positive images generated by the narrators as there are negative ones; about twenty examples of each kind are sprinkled throughout Deledda's prose. Some examples are whimsical, such as when the farmer, Osea, gets a new plow in *Annalena Bilsini*; fondling it, he touches "tutti i congegni dello strumento come un bambino col suo giocattolo nuovo" [all the mechanisms of the instrument like a boy with his new plaything] (658). The Freudian implications of this plow-fondling scene also suggest the man's experience with self-gratification (a subsequent discussion will show how this description fits into a more intricate description of Osea). Some of the images are even more complex and pertinent to the emplotment of the novel, such as in *Marianna Sirca* when Simone Sole's companion-bandit, Costantino, returns to their shared hideout. "Erano come due fratelli bambini che si vogliono bene ma questionano di continuo e il maggiore è il tiranno ma anche il protettore" [They were like two little brothers who love each other but quarrel constantly and the older one is the tyrant but also the protector] (761). In fact this juvenile relationship proves to be important to the storyline of the novel.

In addition there are numerous narrator references to men resembling newborns. A man will have an infantile voice (in three different examples), a babyish face (in two separate instances), his expression, curiosity, compassion, and even happiness are also described as neonatal. One man even eats grapes like an infant: in *Marianna Sirca* Simone goes to her fruit basket (the interpretive possibilities of which are self-evident); he bends over to bite off a grape directly from the basket, much as a child would (809). Another of Deledda's men becomes jealous in an infant-like way; a man has babyish agility; another falls asleep like an infant. Instances abound where just an adjective, such as *fanciullesca-mente* [like a little boy], will highlight Deledda's constant references to immaturity.[19] Deledda never explains why these seemingly random images appear, but it is evident that she is building a "composite man" throughout her *opera omnia*. Her vision, her narrators' vision, her characters' vision are all one and the same. In the event, her life's work constructs "the everyman" as she perceived him.

Many of Deledda's men are petulant, emotional weaklings. A convincing number of her heroes are what we would today call spoiled brats—juveniles who vanish as soon as difficulties arise. In *La madre* Paulo thinks of escaping with mama to avoid the scandal of a priest having a dalliance with a parishioner.[20] This is a grown man who as a cleric is a respected pillar of the community; yet he acts like a juvenile. He thinks that running away will get him out of the sticky situation that he has created but cannot control. When that does not work, he wants to be a baby again and rest his head in his mother's lap. He just wants to run away with mama or pretend to be sick; and Paulo is not the only Deleddan male who resorts to playing sick when he cannot face his obligations. Seeing the love of his life, Maddalena, marry his brother makes Elias Portolu physically sick, and he too takes to the bed. During the wedding reception in the next room, from his sick-bed Elias hears the invited guests having fun. He thinks, "non si davano pena per lui" [They're not paying attention to [me]] (89). Ever the narcissistic youth, that no one is paying attention to him and him alone makes Elias feel even worse.

So his sympathetic mama makes him *un brodo* [some broth] which, *infantilmente lamentoso* [whining childishly] (91), he stubbornly refuses to drink. Curled up in his bed, he is playing the sick baby; the enabling mother is acting her part. The scene borders on a chicken-soup parody as his brother's bride, and Elias's future secret lover, Maddalena, comes in to his room from her wedding reception to urge him to drink his mother's *brodo*.

Elias, perchè fai così? Perchè non prendi qualche cosa?—Non sei più un ragazzino. Perchè addolori tua madre? Su, fa il savio, come dice lei (92).

[Elias, why are you acting like this? Why don't you eat something? You're not a little boy anymore. Why are you grieving your mother? Come on, be a good boy, as she says.]

Sulking, Elias agrees to drink his *brodo*, but only for her and no one else. He is an excellent example of the aggregate-man that Deledda's narrators create as an ensemble. For, all in all, the narrative voice presents little boys who on the positive side are cuddly, chubby, happy, satisfied, sweet, elated, inquisitive, innocent, curious, naïve, carefree, and as blissful as if they had a new toy. On the negative side they can be irritable, crying, sobbing, restless, timid, weak, scared, day-dreaming, guilty, fearful, naïve, abandoned, jealous, and childishly peevish, spoiled brats.[21]

Deledda constructs an elaborate narrative architecture based in part on her male characters being victims of arrested maturation and specifically and overwhelmingly depicted as babies. Throughout her prose Grazia Deledda provides these baby images, and she lets them accrue. There is a purpose and a grand design to this piling up of imagery. In some important cases she uses them for a specific narrative reason; the following is an example of what at times Deledda does on a limited level. In *Cenere*, after mistakenly thinking that he has found his mother, Anania sinks into a miserable depression; he feels torn as though he were two people.

> Uno di questi due esseri era un bambino fantastico, appassionato e triste, col sangue malato, . . . l'altro essere, normale e cosciente, cresciuto accanto al bambino incurabile, vedeva la inconsistenza dei fantasmi e dei mostri che tormentavano il suo compagno, ma per quanto combattesse e gridasse non riusciva a liberarlo dalla sua ossessione, e guarirlo dalla sua follìa (153).

> [One of these was an imaginative, passionate and sad little boy with bad blood, . . . the other normal and aware, who had grown up next to the incurable little boy, saw the inconsistency in the ghosts and monsters who tormented his double, but for as much as he fought and screamed, he never succeeded in freeing him from his obsession, in curing him from his folly.]

Unfortunately for Anania's alter ego, the imaginative little boy was the victim and the tyrant "always won the battle" (153). The above is a highly subtle and restrained example of Deledda's thematic need for the man to conceive of himself as a baby so that he can then compare his more mature self to his *doppelganger*. The interesting part in this example is that the baby in him always wins, and Anania knows it. Deledda's narrative strategy is designed to enhance Anania's characterization; and it works. In another representative instance, however, Deledda uses the baby paradigm in a much more grandiose way. Here it forms an integral part of an exquisite (and playful), narrative strategy where her elegant depiction of the male character trumps the very substance of her plot material.

In an incredible scene from *Canne al vento*, Deledda first establishes that the male figure, Giacinto, is a big baby with phrases, adjectives, and implications such as the ones we have seen above. Baby images occur in connection with Giacinto. After this build-up of Giacinto as a *bambino*, his new girlfriend, Grixenda, at an intoxicating and sexually charged outdoor *festa* immediately turns from the inevitable sexual encounter with Giacinto, and redirects her attention to a real baby. She picks up the actual infant,

> e si gettò sopra il bambino che le sorrideva dal giaciglio. . . . Gli baciò le cosce, affondando le labbra nella carne tenera ove i solchi segnavano striscioline rosee e viola; [22] lo sollevò in alto, lo ribassò fino a terra, lo sollevò ancora, lo fece ridere, lo portò fuori stringendoselo forte al petto (96).

> [and she pounced on the baby who was smiling at her from his bed. . . . She kissed his thighs, burying her lips into the tender flesh where creases outlined little pink and violet lines; she lifted him up high, she lowered him to the ground, she lifted him again, she made him laugh, she took him out pressing him tightly to her breast.]

Deledda substitutes the real baby for that other baby-figure, Giacinto, Grixenda's adult boyfriend. She presents this unmistakable scene of oral sex, especially where Grixenda lifts and lowers him repeatedly with her face between his thighs, a spectacle which Deledda *never* could have published uncensored in the early 1900s. The real baby in this scene serves no other narrative purpose, and only appears briefly once again; but the real baby's subsequent appearance is also in connection with Grixenda's sexual desire for Giacinto. For not much after the scene of fellatio, we again see the real baby; "le morsicava i bottoni della camicia" [he was biting the buttons of her blouse] (98).

With these episodes Deledda primes us to use our imagination later in the novel at a time when the real Giacinto and Grixenda eventually do embrace. Deledda cannot and does not need to elaborate upon that electrified and taboo sexual encounter between the two real lovers. For we have already witnessed the unspeakable in the baby scene which provides us with a proscribed spectacle, what could not be printed. Clearly the man is her baby and the aggressive, dominant woman likes it that way. There are other examples as well.

In *Le colpe altrui*, for instance, Andrea takes Vittoria to the garden to talk. He kisses her; she starts to cry; he rests his head in her lap. "Vittoria non parlò. Il petto le si gonfiava per l'ansia e le sue lagrime cadevano sulla testa di Andrea che le si era curvato sul grembo e le baciava la mano quasi succhiandola come le api i fiori" [Vittoria didn't speak. Her chest was swollen from tension and her tears fell on Andrea's head which was curved into her lap and he kissed her hand almost sucking it as bees do to flowers] (51). Andrea needs to be the passive, baby-like boy in order to rest his head in her lap. Without his head in her lap, his ensuing actions would not have meaning. Fairfield Porter has written, "Some art has very open reasoning, and can be written about in terms of this meaning, but the chances are that if the meaning is the most interesting thing about it, it does not stand alone, it does not assert itself. It leans on what it means. An implied meaning is richer."[23] Porter was writing about painting, not literature, but his notion obtains for the written word as well, especially in this case. Oral gratification is Deledda's subject; otherwise why would she include the explicitly sexual simile of the bees and the flowers in connection with Andrea's sucking Vittoria's hand which is resting in her lap; the two characters are even in a garden, flowers themselves being the very icon of the vulva (interestingly, the botanical terminology is the same).

Later in *Le colpe altrui* when Vittoria kisses Mikali, "le labbra di lui erano così molli che a baciarle le pareva di bere del latte appena munto: caldo e dolce. . . . Come non bere quando si muore di sete?" [his lips were so moist that to kiss them seemed to her was like drinking fresh milk right from the udder: hot and sweet. . . . How can you not drink when you're dying of thirst?] (172). Deledda must refer to his "lips" for censorial reasons, but the scene constitutes a clear reference to fellatio and subsequent ejaculation. In *Il segreto dell'uomo solitario* when Cristiano finally declares his love to Sarina, socially and sexually unable to go any farther, he settles for stroking the fur on her coat near her neck and then kissing her. In any other set of literary circumstances, one could argue that in some cases a kiss is just a kiss and a cigar is just a cigar. But with Deledda, in certain instances, it is clear that she was searching for (and indeed found) ways to say what could not otherwise be mentioned. Here she substitutes the fur collar for the woman's pubic area; her lips are genitalia.

Along these same lines we will see later in this study the many other instances where Grazia Deledda has the boyish man rest his head in his woman's lap. Primarily these episodes mean to show his dependence on her and his subjugation to her mothering impulses, but they also function as a subtextual code, as another way for Deledda to hint at sexual taboos while not actually taking that explicit, narrative step. Deledda was so subtle and sophisticated in her ability to plant these quasi-subliminal messages into her prose that not one of her many negative critics ever realized it. It is playfully ironic that Deledda found a way to talk about such matters without her editorial censors detecting it. The incongruity of Grazia Deledda—a little old lady, the gray-haired, bookish writer, demure and respected, the soft-spoken and dignified Nobel Prize winner—who hints openly and quite playfully even about fellatio and cunnilingus, when few others could (or wanted to) do so! (To think that her acrimonious critic, Father Pietro Casu, found her love scenes benign!) It would be reasonable to believe that Deledda remained above such risqué topics. Maybe not. In her clever way she was indeed quite the subversive.

4

The Woman He Loves

SUFFERERS OF ARRESTED MATURATION ARE UNUSUALLY MANIPULA-
tive. They are con artists, and they know it. They beguile others
deliberately in order to obtain what they want, especially from
those women who are most susceptible to the emotional machina-
tions of a boyishly enchanting man. They rely on their personal
charisma with women to sail them through life's problems and to
avoid shouldering the blame for the disasters of their own making. As adults these emotionally immature men are attracted sexually to assertive yet nurturing women who through their own
cossetting behavior abet and enourage the self-absorbed irresponsibility of their partners and who invariably rescue the men
from their problems by offering a sympathetic lap in which to cradle their heads.

The eminent psychologist, Peter Blos, writes about the women
who attract adult-adolescents: "The girl chosen is often a fitting
challenge to the boy's incestuous attachment: she presents traits
of striking difference or similarity to significant family members,
be it mother, father, sister or brother. The girl chosen is usually
condemned by the boy's family. It appears that the adolescent,
through the choice of his love object, has made a convulsive effort
to extricate himself from an infantile involvement."[1] Kiley agrees
that a "Peter Pan" wants a woman to act as his mother. (He also
points out that there is no dearth of mothering "Wendys" to fill
his needs). The adult-adolescent is preoccupied with maternal acceptance and approval (*Wendy* 107). Unwittingly the couple together forms an emotional codependency of the strong and
dominating woman who needs for her psychological fulfillment
the petulant, self-centered, overly dependent, baby-figure of her
man.[2] He is helpless; life overwhelms him. His woman is com-
pelled to rescue him from problems of his own making. It is the
woman who keeps him on the straight and narrow. Once married
to a stronger woman, after a period of time the men are then in-

clined to take their wives' love for granted; eventually they treat them more like mother–servants than lover–partners. Because of his boyhood deficit, he cannot allow himself to believe in love. He does not trust the concept. He is faithless as an adult. He will never indulge himself in what he has learned not to trust.[3]

In *L'argine* [The Embankment], Franco writes to Noemi about a book he is reading by Otto Weininger, a noted *nemico delle donne* [misogynist] in which Weininger proposes that:

> Ci sono uomini con caratteri spiccatamente femminei, e donne con vividi segni di mascolinità. Perchè una donna e un uomo si ritrovino in amore e si uniscano felicemente è necessario che l'uomo debole trovi la donna forte, e viceversa. Ma egli nega alla maggioranza delle donne le qualità utili per rinforzare nel carattere dell'uomo la sua parte di debolezza: di cui gli infiniti disastri, i malintesi, le tragedie d'amore (94).

> [There are men with decidedly feminine traits and women with vivid signs of masculinity. In order for a woman and a man to be in love and to be together happily, a weak man must find a strong woman and vice versa. But he does not see in the majority of women the qualities useful to shore up the character of the weak man: from which arise his endless disasters, misunderstandings, and amorous tragedies.]

Naturally, in the words of this *libro terribile* [terrible book], written by a man (Weininger) and paraphrased for his girlfriend by another man (Franco), a man's failure is all a woman's fault. She does not have the right qualities to bolster his deficiencies (assuming that were her primary *raison d'être*). The one thing Weininger got right was his reference to weakness attracting strength. Deledda discredits Otto Weininger in this double, back-handed way: she has a weak man, Franco, interpret a discredited misogynist and at the same time make an absurd pronouncement of his own. Thus, one of Deledda's themes of male/female relationships, perhaps not immediately apparent at first reading, becomes crystalline with the emergence of a convincing pattern, coupled with clever use of characters functioning as her mouthpiece.

In the short story, "Chiaroscuro," one of Sabèra's pretenders provides some wry commentary on these mother-nurturers, but Deledda's own voice resonates.

> Perchè, vedi, tu prendi un galantuomo e un malfattore e li metti davanti a una donna: se essa ha gli occhi bendati può darsi che per sbaglio scelga il galantuomo, ma se ci vede prende sempre l'altro (562).

[Because, you see, take a gentleman and a bum, and put them in front of a woman: if she's blindfolded, perhaps by mistake she'll choose the gentleman; but if she can see, she'll always take the bum.]

And he hits it right on the head for almost all of Deledda's women: they have a special knack for picking just the wrong man.[4] In many instances Deledda's men are mama's boys in relation to the women with whom they consort. Even today at the turn of our own century the ancient topic of the need for separation is an issue that remains unresolved among psychologists.[5] While it is unwise to tar all of Deledda's men with the same brush, the fact remains that very few of her main male characters escape this categorization.

Kiley has devised a psychological profile of a typical sufferer of arrested maturation (*Peter* 8–9). He is a man usually characterized by emotional uproar. For him anger is not just anger but rage. He is perpetually furious: he throws frequent temper tantrums. His mild panic becomes exaggerated as hysteria; it is then punctuated by self pity. When confronted for his failure to fulfill his obligations, he engages in indignant assertion; he mounts a high-horse of raging bluster and splenetic outbursts of wrath. He is easily provoked. He fulminates over a woman's assertiveness or independence, but he sees his own outbursts as just being masculine. Fear of rejection makes him hide his sensitivity behind a macho attitude which conceals his sexual problems. When he settles on one woman, he attaches himself completely. Then his jealousy is only outshone by his ability to elicit pity from her. He needs a woman to be dependent upon him, so he can feel he is protecting her. In truth, he is impotent to deal with an assertive female on equal footing; so he attempts to subjugate her.[6]

In his preface to *The Peter Pan Syndrome*, Kiley calls the problem "a novel psychological phenomenon," but anyone who has read all of Grazia Deledda's prose is probably not so convinced of the "phenomenon's" newness. The expectation in Sardinia, or anywhere else for that matter, is for growing boys to begin to behave maturely at some point in their young adulthood. We can see this in some of Deledda's minor characters who serve unidimensionally as mature role models in contrast to the delinquent adult-adolescents. Significantly the minor characters do *not* suffer from arrested maturation. It is mostly the male protagonists who behave non-normatively; and Deledda focuses on them, using the less consequential characters as terms of comparison.

Luigi Russo clearly situates Deledda as a modern writer, but he sees her world as "psychologically remote." Russo believes that Deledda's is:

a crude world, elementary and mystical, psychologically remote, if you will, from our intellectual experiences, but felt not as a provincial from Manzoni's time could feel it, but as a modern spirit can feel it, someone who has gone through the prior experience of our realism and of the religious romanticism of the Russians.[7]

Russo leaves room for healthy skepticism when he describes her world as being "psychologically remote." Grazia Deledda takes up a timeless theme and examines it trenchantly through the filter of her own perceptions. Her experience in Sardinia may have been "remote," as Russo calls it, but it was also indicative of universal occurrences; and as such the focus of her attention is as contemporary as modern clinical psychology.[8]

MAMMISMO

Sardinia is a complex island; it is complicated by the layering of Western culture atop a Nuraghic culture. Along the lines of Blos and Kiley, Giovanni Lilliu discusses the artistic manifestations of various, Sardinian pre-Nuraghic cults dedicated to the concept of "the mother;" and he wonders "if the Mediterranean and especially the Latin man's fixation on his mother does not go back to these prehistoric mental paradigms" (16). Lilliu's question prompts another one: could those cave dwellers of 2000 B.C. have predicted that millennia later an intrepid Sardinian woman would continue their tradition in her own art? For mothers, lovers, wives, and grown-up little boys have intricate relationships that weave in and out of every page of Grazia Deledda's work. Deledda was an alert judge and interpreter of the human odyssey that played itself out before her eyes every day of her existence. In *Adolescent Psychology* Blos tells us that adolescents emerge into adulthood when they disengage from infantile dependencies (i.e., the mother), and gain emotional, moral, and physical independence by forming a strong sense of self-hood, a self-consciousness (412–20).[9] We have seen how Deledda develops the concept of men as babies, and how she depicts them as such in the eyes of their women and, indeed, in their own self-definitions. One of the razor sharp observations from Deledda's unique perspective is that many infantile Sardinian men are indeed mama's boys; in

her opinion, they never acquire that chimerical selfhood so crucial to their own well-being; she sees that they fail to separate
from their mothers; in her prose they remain dependent their entire lives.

In the first part of this discussion of the syndrome of arrested
maturation, several Deleddan textual examples underscore the
notion that men of delayed transition into adulthood are overly
dependent upon their mothers, especially for the psychological
comfort and security that she offers. For the most part Deledda's
men are incorrigible *mammoni* [mama's boys]. In many cases the
woman for whom the Deleddan man falls is years his senior; it
takes no great leap of the imagination to see that typically he is a
boy who craves to cling again to his mother. Perhaps one of the
clearest and most convincing indications of Deledda's intention
to present grown men as mama's boys (vis-à-vis women who willingly act as their mothers), appears in *La Chiesa della Solitudine*
where the forceful Aroldo reminds Maria Concezione that "a
good wife" should be "a mother to her husband" (60). In turn his
friend, Bartoli, offers an especially appropriate simile to describe
Aroldo: "si poteva paragonare solo a quello dei lattanti, quando
succhiano e poi si staccano dal seno materno" [he could only be
compared to nursing babies when they suckle and then they wean
from the maternal breast] (185). One rarely expects such an astute psychological analysis from a friend, especially a male friend
whose articulation might be clouded by gender, by reluctance to
broach such a "female topic" (given the age in which this was
written), and by loyalty and friendship. When it does emerge
from such an unlikely source, it is even more credible and salient;
and the perception that the Deleddan man is indeed a *mammone*
can be accepted with more confidence.

In *La madre*, when Paulo's mother confronts him about his illicit affair, he reverts to being a little boy caught *in flagrante de-
licto*. Rather than to defend himself or assert his right to privacy
as a man would do, his initial impulse is to "fall into her lap" and
beg her "to take him away" from the village (34). He still feels
the need to be comforted in her lap. Paulo speaks as if he were not
capable of escaping on his own. (In fact, he is not.)[10] Sometimes in
Deledda's characterizations the mother and the dominatrix dovetail. Paulo learns that Agnese is sick; he wants to go to his mis-
tress. But the little boy in him wants to be commanded by his
mother not to go because he knows he will backslide.

'Madre, costringetemi a tenere il giuramento.' Aveva l'impressione
confusa di essere come davanti a un altare, con la madre là sopra,

idolo misterioso; e ricordava quando fanciullo, in Seminario, lo co-
stringevano, dopo la confessione, a baciarle la mano. La stessa ripu-
gnanza e la stessa esaltazione d'allora lo animavano; sentiva che se
fosse stato solo, senza di lei, sarebbe già tornato da Agnese, stanco di
tutta quella giornata di fuga e di lotta; la madre lo frenava, ed egli
non sapeva se gliene era grato o no (105).

['Mother, force me to obey my vows.' He had the confused impression
of being in front of an altar with his mother up on it, a mysterious
idol; and he remembered when he was a boy in the seminary they
forced him after Confession to kiss her hand. The same revulsion and
the same exaltation as back then animated him now; he felt that if he
had been alone, without her, he would have already returned to
Agnese, tired of that whole day of running and of battling; his mother
stopped him and he didn't know whether to be grateful to her or not.]

Aside from the absurdity of a priest having to ask his mother
to help him honor his vows of celibacy, the fascinating part of his
passage is how in Paulo's perception his mother and the statue
of the Madonna of his youth blend together into the one Oedipal
dominator of his life. And through his story, Paulo fails to recognize the problem; instead he remains passive and indecisive.[11]

Agnese gives Paulo an ultimatum: they live together openly or
they run away together.[12] She is very strong; he is commensu-
rately weak; she knows it better than he. She threatens to expose
him publicly during a crowded morning Mass if he does not leave
town that very night. He tries to "talk sense" into her; self-serv-
ingly he attempts to convince her to stick to the present arrangement, but he then reverts to adolescent adoration of his mother
figure.

Le scivolò ai piedi; le pose la fronte sul grembo, le baciò le mani; non
gli importava più che potessero sentirlo: era lì, ai piedi della donna e
del dolore di lei come Gesù deposto sul grembo della Madre (116).

[He slid down to her feet; he put his head in her lap, he kissed her
hands; he didn't care if they could hear him: he was there, at the feet
of the woman and her pain like Jesus deposed in his mother's lap.]

Although he is not with his mother, his reaction to fear is the
same as if he were—to seek maternal comfort; whereas a stronger
man might be otherwise inclined to deal with Agnese forcefully.
Since Agnese is the much stronger partner, she provides the
mother figure's lap. True to her threat to reveal to the entire
town that they are lovers, Agnese indeed appears later at Mass to

expose his hypocrisy. Paulo is beside himself waiting in horror in the sacristy anticipating what she will do when he enters the apse to say Mass. Again he thinks of her as a mother: "pensando che Agnese lo accompagnava al suo calvario come Maria Gesù" [thinking that Agnese accompanied him to his Calvary like Mary did for Jesus] (128).[13] Paulo allows the two women in his life to blend into each other. Each offers him the comfort of her lap. It does not matter that one is mother the other is lover. They assume the same maternal, madonna function for this boy/Jesus.[14]

In *La fuga in Egitto* [The Flight into Egypt], Giuseppe's good-for-nothing son-in-law, Antonio, causes him great emotional anguish. As a consequence, out of sheer nervousness, after dinner Giuseppe craves a smoke. He puffs on his cigarette "tenace e profondamente voluttuoso come un bambino che succhia la mammella materna" [avidly and deeply voluptuous like a baby boy who sucks at his mother's breast] (36). In this novel women not only are nurturers but are highly appreciated as such by their men. He knows that it is not good for his mental well being, but despite himself Giuseppe finds comfort in rehashing his past; "così la madre nella notte offre il seno al bambino inquieto, sebbene sappia che ciò può fargli male" [just as a mother in the night offers her breast to her restless baby, even though she knows that it could harm him] (133). Giuseppe is particularly fixated on his mother's breasts. In that he is much more *literally* attached to his mother, while Elias Portolu is more of a mama's boy prone to abstractions. Having fathered Maddalena's child and having become increasingly involved emotionally with her, Elias Portolu, ever the immature boy, contemplates his sister-in-law. In his mind she changes now from incestuous lover into mother—more to the point, into *his* mother. "Ma adesso non la sognava come l'anno passato, con passione fremente; no, la vedeva accanto ad una culla, e sentiva una ninna-nanna nostalgica che gli ricordava quelle della sua infanzia" [But now he didn't dream of her as he did last year with trembling passion; no, he saw her next to a cradle, and he heard a nostalgic lullaby recalling those of his youth] (136).

Elias is the arch-*mammone*. He cannot enjoy the sight of Maddalena's maternal bliss without immediately extrapolating from the scene a Proustian memory of his own mother to whom he is still hopelessly attached. This is not surprising; for, previously we have seen him on horseback, on the way to a religious festival. He would like to break loose like the other guys, and race his horse,

yell and whoop and holler. But his mother, *zia* Annedda, riding
behind him restrains his boyish impulses.

Il braccio sottile di zia Annedda gli legava la vita, ed egli non solo frenava il suo istinto d'uomo primitivo, ma rimaneva assai indietro a
tutti i cavalieri, perchè la polvere da essi sollevata non offendesse la
vecchietta (33).

[The frail arm of *zia* Annedda was entwined around his waist and he
not only reined in his primitive, male instincts, but he remained well
behind all the other horsemen so that their dust wouldn't bother the
old woman.]

To protect and to be near his mother, Elias once again rejects
his opportunity for manhood. He lets the other horse riders be
men; he chooses to lag behind, his mother's arm symbolically re-
straining him from maturity and full masculinity, just as his deliberate but ill-fated choice of the priesthood shields him from a
normal life lived as a whole man.[15]
Perhaps one of the least surprising manifestations of the *mammone* in relation to his mother appears in *Il vecchio e i fanciulli*.
Luca shoots himself to defend his honor; when he awakes from a
coma, he tries to talk; "finalmente la [parola] trovò, la ripeté due
volte, spezzata, incerta, come fanno i bambini che la traggono al-
l'anima loro la prima volta" [finally he found the right word, he
repeated it twice haltingly, uncertain, like babies do when they
dredge their first word up from their souls] (679). Luca's first
word upon awakening from his coma is *mamma*. Wisely Deledda
emphasizes the crucial word by prolonging the description of his
utterance. She leads us into suspense with phrases such as "he
repeated it" and "like babies do" before she tells us what the actual word is.
Cristiano confesses that he is afraid of losing Sarina, the main
female character of *Il segreto dell'uomo solitario*. Her love for him
is "paragonabile solo a quello che la madre, pure spasimante di
dolore, sente per la sua creatura che nasce" [comparable only to
that which a mother, trembling in pain, feels for her baby being
born] (583). Cristiano tells Sarina his story. He lived with his
mother for many years.

Siamo stati molto felici, io e la mamma, allegri come uccelli. Mi faceva
dormire con lei; o meglio ero io che volevo dormire con lei, ancora at-
taccato alle sue viscere, ancora un'anima sola in due corpi (503).

[We were really happy, me and mom, happy as a pair of birds. She had me sleep with her; or better yet it was I who wanted to sleep with her, still attached to the womb, still one soul in two bodies.]

Later he refers to his rapport with her as "come quando ero bambino e dormivo ancora con lei tutti e due puri come la rosa col boccio" [as when I was a little boy and still slept with her, both of us pure as a rose bud] (565). Interestingly Cristiano evinces no hesitation in describing his previous sleeping arrangements with his mother. On the contrary, the imagery he uses reveals a positive experience: "one soul as two bodies," "pure as a rose bud." There is no awareness on his part of an eventual need to separate from his mother (neither is he aware of the interpretive possibilities inherent in his choice of floral metaphors). Cristiano's is not an isolated example. Throughout Deledda's prose there are several references to grown men recalling fondly the comforting effects of sleeping with their mothers. (Anania of *Cenere* regularly slept with his mother before she abandoned him.)[16] And Cristiano is not Deledda's first grown man to look back with undiluted pleasure upon those idyllic days. In "La porta aperta," in order to expiate one of his bigger sins, the protagonist of the short story marries the offended woman. She is ten years his senior. After his marriage to this new mother figure, he realizes what a wise choice he has made:

In poco tempo, infatti, la casa del giovine parve un'altra, ripulita, col forno spesso acceso e il cortiletto animato di galline, come quando era viva sua madre (590). . . . Lui pareva di essere tornato ai tempi felici quando viveva sua madre ed egli, ancora innocente a vent'anni, andava a letto con lei e ripeteva le preghiere che ella gli suggeriva (591).

[In just a short time, in fact, the young man's house seemed totally different, all cleaned up, often with the oven lit and the courtyard alive with chickens, just like when his mother was alive. . . . It seemed like the good old days had returned when his mother was alive and he, still innocent at age twenty, used to go to bed with her to say the prayers that she suggested.]

Rather than growing up, he merely finds himself another psychologically nurturing mother. One of the benefits of such an arrangement is that the house gets cleaned, the fire started, the chickens fed and the bed warmed by an acceptable substitute for mama.

One interesting twist to these numerous, maternal, bedtime relationships is that the men take immense comfort in the security of their mothers' laps. A closely related recurrence in Deledda's prose is that of a man resting his head on a woman's thighs—undeniably an image loaded with symbolism, psychological weight, and thematic baggage. As noted earlier, Deledda surreptitiously inserts scenes of oral sex and other socially proscribed acts into her novels through such seemingly platonic actions. Inextricably tied to that notion, however, are her many references to the archetypical concept of the return to the womb. Scenes of men curled into a fetal position with their faces burrowing into a woman's lap or between her thighs are common in Deledda's prose. A few have already been cited as examples in other contexts. There are more. For example, it is the last night of carnival; Elias Portolu and Maddalena make illicit, incestuous love; the next day he returns to the solitude of the grazing lands. Lonely among his sheep, he desires only to see Maddalena again. He thinks back on the festivities, much as a child would. All he wants is to lay his head in her lap "and cry like a baby" (121). In *Canne al vento* when Giacinto dreams of his mother figure, the stern *zia* Noemi, he turns into a child who also wants "to lay his head in her lap" (157). He regresses to being the little boy who needs comforting, inexplicably unaware that he is a grown man who again has turned his back on his adult responsibilities. With a new twist on seeking one's mother for comfort, Deledda offers Jorgj of *Colombi e sparvieri*. Jorgj's fiancée has treated him coldly and he is feeling insecure. "Come il bimbo in grembo alla madre io mi sentivo cullato e sicuro quando sedevo sulle roccie o posavo la testa sull'erba" [Like a baby in his mother's lap, I felt cuddled and safe when I sat on the boulders or rested my head on the grass] (76).

Jorgj substitutes "mother earth" for the comfort he feels in his own mother's lap. The essential element in his and the maternal cravings of other men is the classically Freudian enclosed space which offers refuge from the problems that the adult adolescent cannot face. There is no evidence that Deledda was familiar with the "return to the womb" theories, but at least on a precognizant level, she incorporates these archetypical ideas into her prose with adroitness. Consider what she accomplishes in *Marianna Sirca* who provides some of the most vivid examples of the *mammone*. (For Marianna is a major player in the master/slave—mother/son paradigm.) In fact at the end of the novel, the act of Simone Sole's putting his head in Marianna Sirca's lap carries not insignificant thematic consequences. Marianna Sirca's reaction to Simone's agony is consistent with his need for mothering:

"lo amò come un bambino addormentato; le sembrò di poterlo proteggere, di salvarlo, di accoglierlo entro le sue viscere come un suo figlio stesso" [She loved him like a sleeping baby; she thought she could protect him, save him, welcome him into her womb like her own son] (752). He is a boy in trouble; she is the willing mother. He stirs and "con un tremito nel collo tentò di affondare meglio la testa fra le ginocchia di lei" [with a tremble of his neck he tried to bury his head deeper between her knees] (752). One ventures to guess that few other literary returns to the womb could be more unambiguous than this one.[17] Later Simone reassures Marianna that he is still her servant.

> Marianna! Sono qui, invece, lo vedi, sono ancora il tuo servo; ti metto la testa in grembo, e tu puoi prenderla fra le tue mani come il frutto del castagno che fuori è tutto spine e dentro è dolce come il pane (753).

> [Marianna, I'm here, instead, see; I'm still your servant; I put my head in your lap, and you can take it in your hands like the fruit of the chestnut tree which on the outside is thorny and on the inside is sweet as bread.]

Simone and Marianna quarrel. She is calm; he overreacts and then in remorse for his reaction he would like nothing more than "to lay his head on Marianna's knees and go to sleep" (759). He cannot face adulthood. He needs the solace of her lap. When Simone fantasizes, he has illusions about Marianna; in his dreams he again envisions his head between her thighs: "gli pareva di affondare il viso fra le ginocchia di lei e aveva desiderio di mordergliele" [for him it was like burying his face between her knees and he wanted to bite them] (760). In this sequence, for example, Simone undergoes a transition from seeking compassion to pursuing a more erotic experience. These postures illustrate that the man wants sex, that the woman wants to nurture, and that both are working at cross purposes.[18]

Deledda's many lap scenes acquire a subtle thematic significance at the end of *Marianna Sirca* when Simone has been fatally shot. Marianna rushes to him. His blood soaks onto her legs, but more to the point, "le bagnava il grembo" [it wet her lap] (860). Deciphering the interlinear, one can presume that in previous lap scenes Simone's head insinuated itself between Marianna's thighs and at a certain point elicited a discernible, sexual response in her (along with some measure for him of Oedipal reassurance in a return to the womb). In this instance of bloodshed and death, however, Deledda substitutes blood for erotically produced moisture in order to present a kind of anti-love-making scene and the antithesis of a comforting return to the womb. In this case the "baby" dies as a victim of violence, perhaps proving the adage that there is no return to the womb for Simone Sole. There is also no possibility for rebirth; he is about to die. The author creates an allegory with this lap scene, a story of the dead-end for Simone Sole. Deledda develops a shadow theme where she adeptly teases out the notion that female assertiveness and illicit love with bandits will not and cannot flourish in this society. By situating Simone and Marianna in this predicament, Deledda fashions a literary double helix where for punishment Simone Sole must perish and Marianna Sirca must remain alone. The pathology of arrested adolescence comes in handy; it does its thematic work. Using this elegant narrative strategy, Grazia Deledda coaxes us into realizing that Marianna's independent streak will not be rewarded in the society in which she lives.

It is not just the men who contrive and even welcome a return to the matrix. In some cases the women are more than willing participants. In *Il dio dei viventi*, Bellia is fully sixteen years old, but Bellia's mother considers him "sempre un fanciullo per lei" [always a little boy for her] (56). She takes him to the beach; when Bellia eventually emerges from the water, his mother meets him with a towel.

Glielo avvolse bene intorno al corpo; e ancora una volta avrebbe voluto prendersi in collo il suo ragazzo per asciugarlo e scaldarlo contro il suo seno. Gli diede subito da bere un uovo, poi un bicchiere di vino bianco; poi si piegò a togliere i sassolini dalla sabbia dove egli si stendeva e gli coprì i piedi con la rena calda; infine sedette in modo che la testa di lui riposasse sull'ombra di lei come sul suo grembo stesso (207).

[She put it around him snugly; and once again she would have liked to take her boy in her arms to dry him and warm him at her breast. She quickly gave him an egg to drink, then a glass of white wine; then she bent over to remove the pebbles in the sand where he lay and she covered his feet with warm sand; finally she sat in such a way so that his head would rest in her shadow, as if it were in her very lap.]

Bellia's mother offers him her breast for nourishment, her fertility in the form of an egg to consume, her inebriating liquors in the guise of wine; she makes a comfortable bed for his body and offers the shelter of her lap/womb for his head. Willing women like Bellia's mother abound in Deledda's prose—women who do not wait for the man to make the first lap-seeking move. And despite all their juvenile behavior, it still takes a willing mother or maternal partner to enable a *mammone* to continue in his ways; and Deledda's women buy into this paradigm unquestioningly.

In *La madre* Paulo's mother pampers him incessantly, idolizing and protecting him, even willing her own public death to save his shabby reputation. Paulo's mother's *de facto* suicide is not the only case of maternal self-destruction in Deledda's writing. Vittorio Spinazzola remarks, "In this as in other novels, Deledda gives the male characters the initiative to live real life, but she assigns to the women the task of enduring the consequences of their inevitable mistakes and of bringing them back to paying attention to their consciences: see the novel entitled precisely "The Mother," which also ends with the death of the mother who pays the price for the spiritual resurrection of her son" (XV).[19] Spinazzola writes primarily of *La madre*, but his idea is valid as well for *Cenere* where Anania's mother, a prostitute, commits suicide to save his reputation, and in doing so, solves his immediate problem of having a socially unacceptable mother.

EFFEMINATES, CROSS-DRESSERS, AND HOMOSEXUALS

Deledda had very clear ideas on men and women and how they choose their mates. Consonant with the wastrels and weaklings, the irresolute and the irresponsible, she describes a large contingent of men as effeminate, as wanting to dress like women, even alluding at times to homosexual leanings. And as her men adopt more feminine qualities, her women begin to take on increasingly masculine qualities.

In western culture at least, perceived male weakness is often described with the hackneyed traits of a helpless woman. Deledda does not deviate from that model. Many of Deledda's men are not only weak-willed in the different ways examined above, but at the same time are presented as effeminate. We see this not only in their stereotypically feminine behavior and in what others think and say about them, but in their physical characteristics. Moreover, Deledda reshuffles the gender deck by depicting girlish men who in some instances choose to dress like women and in other instances are tagged with certain conventionally accepted homosexual marks and labels. Incredibly, for a woman of her times,

Deledda is not shy about dealing with this topic; she seems to know a lot about it; and, in fact, she treats the whole matter with an astounding modernity, with an ease and familiarity that belies both her sheltered upbringing and the mores of the age in which she was writing.[20]

Effeminacy emerges so often in Deledda's men that its absence is remarkable, not its appearance. It is commonplace to encounter such descriptions in just about every male main character. For example, in *Marianna Sirca* Simone's bandit friend and associate, Costantino, as a young boy was tied to his mother "like a daughter" (738). Later Simone bathes nude in a stream; his chest is "white like a woman's" (759). When stripped for medication, her father's chest is also "white like a woman's," exactly like her lover's (860). In a climactic episode, Marianna Sirca's father fears an imminent, violent scene; gripped by terror, his heart "beat like a woman's" (842). It is especially salient that the three men most closely associated with the assertive and strong Marianna are all effeminate. Moreover, in proportion as she gains the upper hand in their relationships, they take on the traits of fragility. Deledda's depiction of men, not just as emotionally immature but physically undeveloped as well, underlines her deliberate dramatizing of the totally helpless boy-man. In all cases the use of "like a woman's" conveys the notion of weakness and frailty, both physical and emotional. In some cases the comparisons are more abstractly nuanced. For example, in one of those rare instances of self-awareness, Franco of *L'argine* arrives at a conclusion about himself.

> Sono un debole anche io. Questa mia facilità di commozione, questa superstizione, questa illusione di potermi sollevare e di sollevare gli altri, sono segni evidentissimi della mia femminilità (94).

> [I too am a weakling. This promptness of mine to get emotional, my superstition, my illusion that I can lift myself up and lift up others are very clear signs of my femininity.]

Within the context of the novel, he uses this illumination not for self-edification, but to explain away his wife's inability to help him and her subsequent suicide. Nevertheless, it represents an uncommon moment of self-recognition on the part of the juvenile hero. Later when Franco and his friend, Antioco, sit down together for dinner, they have "discorsi innocenti come quelli di due signorine intellettuali" [innocent talks like those of two intellectual young girls] (109). Deledda could have easily chosen to describe them as "two intellectual young *boys*;" instead, in order to underline Franco's girlish traits, she opts to smudge the lines of gender differentiation.[21]

Elias Portolu's father constantly derides him for being a *femminuccia* [weak, little woman] and for not being strong and masculine.[22] Elias goes to visit *zio* Martinu who sees him "beautiful and weak as a woman."[23] The effects of his powerful, unbending, crude father are softened by the sensitive, gentle, understanding mentor, but the value judgment is always the same in their eyes: Elias is as weak as a woman. The only changeable element is their manner of delivering the similes and metaphors.

It takes Deledda exactly two pages to begin pointing up Paulo's effeminacy in *La madre*. Paulo's mother remembers having surprised him looking in the mirror, preening himself at length "like a woman" (10). His room is "like a girl's room" (23). Paulo's hands are even delicate and unroughened by manly work (95). On his way back from a tryst with Agnese, Paulo has a surprisingly feminine reaction to having made love. "Gli mancava il respiro; provò un senso di vertigine come sua madre sulla china della valle quando s'era accorta d'essere incinta" [He was breathless; he felt a dizziness as his mother did on a precipice when she realized she was pregnant] (31). This perhaps is one of the most interesting of Deledda's feminizations. It truly places Paulo in the traditional woman's place—capable of getting pregnant, passively transported by lovemaking with breathlessness and vertigo, not showing any stereotypically male gestures or ostentatious signs of roostering triumph after a dangerous assignation. Paulo's womanly reaction ties together as well with the many other references to his being an ineffectual weakling. As Deledda weaves these allusions in and out of her prose, she slowly builds a picture of him as unmanly in every respect.

Not to be outdone by Paulo, Jorgi Nieddu of *Colombi e sparvieri* languishes in his sickbed. The reader is confronted with this ambiguous scene:

> Con un fazzoletto bianco intorno alle orecchie, dormiva una persona che a tutta prima sembrava una donna. I lineamenti erano delicati, la fronte alta nascosta sulle tempia da due bande di capelli neri finissimi: sotto la pelle di un grigio azzurrognolo si delineavano le ossa, e le palpebre larghe dalle lunghe ciglia sembravano tinte col bistro. Ma la lieve peluria che anneriva il labbro superiore, sotto cui si notavano i denti, rivelava il sesso del dormiente (10).

[With a white kerchief around the ears, there slept a person who at first glance looked like a woman. The features were delicate, a high forehead hidden at the temples by two burns of very fine, dark hair: the bones were delineated under a blue-ish grey skin and the large eyelids with long lashes looked as though they had been made up with mascara. But the light peach fuzz that darkened the upper lip, under which teeth could be seen, revealed the sex of the sleeping person.]

Doubtless Deledda means for the reader to think "woman" throughout this description. She relies on the grammatical possibilities of Italian which allow her to obfuscate the gender of her subject by using body parts whose definite articles and possessive adjectives fail to reveal the sex of the sleeping person. So through a kind of grammatical smokescreen, we are led to believe that this is a woman. (The English translation, in fact, is rather stilted when rendered here in the Italian way of forming possessives. English forces the writer to make a choice: "his ears" or "her ears;" "his features" or "her features;" etc.) Teasingly Deledda withholds the fact that the individual is a man until the end of the description where her lexical embroideries blur the edges of gender.[24]

In *Nostalgie*, suspicious that her husband has been having a dalliance with a certain Roman aristocrat, Regina thinks back on how distant Antonio was when he came to reclaim her in Parma. "Egli tornava a lei contaminato, fremente di angoscia come una fanciulla che s'è appena venduta a un lurido vecchione" [He came back to her tainted, trembling with anguish like a young girl who has just sold herself to a dirty old man] (223). It is literarily engaging that consciously she compares her husband to a young woman consorting with a disgusting, elderly, male suitor; but specifically she does not compare him, as one would expect, to a young man who has sold himself to a randy, older woman. Feminine descriptions applied to men are second nature to Deledda, with dozens upon dozens of references to men with feminine characteristics. In fact in *Cenere* Deledda is so accustomed to depicting men in this way that effeminization is a given. In a school play, for example, the director wants Anania Jr. to play the part of a woman (87). Nothing more is made overtly of this fact; it seems thematically unnecessary and just there without other significance.[25] Feminization is a habit for the author who sprinkles references throughout her work. At times the men *want* to act and to be treated like women. In *Cenere* Anania's mentor says that he would like to see a school play presented where the men get to go to bed and receive the same treatment "as their wives while in childbirth" (91). In several episodes men choose to wear women's clothes or deliberately to dress with feminine touches. For example, *La madre* abounds with allusions to Paulo's delicate taste.

> Il rumore del vento accompagnava il fruscio della sua veste; ed era un fruscio come di vesti da donna, perch'egli s'era fatto fare la sottana di seta e il mantello di stoffa finissima (36).

> [The sound of the wind accompanied the rustle of his vestments; it was the swish of a woman's dress, because he had had made for himself a cassock of silk and a cape of the finest material.]

Paulo's choice to spend his limited money on the "finest material" for his dandy cassock and cape is telling. Clearly he is pleased by the "swish" made by his womanly attire. But Deledda's mention of "a woman's dress" is not really important for a clear understanding of Paulo's problems, nor is the fact that he is intensely interested in his own clothing (a rarity for a priest to be so vain). For, his troubles have nothing to do with gender identification; on the contrary—he is having a heterosexual affair. His predicament relates only to his conscience. Deledda purposely chooses to effeminize him when just as easily she could avoid the whole question, unless concomitantly she is imbedding a sort of "shadow story" into the text of the novel.[26]

In another interesting case, Deledda goes considerably beyond simply making mention of feminine traits. *Il paese del vento*'s female narrator thinks back on Gabriele, one of her first loves. She tells us an interesting story about the ease with which Gabriele deliberately passes for female.

> Questo scorso carnevale, quando venne in vacanza, ne fece una straordinaria. La domenica, dunque, unica persona che scese dalla diligenza, fu una giovane straniera, una di quelle che capitano ogni tanto nel nostro paese per visitare l'antica basilica. Questa signorina, però, non aveva, al solito, gli occhiali e non era vestita goffamente: era bella, elegante, pitturata, con la pelliccia ed i veli. Depositò la valigia nella locanda ed andò subito a visitare la basilica; poi domandò dove si poteva veder ballare all'uso del paese. L'accompagnarono in una casa dove si ballavano danze antiche e moderne: e fu subito un grande subbuglio, non solo per la presenza di lei, ma per il suo modo di comportarsi. Ella cominciò a guardare i giovanotti borghesi, in modo che essi abbandonarono le loro dame per occuparsi di lei. Ballò,

anche, e ricevette subito parecchie dichiarazioni d'amore. Finchè, av-
vertito da un amico, non sopraggiunse un mio giovane nipote, il quale,
osservata bene la straniera, gridò: "Ma non vedete, babbei, che quello
è il mio cugino Gabriele?" (29)

[This last carnival when he came here on vacation, he really pulled
off a good one. Sunday, the only person who got off the public carriage
was a young woman, an outsider, one of those who turns up every
now and then in our town to visit the old basilica. This young girl,
however, did not have the usual glasses, and she wasn't dressed awk-
wardly: she was beautiful, elegant, well made up, with furs and veils.
She left her suitcase at the *pensione* and went immediately to visit
the basilica; then she asked where she could see our folkloric dances
performed. They took her to a home where they did old and new
dances: and there was immediately a hubbub, not only because of her
presence, but because of her way of behaving. She began looking at
all the middle class young men in such a way that they left their girls
to pay attention to her. She danced too and she immediately received
many declarations of love. Until, alerted by a friend, a young nephew
of mine arrived who, having looked closely at the outsider, exclaimed,
"Can't you jerks see that that's my cousin, Gabriel?"]

Patently Deledda is describing this scene where numerous
would-be suitors at the dance are forced to come to terms with
their taste in "women." She exposes them as victims of the ambiguity and irony of sexual attraction. Indeed Deledda creates many
scenes where there is some question about the full masculinity of
her men; yet, she has them performing all their husbandly duties
(without overt complaint from their wives) or she embroils them
in heterosexual affairs without questioning their sincere interest
in healthy sexual escapades. With this recurrent *leitmotiv*
Deledda clearly is questioning conventional assumptions about
how men and women should behave, what they should look like
and whom they should love.

She brings up the topic again in *Elias Portolu* when for carnival
Elias Portolu chooses a "travestimento femmineo" [feminine cos-
tume]. He even wears a "corsetto femminile" (110) [a woman's
bodice]. In his introduction to the English translation of *La
madre*, D. H. Lawrence explains why Elias masquerades as a
woman for carnival—all the men do: "The maskers were nearly
all women—the street was full of women: so we thought at first.
Then we saw, looking closer, that most of the women were young
men dressed up. All the maskers were young men, and most of
these young men, of course, were, masquerading as women"

(149). Lawrence goes on to describe how the women are men and the men are women during carnival time; he points out that when women dress as men, it is a sign of their desire to protect their virginity; when men dress as women, it is a sign of heightened sexual activity. Michèle Perret agrees; and he adds that women in men's attire also can also profit from men's privileges.[27]

Surely Elias's transvestitism is primarily a normal part of carnival time; secondarily it is certainly part of his heightened sexuality, as Lawrence and Perret contend. But within the context of all the other men in Deledda's works who dress with effeminate taste outside of the context of carnival, it is also an intrinsic allusion to Elias's feminine side, especially given the many other descriptions of him as a weakling. Deledda's text is multi-layered; we watch her slowly peel the onion of gender-bending possibilities. She was constrained by the rules of propriety in her day and age. Nevertheless, Deledda found effective ways to address at least a few topics that were supposedly forbidden. The murkiness of sexuality is one of them.

Pivoting effortlessly from simple effeminacy through cross-dressing, Grazia Deledda delves as well into the topic of implicit homosexual behavior.[28] She is not so intrepid, however, with this topic as she is with the relatively mundane matters of oral sex, masturbation, effeminacy, and refined taste in clothes. Deledda subtly flies just below the radar of homosexuality as a *leitmotiv* with Franco of *L'argine*, who dreams of his extremely effeminate friend, Antioco, "come la fanciulla sogna lo sposo" [as a young girl dreams of her future husband] (76). She becomes a bit more explicit, however, when she describes Costantino, Simone Sole's trusted servant and fellow bandit in *Marianna Sirca*. Costantino has been Simone's best friend and intimate companion since boyhood. When Simone begins his love affair with Marianna Sirca, however, Costantino becomes possessive and jealous of Simone; he feels as betrayed as a spurned lover. The two men have an altercation; later in their secluded cave while sleeping in close proximity, Costantino deliberately and tentatively reaches out his foot to make contact with Simone's in a blatantly sexual, reconcilliatory gesture after their minor spat. Sensing that he is losing his friend's affection to a woman, Costantino makes it a point again to sleep close to Simone when afterward the two bandits are alone in their mountain hide-out. As Costantino envisions them, they are like "uccellini nel nido" [little birds in their nest] (766). Costantino feels Simone emotionally slipping away from him. He cherishes their former closeness and relishes in his mind the good old days when it was just the pair of them alone together (776). At one point Costantino even becomes jealous of the dog sleeping between them. But in perhaps the most telling comment, in his passionate desperation Costantino reminds Simone that they are blood brothers: "compari di San Giovanni," which carries tremendous importance: "più che la sposa, più che l'amante" [more than a wife, more than a lover]. Clearly Costantino is the image of a spurned wife; at minimum he is an icon of extreme male bonding. The hint of a homoerotic attachment, however, only applies to Costantino's half of their friendship. Simone is too preoccupied with Marianna Sirca even to notice Costantino's emotional panic and jealous despair.[29] The parameters of sexual identity are only clouded for Costantino.

At the turn of the last century, there was little if any knowledge of the complexities of gender identification comparable to the flurry of studies being conducted today. Even if there had been public dialogue on homosexuality and cross-dressing, Deledda's reticence, sense of propriety, educational lacunae, and sheltered upbringing surely would have precluded her being in the forefront of any plausible, common discourse of these matters. Absent any evidence of such open discussion or even acknowledged awareness of these issues, we can only assume that Deledda's interest is "literarily instinctual." That is to say, she somehow sensed that the adult-adolescent was something less than a whole man; therefore, he must tend toward womanliness, the extreme cases being those who wished to dress the part of a woman or take their feelings a step further by engaging in the simulation of male-female relationships, à la Costantino vis-à-vis Simone Sole. Deledda deliberately obfuscates the differences between her male and female characters in some cases. She affirms masculine qualities in women and does the opposite for men, where feminine qualities define them as juveniles and adolescents who have not yet (and never will) attain full manhood. It is an interesting paradox and yet another example of her tendency to subvert the system into which she was trapped. That hidden feminist in Deledda resurfaces to point out how men's prolonged dependence upon their mothers in a sense works to the woman's advantage. The effeminized men inevitably choose masculinized women, allowing the women ultimately to control that part of their lives which was otherwise uncontrollable. The reversal of roles, where the mama's boy becomes the "girl" to his lover's metamorphosis into a traditionally masculine authority figure, works to the clear advantage of the woman who finally is allowed to experience some of the perquisites of being a man—exactly what Deledda wanted for herself.

At first glance Deledda's composite hero may appear to be the typically "Romantic" young man of European literature, one of whose salient characteristics is immaturity and a stereotypical effeminate sensitivity. Indeed, Grazia Deledda was a budding teenage writer and promising young adult during the height and aftermath of Romanticism; she read only what was available in her culturally and geographically remote hometown. Before she found her own literary voice (strongly grounded by her insatiable reader's interest in the post-Romantics, especially Verga and the French naturalists), perforce she fed herself a steady diet of "women's novels" and "bodice-ripping" short stories, replete with all the verbal debris and lovers' brooding melancholy of the age. These works comprised the only modern literature obtainable in Nuoro on a consistent basis. The Romantic influence, however, only in small part accounts for Deledda's conception of what men are like, vis-à-vis their women. Moreover, very little of her writerly style can be otherwise characterized as "Romantic." In his preface to *Romanzi e novelle di Grazia Deledda*, Natalino Sapegno stresses that Grazia Deledda had very little contact with her contemporaries in literature. He recognizes that of all the different contemporary literary movements (Naturalism, Idealism, Esthetism, Anti-Naturalism, Modernism), one cannot find a trace in her novels. While she could not have ignored these poetics, she remained

> always an outsider and like a refraction, closed in the hull of her own inspiration, with the passage of time, she eventually seemed even more removed, remote and archaic. Closed in an area of experiences more kindred to her, one can say that she was not even touched by the events which comprised the foundation of the changes in European and Italian themes and literary strategies (from Panzini to Pirandello to the first works of Tozzi [xii]).

Deledda worked diligently to develop her own style, quite apart from what she read as a girl. In her preface to *Grazia Deledda: Novelle*, Giovanna Cerina quotes a letter from Grazia Deledda to Stanis Manca written in 1892, where Deledda describes a "spiritual revolution" taking place within herself which was "sharpening her perceptions." She vowed that he would see a much different writer with the passage of time.[30] More likely than slavish adherence to Romanticism, first-hand observance (and sometimes deliberate surveillance in the case of watching her brothers' behavior) played a much larger role in Deledda's social depictions and conclusions. This is obvious both from her autobiography, *Cosima*, and from what is known about the people with whom she interacted almost daily. To be sure, there are traces of her Romantic, autodidactic youth, but Deledda was not a copyist. She was not an erstwhile Romantic who never got over it. Deledda does not simply orchestrate a parade of effeminate D'Annunzian heroes replete with all their Romantic traits.[31] Romanticism is not enough to explain away her life-long interest in much broader issues.[32]

Grazia Deledda saw something much grander at play. During her life she watched people; she listened to their stories, problems, crises and disasters; in her prose she analyzes their behavior and writes about what she saw transpire in reality. And what she saw in the relationships between men and women was sometimes tinged with disturbing characteristics and patterns which in some instances led to the depiction of sins and crimes needing redemption. She also knew that when one fails to grow up and reason like an adult, crimes and sins do indeed get commited, and the repercussions involve the lives of others in very dramatic ways. The critics who dwell on the themes of expiation and redemption are right; but they never look into *why* those transgressions happened in the first place. Grazia Deledda provides various facets of wrongdoing in her different novels. All transgressors receive their just punishment and they must atone for their sins in different ways. What is constant for most of them, however, are the underpinnings of their weakness—their inability to function as mature adults. And perhaps the most serious evidence of that problem appears in the adult-adolescent's tortured and troubled relationships with women.

5

Manifestations of the Syndrome: Relationships

... l'uomo fosco ed impenetrabile, il caotico uomo sardo, con
tutti i suoi sogni infantili, con tutte le sue turbolente chimere:
non avevano per lei niente d'inesplorato.[1]

[... the brooding and unfathomable man, the chaotic Sardinian man, with all of his childish dreams, with all of his turbulent pipe-dreams: for her there was nothing about them left
unexplored.]

WOMEN IN THE ASCENDANCY

DELEDDA'S ADOLESCENT MEN HAVE THEIR SHORTCOMINGS, MANY OF
which are self-inflicted. Because of their immaturity, they suffer
from varying degrees of emotional destitution. But by the same
token the women with whom these ill-starred men consort often
unwittingly supplement their woes by being mismatched personality types who find themselves in the worst place at precisely the
wrong time.[2] Very few of the women evince any serious psychological maladies (in comparison with the men who in most cases
are paradigmatic of arrested maturation). Deledda's females
function relatively well in society, whereas the men are almost
always in some kind of trouble. They are either in spiritual anguish or in a drunken crisis. They are in jail or living outside the
law. They are gamblers, dissipaters, murderers, spendthrifts, or
delinquents. Someone usually has to die before they are jolted
into a murky half-awareness of their own serious problems. While
they rarely are in a state of blissful contentment, the majority of
women do fine on their own; and, for the most part, they are well-
adjusted individuals without much mental clutter. Deledda's
women are simply not compatible with their men. Inevitably both

parties come to this realization too late; yet it is that fatal mix which makes for such gripping stories. Deledda's characters operate within the framing structure of prolonged male adolescence undergirded by seemingly perpetual female tolerance for the manifestations of narcissistic despair. We have seen numerous examples of the spiritual anguish of the male, but who is the woman who appeals to that juvenile, self-centered Deleddan man?

One's first temptation might be to think that only a weak, submissive, "doormat" of a woman, lacking an identity of her own, would or could put up with some of the adolescent-male behavior patterns evidenced above. Yet, perhaps one of the most ironic features of Deledda's prose is that her most representative (and interesting) woman is one who dominates men, who will not be subjugated by anyone, and who struggles to be the master of her own fate. The most salient example of the strong, proud, Deleddan woman who commands an ascendancy over the men in her life, despite the stifling Sardinian patriarchy, is Marianna Sirca, who protagonizes the homonymous novel. Marianna is a pillar of strength: "sostenuta dal calcagno alla nuca da una verga di orgoglio" [supported from her heels to the knape of her neck by a rod of pride] (846). Fiercely her own woman, Marianna is dominated by no one.

Marianna Sirca is the story of a thirty-year-old woman of inherited wealth who spurns a convenient marriage with a distant relative, Sebastiano. Instead she opts to consort with a dashing bandit, tantalizingly named Simone Sole. Marianna Sirca is an independent woman who will not be told what to do with her life, not by anyone. One suspects that Marianna wants to marry Simone because such a step would fly in the face of social canon. For marriage, in particular to a notorious bandit, is the ultimate slap in the face to those in her family who would forcibly marry her off to a relative only to keep Sirca money in the Sirca family. Yes, she will marry, but only the most socially unacceptable person she can find. Above all, Marianna wants to do things her way. In her heart, Marianna considers marriage nothing short of institutionalized slavery. She much prefers to have a dalliance outside of the law rather than to submit to social convention. She asserts herself early and often on this topic, for example when she delivers her signature statement—off-handedly she dismisses her adamant suitor, Sebastiano, as a man "like all the rest."[3]

When Sebastiano asks for the "key to her heart," she tersely replies that he never loved her before she inherited, now suddenly he wants to take away what is hers.[4] When she tells Sebastiano that she is in love with Simone Sole, Sebastiano launches into a flurry of unmitigated histrionics. During his big scene, Marianna feels nothing but pity for him, "not devoid of derision" (820). When a subsequently calmer Sebastiano insists on protecting her from Simone, Marianna issues a ravenously assertive, self-defining speech to squelch his protestations.

> E allora mi devi dire almeno che cosa ti importa. Che cosa ti importa? Che importa a te ed agli altri? Se è per i beni prendeteveli pure; tutto prendetevi, anche la cenere del focolare. Io non voglio nulla, null'altro che la mia libertà. Ma perchè non posso essere libera di fare quello che voglio? Parenti! I parenti! Chi si è mai curato di me? Non mi avete cercato mai perchè non avevate amore per me. Solo forse un poco d'invidia. E adesso vi ricordate di me, adesso? Per togliermi quello che a voi sembra di troppo: la mia felicità. Mio padre non è buono a nulla, hai ragione: mi ha buttato fuori di casa bambina perchè non si sentiva capace di bastare a sua figlia; ma lui almeno riconosce il suo errore (821).

> [And now at least you have to tell me what business is it of yours? What do you care? What do you and the others care? If it's for my possessions, take them; take everything, even the ashes from the fireplace. I want nothing, nothing but my freedom. Why can't I be free to do what I want? You say we're relatives! Relatives! Who ever cared about me? You never looked me up because you didn't love me. Maybe you envied me a bit. And now you remember me, *now*? To take away from me what you think is excessive: my happiness. My father is a good-for-nothing, you're right: he threw me out when I was a child because he didn't feel he could live up to his daughter's expectations; but he at least recognizes his mistake.]

Marianna always maintains the upper hand in her relationships.[5] At an especially dangerous juncture in the story line, she receives a physical threat, but she refuses male protection; she insists that she does not need anyone's guardianship, that she is her own woman, and that not even her father can tell her what to do (845). One of her major fears is helplessness, what she calls an "impotenza a muoversi" [an inability to function]. She feels constrained by a genetic destiny which denies her the freedom she craves; she wants to break free; she feels like a caged animal gnawing on a binding chain, as though she were constantly searching to escape her preordained role in life (823).

This is one of the topics that Deledda handles exceptionally well—the depiction of a capable and powerful woman constrained by social convention (*Annalena Bilsini* is another). The effects of the patronistic, Sardinian society weigh heavily indeed in this novel which mirrors in many ways the author's own obsessions with being free to write, to have her own voice, to live a life outside the limits already circumscribed for her before she was born. Clearly much of what Marianna Sirca feels is exactly what Grazia Deledda must have experienced living in similar circumstances. It is no wonder that Grazia's own voice resonates so clearly in Marianna's.

Sharon Wood correctly interprets a Marianna who seeks "escape from a role imposed upon her. Refusing the position of woman as exchangeable currency or goods . . . , an item of value in a patriarchal society, she will dispose of her wealth—and her body—as she wishes" (70). For, surely as one of Deledda's most powerful figures, Marianna relishes being in control and having an ascendancy over her lover. At one point in the novel when Simone is resting his head in her lap, Marianna thinks, "Era sul suo grembo, ritornato davvero bambino. Era l'uomo in grembo alla donna; il fanciullo innocente al quale la madre insegna la buona strada" [He was in her lap, truly reverted to being a little boy. It was man in woman's womb; the innocent boy whom the mother teaches the right path] (753). Marianna feels both the didactic responsibility and the exhilarating power of the moment. She knows she is in full control of him. He is the boy who needs her protection; she is the genetrix, the nurturer and later the strict teacher to his adolescent boy. "Un uomo era là, ai suoi piedi; ella poteva stroncarlo come un fiore, servirsi di lui come di un'arma; poche parole e il destino di lui era mutato" [A man was there at her feet; she could cut him off like a flower, use him like a weapon; just a few words from her and his destiny would change] (753).

In the two instances above, Marianna vacillates between manifesting her tenderness toward him and exercising her power over him. She knows she is in full charge and takes advantage of his being an adolescent. Later when Marianna finds Simone grovelling at her feet; she conceives of him benignly as "an infant in her arms" (767–68). Simone may be infantile, but Marianna is just as encouraging of his adult-adolescence as Simone is immature; moreover she likes it that way.

On the one hand, Simone protests to Marianna that all he wants is to be free; yet his psychological dependence upon her gives the lie to that yearning. Simone again humiliates himself: "Essere il tuo servo; scaverei la terra ai tuoi piedi perchè non ti fosse dura"[6] [To be your servant; I would scrape the dirt under your feet so that it wouldn't be hard] (797). Despite his own vigorous protests about his lack of freedom, he then puts his head on her breast and lets it slide into her lap. When he thinks of her, he wants to fall at her feet (849). He may adore her as his madonna-mother, but Marianna considers Simone a prodigal son. His many scenes of servitude, of self-humiliation at her feet, and abnegation reflect not only his immaturity but her willingness to play the part of stern mother. She loves him for her own reasons, but she never grovels for his love as he does for hers. While Marianna is emotionally underinvested in the relationship, Simone is over-involved to the point of obsession. She does not need him in order to function as a whole person, but he needs her for psychological validation.

Simone patently wants to be dominated; Marianna Sirca is just the woman to comply with his desires. Together they form an unshakeable and seamless symbiosis. Early in the novel, Simone and Costantino (his intimate friend and associate in banditry) are discussing Marianna's ultimatum that Simone give himself up to the law and face the consequences of his criminal actions before she will marry him. The loyal but jealous Costantino is quick to see the emasculating effect that Marianna has on Simone. "Marianna lo dominava, gli premeva sulle spalle" [Marianna dominated him, she weighed heavily on his shoulders] (765). Dating back to the very beginning of their affair, Simone had always acknowledged Marianna's power over him, her role of mother to his weak baby. When once they were alone in a meadow, he lowered his head in her lap boyishly (752). And Marianna's reaction to his boyish gesture? "Lo amò come un bambino addormentato; le sembrò di poterlo proteggere, di salvarlo, di raccoglierlo entro le sue viscere come un suo figlio stesso" [She loved him like a sleeping baby; it seemed to her that she could protect him, save him, gather him up in her womb like her own son] (752).

Deledda uses Simone's puerile behavior as a lens for focusing on Marianna and her reactions to him. When he is her baby, lovingly she protects him. Yet, when he is her 'bad little boy,' she can be as severe as the dominatrix he craves. Objectively she is a blend of the madonna and the prostitute; but his immature conception of women precludes a healthy acceptance of that mixture.

Often, different Deleddan men are merely refractions of the same psychological prism. It ensues that Marianna has a cowering effect on almost all of them, even on her own father who is understandably dumbfounded when he learns the identity of the person she wants to marry.[7] Yet despite his horror over the prospect of having a bandit for a son-in-law, he too falls at her feet "like a dog licking her hands" (816). And dog/master images do not end with this improbable scene where a patronistic Sardinian father subjugates himself to his daughter in such a demeaning way. Simone reproaches Marianna for wanting to take away his freedom. He accuses her of wanting to put him "on a leash like a dog" (856). Then immediately regretting his harsh words, he falls at her feet. Clearly he likes and needs to be the subservient canine and he begs her forgiveness.[8]

Marianna's men may see themselves as dogs at her feet, but Marianna, herself, is not above such metaphoric conceptualization either. At the end of the novel, her other, more socially conventional suitor, Sebastiano, fatally shoots Simone Sole. Marianna becomes hysterical, beside herself with rage; she wants in turn to kill Sebastiano "lì, ai suoi piedi, come un cane arrabbiato" [there at her feet, like a rabid dog] (809). Marianna really does want to see men grovel.[9] Inevitably their type of dog/master relationship is a mutual reliance that must be interrupted if they want the troubled partnership to flourish, but in some instances the characters do not opt for change. They choose instead to live in a harmonious balance of power and weakness that seems to please both entities.[10]

Marianna relishes her ascendancy over the juvenile Simone. She constantly reassures herself that she is in control and if necessary could take any appropriate action. She views his behavioral problems through a private glass that bends his significance to her concerns—heady stuff indeed for a Sardinian woman in a supposedly patronistic society.

When viewed through Wood's grid of social institutions, the ending of *Marianna Sirca* is "a tragedy for Marianna; for when Sebastiano kills Simone, he also kills the rebellion (interpreted at any level) in him, (Sebastiano representing the patriarchy); Marianna thus is without love, sex, and now belongs to "the legitimate social order" (71). This is true when imposing a sociological interpretation upon the novel (which Wood does with unqualified success); but it is difficult to conceive of *Marianna Sirca* as a "tragedy" when we remember that Marianna has accomplished what few of her cohort could have ever dreamed of doing. In one of the most socially conservative societies of Western Europe, Marianna defines a life for herself on her own terms. In this both Marianna and her creator are very unlike the majority of women in the Italian fiction of her time. As Anna Nozzoli describes the turn-of-the-century women, they are:

Vain, capricious, excitable, falsely sentimental, conceitedly spiritual, foolishly hysterical, decadent or academic,' as Sibilla Aleramo defined them, the female prose figures between the nineteenth and twentieth centuries conform without doubt to a very precise typology, codified in the pages of the most popular authors (1).

Nozzoli's description may be accurate for most female characters of that era; but with Deledda's women, just one look at *Marianna Sirca* dispells the notion that Italian fictive women of that epoch were all of a piece. For Deledda's women stretch far beyond the previous boundaries of Italian "women's" literature.

Reminiscent of *Marianna Sirca*, many of Deledda's other novels present men and women, often in a similarly conceived mother-son relationship, where he is just a boy and the mother figure is nurturing, but strong and emotionally controlling. Marianna may be the most striking example of a Deleddan woman in the ascendancy, but Grazia Deledda's other novels weave an intricate pattern where similar women dominate—more than enough to comprise a convincing matrix. For example, in *La madre* Agnese has the same powers over Paulo. "Ella aveva la potenza terribile di trascinarlo in fondo al mare, di sollevarlo sull'abisso del cielo, di fare di lui un essere senza volontà" [She had the terrible power to drag him to the bottom of the sea, to lift him over the abyss of the sky, to turn him into a being without will] (112).

Agnese is for Paulo the rabbit trap alluded to early in the novel where her breath "encircled his neck like a snare" (112). She is the ensnarer for him; he is prostrate in the face of her power.[11] In Grazia Deledda's prose, the women are pillars of strength, ever controlling the ineffectually hapless male protagonists.[12]

Like the rest of the Deleddan fraternity, Elias Portolu imbues his sister-in-law, Maddalena, with the powers of a temptress; he does not consider himself the forceful actor, the potential aggressor, the principal character of his own drama. He is content to be acted upon by Maddalena. "Lasciamo star le donne, che fanno diventar matti" [Let's leave women out of it; they make a guy crazy] (46). Talking to himself, he mentally reassures his brother that he, Elias, will not steal his brother's wife; he does not say to himself that he will not aggressively take her away from his brother; he says that in effect, 'even if she tempted me beyond endurance, I would resist.' With such an averral, subtly he ascribes to her the greater power. He does not see himself as the hawkish, male seducer but as a weak resister.

For the Portolu family it is time to shear the flock. The whole clan gathers for their annual ritual in the sheep meadows. For this festive occasion Maddalena is looking especially gorgeous. "Appena se la vide vicina e fu sotto l'impero di quegli occhi ardenti, Elias si sentì perduto" [As soon as he saw her nearby and was under the spell of those burning eyes, Elias felt himself lost] (71). Again, for him it is an external matter; her fiery eyes have a near fatal effect.[13] The governing strength is not within Elias; it is outside of his power. Later Elias is working in the fields; unexpectedly as though out of the blue, he sees Maddalena coming toward him with an air of determination. He sits passively on the stone fence; he lets her approach without taking action. Inexorably she nears, drawing closer and closer. He remains seated; she arrives and significantly stands over him in the superior position to this man-child. They embrace. She is the aggressor; she comes to him. Unwillingly (but not really), he dances the dance choreographed by the dominant Maddalena; he cannot resist; and their miserable fate is determined by her ascendancy over him. The approaching Maddalena's dignified carriage and air of confident self-composure reflect Lilliu's thoughts on women's role in Sardinian society which he traces back even to Nuraghic times. Lilliu expatiates upon certain cave drawings which illustrate clearly that prehistoric Sardinian women also carried themselves with a note of "severe composure, sometimes with a solemn and unspoken tragicity: like the Sardinian woman still has today" (28). Evidently that same female ascendancy has roots which predate by millennia Deledda's literary depictions. Women for a Deleddan man are larger than life; they stand taller; women are the focalizers; they have a commanding presence.[14]

In *Il segreto dell'uomo solitario*, when Cristiano declares his love to Sarina, he amalgamates with almost all of his fictive, male counterparts. Cristiano gets down on his knees; he tells Sarina to do with him whatever she wishes; he throws himself at her feet and likens himself to "the dust you walk on" (583; see also 540 and 579). His words are almost identical to those spoken to the indomitable Marianna Sirca by her own submissive lover. Deledda's men love to snivel in positions of surrender. In *Le colpe altrui* Andrea wants Vittoria at any cost; and what a price he is willing to pay!

Vittoria, dolcezza, amore, oblio, ecco il soldato steso ai tuoi piedi, tu puoi calpestarlo, basta che gli lasci lambire il tuo piede; e se gli prometti ancora una goccia d'acqua, un pezzo di pane, egli tradirà per te il suo destino, e suo padre e sua madre, e sè stesso (82).

[Vittoria, sweetness, love, forgetfulness, here is the soldier prostrate at your feet, you can kick him, but it's enough for him that you let him lick your foot; and if you promise him a drop of water, a crust of bread, for you he will betray his own destiny, his father, his mother and himself.]

No matter how ridiculously low the man sinks in his servility, the women revel in their superior position over the men; they always choose the groveller, but then disdain him for being weak. When Deledda's men are not licking their women's feet, they are behaving like lap dogs; and the women love them for it.

Mundula describes the typical Sardinian woman throughout history where the mother always had a strong role to play, but men were the absolute *padroni* [masters]. Wives were expected to be a "wise housewife, administrator of her husband's goods" (59). Mundula continues: "Moreover, formally the woman is downtrodden, humble, housewifely, but in reality at times she dominates the whole situation with her personality, and it is the husband who effectively is demoted to second place" (59). And he is not exaggerating, especially in the Deleddan context. When we read Deledda, we are forced to ask how a stereotypically unshakeable patriarchy can sustain the consistently bizarre behavior of such male juveniles, yet continue to produce strong women who themselves display little evidence of serious misandry and who ironically seem to foster and abet that very patriarcal system which is ultimately so detrimental to their lives? The answer resides in recent research.

In *The Cinderella Complex*, Colette Dowling elaborates on the men-as-passive model from the woman's point of view.[15] She answers a common question that arises in the literature of psychology: Why would a woman put up with all this swinish behavior? Because by sharing with one another the comforting 'all-men-are-babies' clichè, women can vent some of the pain of their girlish disillusionment without risking change.[16]

They never have to do anything about their lives. They simply, comfortingly, complain. The dependent wife often veers back and forth between building her husband up and tearing him down. . . . As Big Nurse, a woman whose self-confidence is a slender reed can gain an illusory potency.[17] 'See how well I cope?' her every act demands. 'Trust me. Rely on me.' Under the guise of helping their husbands, many women have an emotional investment in keeping their husbands weak. Weak, men will always need their wives. Weak, they will never leave (156).

This explanation obtains for most of Deledda's novels where the women fall squarely into this paradigm. For in a society where—no matter how strong and assertive—women without financial security plainly could not support themselves, it makes sense that they would both disdain their men's childish behavior and at the same time strive to keep them from ever abandoning the family. The collective result for the male/female relationship is a lifelong pattern that gets rehearsed by both partners who execute their assigned roles without deviation, each for his or her own tacit reasons. In a riveting analysis of this very phenomenon, *The Dance of Anger*, Harriet Lerner discusses at length the notion that human relationships equivalate to a "dance" where each partner learns the steps and sticks to the script, if the alliance is to endure. She analyzes, for example, a typical quarrel where each person recites the same objections, defenses, and excuses and knows from much experience what the partner's rebuttal will be. Each individual learns to rely on the other's position to keep the disagreement evenly balanced within those comfortable and well-rehearsed confines. Because if they were to argue about the real, deeper issues of basic incompatibility, they would have to face certain raw truths which neither wants to confront. No matter how outrageous certain behaviors are, problems only arise in the relationship when one of the parties refuses "to dance the dance."[18] If in the desirable equilibrium of the sexes each party performs according to the reassuring, tried and true script, then the status quo is preserved and the frightening notion of radical change is circumvented. With the same general notion in mind, Deledda maps out in male/female relationships the tenuous balance that keeps the Sardinian system in harmony. Thus one sex abets the other in an endless roundelay where nothing is ever discussed in depth for fear of having to adjust offending behaviors, where nothing is lost, nothing is won, and most important, nothing ever changes.

MISOGYNISTS

While the idea of the eternal adolescent is an important organizing principle of Deledda's works, it is not the only filter through which she looks at life. It in itself is not her obsession. Her fascination does not end with merely *depicting* it. Something broader is in play, especially considering her works as a *quadro d'insieme*. In *The Wendy Dilemma*, Kiley has a serviceable, contemporary explanation for what also transpires in Deledda's novels. "Mothering a man encourages immature behavior" (11–12); yet "mothering him sometimes seems like the best way to express love. . . . Women trapped in this dilemma . . . face several internal battles: the traditional feminine role versus personal freedom, self-promotion versus self-sacrifice" (12); because some of these women have not yet gained control over their own lives, "they adopt attitudes and behaviors that make them feel they are controlling the lives of others. Mothering becomes the key strategy in their attempt to gain some semblance of adult control" (12). Kiley points out that most overly nurturing mother figures are filled with self-doubt; they must please others out of fear and insecurity; they feel inferior to others; others control their destiny" (24–25). Along the same lines, Dowling suggests that female enablers and nurturers subconsciously may be joining up with men of arrested maturation precisely to avoid striking out on their own. Some women evidently have a hidden fear of independence.[19] This interpretation does not make for especially comforting reading; nevertheless, in Deledda's work it accounts for the *seemingly* random details stressing the mother–son relationships of numerous episodes. This may be helpful information at the beginning of the third millennium, but in the late nineteenth-century culture into which Deledda's women were born, functioning independently as a single woman by choice, exercising a profession, or even contemplating a career were *not* options (*Marianna Sirca* notwithstanding). Grazia Deledda's own life of constant vilification is an excellent example of what happened to women who tried to fashion fulfilling lives for themselves. They were lambasted beyond endurance. In Deledda's case, in exasperation she was forced to leave her island in order to find the relative peace in which to write; yet even that drastic action did not solve her problems with the literary critics. Deledda's women do infantilize their men; but in some instances, it seems to be a successful strategy to keep the men dependent and at home. In doing so, the women also gain a certain reassuring (albeit false) sense of being in control of their own future. Given the place, time, and lack of other options for Sardinian women, what else could they do?

Unfortunately the consequences of strong women pairing off with inneffectual men are that the stalwart women suffer in more than obvious ways when their men are effeminized. The men who find themselves in an untraditional position of inferiority within a traditional society sometimes deal with it in socially proscribed ways. Perhaps at least partly because of their intensely close, yet ultimately unsatisfying relationships with their mothers, wives and mother-figures (but no matter what the reason), many of Deledda's grown-up boys eventually reveal distinct evidence of misogyny. [20] Marilyn Migiel sees this in the last pages of *Cenere*.

> We begin to see how much Anania's actions are motivated by his desire for power, for it is only here that Anania comes into real conflict both with Margherita and with his mother. He is involved in a desperate play for power with both these women, since he perceives both of them as being at times weaker than he is, at times irritatingly stronger, more generous, and more aware than he is. The latter qualities he can in no way tolerate. Despite his tendencies toward pettiness and cruelty, Anania depicts himself as victim to Margherita; actually she turns out to be a scary figure because she has at times a threatening voice (a voice that in some instances lacks the maternal tones of compassion and generosity, a voice that does not speak in simple tones, but has recourse to rhetoric), and she writes with 'caratteri rotondi, quasi maschili' (117) [rounded, almost masculine letters] (69).

Anania suffers pangs of distaste over the power struggle with the two women in his life, but other protagonists escalate the battle into unmitigated loathing. At times the Deleddan males' hate for women is so strong that they actively engage in vivid fantasies of violence. They day dream of overpowering their women in chimerical scenes of rage and force, most often brought about by their powerlessness over those very dominating women whom they have actively pursued and chosen to love. In *Marianna Sirca*, Marianna personifies all of Simone's loathing for the Sardinian class system that he thinks forced him into banditry and emarginated him from society. He does not love her, but he needs to ravish her, to possess her, to violate her, to wreak revenge on a system that he believes has kept him poor, on the outskirts of society and in his place. She suffers at his hand just by existing as an independent woman in a man's world.

Simone takes great pleasure in making Marianna cry: "provava in fondo un piacere crudele a vederla così umiliata e vinta"[21] [down deep he felt a cruel pleasure in seeing her so humiliated and vanquished] (822). The need to put her in her place overrides Simone's rationality; but Simone's rival-in-love, Sebastiano has plans of his own for Marianna. "Fossero stati soli! Si sentiva capace di afferrarla per la vita e spezzarla sul suo ginocchio come una canna" [If they had only been alone! He felt capable of seizing her by the waist and breaking her over his knee like a reed] (841).

The sexual overtones are evident in this fantasy of violence in a spanking position. Sebastiano is clearly enraged and wants only to harm Marianna. His frustration with her strong will plays out not with rational, adult behavior, but with outbursts of dangerous fury. At times various men think about dominating Marianna in situations of rage, usually brought about immediately after a manifestation of Marianna's powerful, controlling personality. Unused to women with an independent streak, Marianna's men can devise only one solution to this female anomaly: sexual battery.[22]

Similarly, in *Cenere* Anania eventually grows to detest Margherita. Deledda puts into his mouth all the misogyny one would expect from this particular adult-adolescent (who also evinces many of the symptoms of the syndrome in general).

> Come ella era vile! Vile sino alla spudoratezza. Vile e coscientemente vile. La Dea ammantata di maestà e di bontà aveva sciolto i suoi veli aurei e appariva ignuda, impastata d'egoismo e di crudeltà; La Minerva taciturna apriva le labbra per bestemmiare: il simbolo s'apriva, si spaccava come un frutto, roseo al di fuori, nero e velenoso all'interno. Ella era la Donna, completa, con tutte le sue feroci astuzie (229).

> [How vile she was! Vile to the point of shamelessness. Vile and consciously vile. The Goddess cloaked in majesty and goodness had unfurled her golden veils and was naked, full of egoism and cruelty. The taciturn Minerva parted her lips to curse: the icon was splitting open like a piece of fruit, pink on the outside, inside black and poisonous. She was Woman, complete with all her ferocious craftiness.]

Anania's vitriol is conveyed through the tone and imagery of his monologue, dripping with sarcasm and fury; the sexual innuendo in his "split open fruit" simile is especially disturbing when we learn in addition that he considers the inside of the fruit a black poison.[23] His misogyny bubbles to the surface with a vivid, figurative language that speaks volumes about his attitudes toward Margherita. Minerva, the Roman goddess (Athena in Greek mythology) was famous for her beauty and her undefiled virginity. She was also a fierce and ruthless battle goddess. This is how Ananias envisions Margherita.

When Elias Portolu announces that he wants to be a priest,

concomitantly he admits his dislike for women. "Per me donne e uomini sono la stessa cosa, anzi le donne sono più spregevoli degli uomini" [For me men and women are all the same, on the contrary, women are more despicable than men] (49). Elias establishes a connection between the priesthood and his difficulty with people in general, but especially with women.[24] Being a priest will provide him with an effective shield against having to deal with what makes him uncomfortable. In *La via del male* Pietro cruelly wants Maria to believe that he is in love with her for his own reasons, specifically to obtain revenge on all the women who have treated him badly. His misogyny takes the form of vendetta.

> E avrebbe riso. Le donne si beffavano di lui; egli voleva ridersi delle donne (239). . . . Bisogna essere astuti; astuti come le donne . . . Bisognava che anch'io diventi maligno, calcolatore, astuto (315).

> [And he would have laughed. Women made fun of him; he wanted to have a laugh over them. . . . One must be shrewd, astute like women . . . I too have to become nasty, calculating, cunning.]

Pietro wants to make up for what he believes are past injustices and he will effect his plan at the expense of Maria. Cristiano of *Il segreto dell'uomo solitario* takes that concept a step further; he is furious with Ghiana for blackmailing him and complicating his affair with Sarina. He thinks to himself. "Ah, bisogna essere duro con le donne, Cristiano: duro come il domatore che solo con la minaccia della sofferenza e della morte tiene fermo l'istinto cieco delle belve" [Ah, a guy has to be tough with women, Christian: tough like an animal tamer who only dominates the blind instinct of wild animals with the threat of suffering and death] (554). Whereas Pietro above chooses to combat women with simple revenge, Cristiano raises his hatred to the level of intimidation with the threat of physical harm and even death to the woman.

The topic of misogyny was not a late discovery for Deledda; it is one that she treated from the very beginning of her career, starting with one of her earliest publications, "Romanzo minimo" ["A Trivial Novel"], written when Deledda was a twenty-one-year-old. With a male voice speaking in the first person, the author creates a protagonist who wants to humiliate a woman and who then admits to his own regression into infancy.

> Mentre nello stesso tempo, provavo una strana gioia, pensando che potevo finalmente umiliarla!—Umiliarla, oh, umiliarla! Veder finalmente chinare quegli occhi altieri e misteriosi, quella fronte fredda e

ironica, innanzi a me! Che vittoria! Che vittoria! E ritornato bambino, senza per nulla ponderare la mia azione odiosa e leggera, lasciai la finestra . . . (31).

[While at the same time I felt a strange joy, thinking that finally I could humiliate her! To humiliate her, oh, to humiliate her! Finally to see her lower those haughty and mysterious eyes, that cold and ironic face in front of me! What a victory! What a victory! And become a little boy again, not at all evaluating my hateful and frivolous actions, I left the window . . .] [25]

Just this sampling of several instances of misogyny dating from the very beginning of her career reveals a whole gamut of the manifestations of an emotionally immature man's hate toward women. Deledda's men choose either to make her cry or to break her in two, to publicly humiliate her, to domesticate her with force, to take revenge or to threaten suffering or even death with the tools of an animal tamer. From the first works of Deledda's career to her last novel, the matter of misogyny was of lifelong, literary interest to her (mostly in the form of *leitmotivs*. There are no novels where the main theme is wife battery, deliberate emotional assault, or mental cruelty). In this matter of misogyny, Deledda was not content to leave the issue with simple scenes of woman bashing. At times her characters gravely escalate their vengeful desires.

RAPE FANTASIES

Some of Deledda's men do not limit themselves, as those above, to daydreams of punishing their women and wishful thinking of retribution, spite, and revenge in general. Not simple cases of innocent, youthful exuberance, these men truly are in an "emotional uproar." George Will bemoans their lives, "lived in subordination to elemental and unedited appetites."[26] In some cases they relish doing serious, specific, physical harm to their women. In certain instances their woolgathering is nothing short of rape fantasy.[27] For example, when Marianna Sirca insists that Simone get right with the law, he promises to return by Christmas with an answer, during which time the rage builds up inside Simone. He goes off to his hideout in the mountains to ruminate on his youth as a servant in the Sirca household and how he was forced to endure constant humiliation at the hands of the powerful, all of whom crystallize into the person of Marianna. The more

Simone thinks about accosting Marianna, the more rabid he becomes emotionally. He feels something akin to a beast within
which elicits pain and spiritual agitation.[28] All of Simone's hate
for the class system that forced him into banditry is personified
in Marianna. He does not love her; but the monster of hate in him
needs to possess her, to violate her in order to exact revenge on a
society that forced him to press his nose against the window of
life. Eventually Simone agrees with Costantino that he cannot
surrender to the law and that Marianna will have to accept him
as he is. If she will not, then he will take her—forcibly (766). He
works himself into a lather of rage, focusing on her; and in a disturbing passage, we learn that there is grave danger lurking
within the powerless Simone Sole. His indirect discourse reveals
just how embittered he is.

> Era diventato padrone come anelava nel tempo della sua servitù.
> Marianna, la sua padrona di quel tempo, quella che neppure lo guar-
> dava in viso, Marianna lo amava e aveva promesso di aspettarlo.
> Come tutto questo era accaduto? Appena l'aveva riveduta lassù da-
> vanti alla casa colonica, nei luoghi ove era stato servo maltrattato dai
> servi, gli erano tornati tutti i suoi desideri violenti di quel tempo, tutti
> personificati in lei. Afferrare lei era afferrare tutte le cose che lei rap-
> presentava: quindi era rimasto in agguato nel bosco intorno a lei, per
> darle la caccia. Ma nell'agguato pensava al come prenderla meglio;
> viva e non morta, in modo da possederla per sempre e non per un is-
> tante solo (759).

> [He had become *someone*, as he craved back in the time of his servi-
> tude. Marianna, his boss back then, the one who wouldn't even look
> him in the face, Marianna now loved him and had promised to wait
> for him. How did all this happen? As soon as he saw her down there
> in front of the [Sirca] country house, in the places where he had been
> a servant abused by other servants, all of his violent desires came
> back to him from those days, all personified in her. To seize her was
> to seize everything that she represented: so he stayed hidden in the
> surrounding woods, as if to stalk her. But while hiding out, he
> thought about how best to get her; alive not dead, in such a way as to
> possess her forever, not for just one instant.]

Simone feels powerless and wants to wrest forcibly Marianna's
love. The following passage from *La via del male* compares with
Simone's vision of the violent payback. In this next case, there
appears yet another instance of a male servant who needs to dominate the *padrona*. She is the boss; in his perception he is the
lowly hireling whom she kicks around. His only source of domina-

tion is sexual and he dreams about overpowering her to teach her a lesson. Deledda presents a frightening pseudo-rape, where the immature Pietro, fantasizes what he would do to the despised Maria: "Vorrei fosse qui ora; la butterei per terra, la bacerei morsicandola. Ecco, vipera: . . . Ecco, a te questi baci cattivi" [I wish she were here now; I would throw her on the ground, I would kiss her, biting her. There, you serpent: . . . Here, these painful kisses are for you.] (226).

This is seemingly an unimportant scene within the context of the novel, but when one takes stock of the power struggle involved, the relatively minor episode takes on greater importance. Handled differently, this could be a scene of a playful lover's cuffing—the proverbial "toss in the hay," which ends with an innocent kiss. But Deledda chooses violent verbs (throwing, biting); she extends the kiss to one which produces pain. Instead of using an endearing nickname for Maria, she is a serpent. Pietro always feels subservient to women, a little shy, a bit inferior (200). This bothers him even more. He contemplates his bashfulness and rues his own feelings of servitude. Later a regretful Pietro knows that he could have raped Maria in the vinyards and forced their marriage; he bewails the fact that he did not choose that strategy; he tells himself that he has been stupid, "like a little boy" (317). Pietro chastizes himself; little boys do not rape, men do; in his mind, therefore, he must not be a real man. A kindred spirit of Simone and Pietro is Mikali of *Le colpe altrui* who wants Vittoria any possible way he can get her. He dreams of conquering her:

E sentiva una smania violenta di arrampicarsi con le unghie sui muri, di penetrare per le fessure e devastare tutto là dentro e portarsi via come un tesoro rubato la donna che non voleva essere sua (172).

[And he felt a violent urge to scale the walls by his fingernails, to penetrate through the opening and to destroy everything inside and to take away like a stolen treasure the woman who refused to be his.]

Deledda's prose is undergirded by sexual allusion; she never makes explicit what is implicit; yet, this scene is clearly one of erotic violence. Mikali's mental image of penetration with the intent to destroy, his desire to steal something of value, the essential objection being her unwillingness to be his (the wall), all point to the classic excuses and justifications for rape. To emphasize his intentions, Mikali boasts to his friends of being a *real* man and of forcibly demanding Vittoria's respect. Immediately, with his audience watching, he then jumps on an unbroken horse (read: the untamed Vittoria), and he flourishes his riding crop "whooping for joy" (185). Waving his phallic symbol for all to see, Mikali engages in the masturbatory/rape scene that Deledda could never have depicted without censorship; but by including the kinky elements of sex fantasy (woman as horse, riding crop), the author plants just enough clues for the agile reader to interpret what she has in mind.[29] Since the literal scene conforms with Mikali's previously established prowess as a horseman, no possible censorial repercussions could obtain.

These male fantasies of rape, battery, and sexual mayhem, however, are mere child's play when compared to Deledda's most extreme case. In a graphic and uncharacteristically gruesome scene, Deledda presents Luca of *Il vecchio e i fanciulli* who, in connection with his archenemy, Francesca, dreams of the first meal he intends to devour upon his recovery from a self-inflicted gunshot wound (significantly caused, in his mind, by a woman).

'Il primo agnello che trovo è mio: lo arrostirò vivo sulle brage e me lo divorerò tutto: gli caverò gli occhi caldi col dito e li manderò giù come acini d'uva nera; sorbirò le cervella come un dolce e il suo sangue come il sacerdote nella messa quello di Cristo; gli leverò la lingua tutta intera e la mangerò in un boccone. E i rognoni che danno forza? In ultimo succhierò la coda, piano piano, suonandola come un flauto di canna.' Egli si godeva già il pasto mostruoso, crudele e vivificante, con un senso di voluttà carnale, come se sognasse di possedere con violenza una donna (683).

["The first lamb I find is mine: I'll roast it alive on the embers and I'll devour it all myself: I'll dig out its hot eyeballs with my finger and I'll gulp them down like black grapes; I'll sip its brains like dessert and its blood like a priest at Mass does with Christ's; I'll cut out its tongue whole and I'll eat it in one mouthful. And its kidneys that make you strong? Lastly I'll suck its tail, very slowly, playing it like a reed flute." He was already enjoying this monstrous, cruel and vivifying meal with a sense of carnal voluptuousness, as if he were dreaming of raping a woman.]

Any representational spectacle of rape or sexual battery that Deledda could provide would be rendered superfluous by her depiction of the unspeakable, ghoulish violence delivered by the allegorical nature of this scene. And it is precisely the *figurative* rendition of rape that makes the episode so vivid. In effect Deledda depicts what Luca would like to do to Francesca. The erotic itinerary of his reverie begins with her (the lamb's) head and works his way to a scene of ersatz cunnilingus; significantly he wants to destroy her sight, her brain, and her ability to speak. He wants to tease her sexually as though playing an instrument, while at the same time retaining the power for himself. Luca will ultimately settle for nothing less than total anihilation of the woman (sacrificial lamb), but he especially fears Francesca's most important senses—her eyes, her intellect, and her ability to articulate her desires; namely, the tools she uses to infuriate him. Just one page after this erotic fantasy, Luca senses a woman near his sick-bed and thinks of Francesca:

> Pensava con soddisfazione alla probabilità d'incontrarsi con lei e guardarla con disprezzo, sentirla umiliata, piccola e stesa sotto il suo sguardo come un compagno vinto che, a volerlo, si può bastonarlo a sangue (684).

> [He thought with satisfaction about the chances of meeting her and of looking at her with disdain, to feel her humiliated, small and supine under his gaze like a vanquished companion who, if one wanted, one could beat to death.]

At first Luca obsessed on how he wanted to rape Francesca; but only one page later, he contemplates beating her to death. Turn another page and when she comes to wash him, he remembers that his mother used to do that when he was a sick child (685). He mentally connects the object of his rape fantasy with his mother. He hates Francesca; he equates Francesca with his mother; he hates his mother. He wants to rape and do violence to women. The two women in his life shade into each other; Francesca and his mother fuse into an Oedipal object of loathing.[30] It all merges into one dysfunctional, psychosexual quagmire for Luca. But Deledda is not finished with the possibilities of this episode. When Luca subsequently tells Ulpiano what the latter's daughter, Francesca, did to him, Ulpiano too wants to do violence to her.

> Era pronto a prenderla per i capelli, legarla ad un albero con le corde di pelo che si usano per il bestiame, e frustarla fino a sangue: che le sue grida risonassero per tutte le terre della contrada, ed anche i cani arrabbiati e le faine crudeli in cerca di cibo ne avessero pietà (686).

> [He was ready to grab her by the hair, tie her to a tree with the fiber ropes that are used for farm animals, and whip her bloody: let her

screams echo throughout the countryside, so that even the mad dogs and vicious martens searching for food would feel sorry for her.]

Even Francesca's father engages in a misogynistic scene of outrage aimed at his own daughter; the father's wrath is only outdone by the viciousness of Luca's own. Deledda deals both with the exaggerated reactions of a spurned lover and with the general principle of woman-bashing, given the father's taste for ropes, whips, animals, and blood. For when even fathers conjecture doing such things to their female offspring, the Deleddan issue explodes into a more universal problem than simply the relations between lovers. When Francesca answers him harshly, Luca thinks to himself:

Ah, come gli sarebbe piaciuto lottare con lei, rotolare assieme avvinghiati sull'erba e fra i cardi spinosi, morderla e schiacciarla come una mandorla fresca (703).

[Ah, how he would have loved to wrestle with her, to roll around tangled up together on the grass and among the prickly cardoons, to bite her and to split her open like a fresh almond.]

This is Luca's fantasy: a retributional rape where he really is not craving fresh almonds at all (just as previously Anania of *Cenere* was hardly talking about "split fruit" when he spewed his hate for Margherita). And these two protagonists are not alone. Still on the topic of mother nature's fruitful bounty, *Annalena Bilsini*'s son, Osea, engages in his own imaginings which are part of yet another clever allegory on Deledda's part. He is plowing the earth and finding it very rough going indeed.

Quando la terra si rifiutava ad aprirsi, simile alla donna che resiste all'atto d'amore, egli se la pigliava con l'aratro, rivolgendogli le più schifose ingiurie; poi lo percuoteva con un suo frustino, aiutandolo però a procedere nella sua opera (546).

[When the earth refused to open up for him, like a woman who resists the act of love, he got angry with the plow, directing the most vulgar insults to it; then he beat it with his whip, helping it to get on with its job.]

Deledda is not an author to waste space bucolicly describing a farmer doing his work. Osea is attempting to rape mother earth and masturbating his own recalcitrant plow in order to achieve penetration. This scene needs to appear here because we find later that Osea's wife has indeed finally become pregnant, of which Osea conceives as "la terra posseduta con violenza dal sole" [earth raped by the sun] (605). Osea equates his plow with his penis; his wife with the earth; and himself with the sun. Not willing to let this metaphoric allegory slip away unnoticed, Deledda tells us later that Osea has bought a new plow; he looks at it lovingly and fondles all the parts "of his new plaything" (658). The onanistic possibilities of Osea's new plow convert the scenes above into resonant messages about his attitudes toward women. Most disturbing are his notions of having to rape in order to conceive a child. Deledda uses this thinly veiled scene to hint at Osea's own sexual problems (so characteristic of arrested maturity) and how he transfers to the woman his rage over his own quasi-impotence.

Grazia Deledda could never have broached this subject openly in her day. Much as she did with the *leitmotivs* of oral sex and homosexuality, for propriety she is forced to camouflage the real issue with an age-old allegory, that of the farmer and the plow.[31] For many of Deledda's men the act of love is not a mutually satisfying, male/female endeavor; instead it is a violent theft, a debasement, a painful punishment for the woman. The Deleddan unhappy man is unable to deal on an equal basis with the assertive woman; so he attempts to subjugate her in the only way he knows.

THE TROUBLE WITH WOMEN

Whatever their own intentions and expectations, unrealistic dreams and desires, whatever the external reasons, many of Deledda's juvenile men inevitably must settle for twisted relationships with women. In *The Wendy Dilemma,* Kiley sees the adult-adolescent's ability to solve problems "disappearing at the cost of unbridled narcissism" (29). As such, it seems that an immature man's failure to grow up elicits in the woman her strongest mothering instincts, creating that vicious circle in which so many Deleddan couples find themselves. Typically the childish man's love is not the true and lasting kind, but one of short-term infatuation followed by the disillusion that has by now become part of the syndrome of arrested maturation. Deledda's men do not discern the difference until it is too late.

At the breathless beginning of their affair, Elias Portolu views

Maddalena descended upon this earth as the incarnation of utter perfection. When *zio* Martinu suggests that his brother's failed marriage to Maddalena may have had the same sorry result if Elias had married her instead, the adult-adolescent in Elias vehemently protests that, unlike his brother, *he* would have worshipped the ground upon which she walks (95). Later, however, well into their incestuous affair when he eventually does tire of her (just as the wise *zio* Martinu had predicted), we are reminded of Elias's earlier protestation of his love for her and how he once adored everything about her.

Elias's psychological problems preclude his experiencing real, enduring, abiding, all-accepting, unconditional, adult love. He is a boy of fleeting passion; his immature way of loving needs to maintain a distance, lest he discover the defects in the object of his idealization. This is a major constituent of Elias Portolu's problem (and that of most sufferers of arrested maturation). Worse yet, he fails to recognize the problem but instead specifically wants Maddalena to stay virginal and pure. When *zio* Martinu insists that Elias will grow weary of Maddalena, when she has children, goes to seed, and no longer takes care of herself, Elias becomes angry. "Voi v'ingannate, zio Martinu. Questo è il guaio: ella non avrà mai dei figli, si conserverà a lungo bella e fresca" [You're dreaming, uncle Martinu. This is the tragedy: she will never have children; she will remain forever beautiful and fresh] (96).

The dreamer in Elias needs a virgin not a prostitute (conveniently named Maddalena). He naïvely predicts that she will remain pure for the rest of her life. He vows he loves her "for herself," not for her beauty (96). *Zio* Martinu is right; as usual Elias does not heed his advice; and not long after, Elias notices that he has begun to feel disgust for Maddalena (133). Despite his averral to "love her for herself," he is put off by her motherhood and her ironic failure to keep herself virginal for him.

Initially, when Maddalena tells Elias that she is pregnant, he is ecstatic. But soon thereafter her impending motherhood ruins his ideal of chaste womanhood. She is either his madonna or his prostitute, but he cannot let her be both.[32] He compromises by thinking about her as the "the mother of his little boy" (135). Their son then takes Maddalena's place in his obsessional heirarchy. Elias needs *someone* to love him; it seems not to matter whom; and ever the narcissistic Deleddan man, he will do anything to get that love.[33] By the end of the novel his love for Maddalena is only in connection with their baby; and his love for the baby is only in association with himself.[34]

Both Bruno of *Il nostro padrone* [Our Master], and Anania of *Cenere* suffer much the same problem—they have an unworldly conception of their women, Sebastiana for Bruno and Margherita for Anania. They both want someone they cannot have; and they both conceptualize the object of their love in saintly terms.

> *Bruno*: "Come la desiderava, adesso che era lontana e il desiderarla non portava pericolo" [How he wanted her, now that she was far away and desiring her brought no danger] (262).

> *Anania*: "Pensavo a te come a una santa, soave, pura, fresca e bella" [I thought about you like a saint, sweet, pure, fresh and beautiful] (164).

In both cases the woman is their *donna-angelo*, their madonna figure to offset their mothers who, interestingly, were both prostitutes. In the end almost all of Deledda's male protagonists are left with neither the virgin nor the whore; and they remain befuddled, their emotional problems surpassing neurosis but not quite approaching certifiably psychotic disorders. The men in Deledda's prose for the most part manage to function (however badly) in society; but it is their rapport with women that causes the most distress.

WHAT DO WOMEN WANT?

> Questi mariti della Deledda sono figure quasi sempre infelicissime, spesso funzionari di grassa borghesia ma forniti di deteriori caratteristiche spirituali. È triste che la scrittrice che così palesemente dedica la sua attenzione alle donne, senta sempre il bisogno di porre loro accanto tali disturbanti fantocci.[35]

> [Deledda's husbands are almost always very sad figures, often comfortable bourgeois functionaries, but endowed with flawed spiritual characteristics. It is sad that the writer who so openly dedicates her attention to women always feels the need to pair them with such disturbing puppets.]

Deledda's women command superiority over their men; they are imposingly strong characters who attract their opposites in the men who court them. It would not be surprising to find many women who take advantage of their upper hand. Yet there is no evidence in Deledda's prose that the typical woman lays traps for the first weak man who stumbles onto the scene; for the most part Deledda normally offers common, human situations where ordinarily a man has certain qualities and a woman has precisely the opposite characteristics to make for an interesting match where something is to be gained for both. But at least two of Deledda's women consciously finesse the ascendancy factor to work in their favor, where the woman recognizes the flaws in her man and cynically takes advantage of the occasions presented to her. Given the lack of options in life for Deledda's women, it is not shocking that a few devise less than scrupulous strategies to obtain what they need: financial security, social approbation, children as a safety net for their old age.[36] The only two clear examples of this sort of opportunism do illustrate the point that not *all* Deledda's women are blameless martyrs on the altar of arrested maturation.

For instance, in order to marry Stefano, Maria of *La giustizia* [Justice], needs to win over her future father-in-law. She homes in on Stefano's father's soft spot and does exactly what is necessary to place herself in good light. Maria discovers that while Stefano's father is indeed the ogre she had imagined him to be, nevertheless he does have a weakness:

Anzi gli scoprì subito il debole più evidente, che era un formidabile egoismo infantile, e s'avvide che per conquistare quel piccolo animo, bisognava lusingarlo e dargli sempre ragione (36).

[On the contrary, she immediately discovered his most obvious weakness, which was a formidable juvenile egoism, and she became aware that to conquer that little soul, she had to flatter him and always agree with him.]

Maria's cynicism eventually works in her favor; she takes advantage of his "formidable juvenile egoism" and gets what she wants. Similarly in *Il segreto dell'uomo solitario* there appears another woman like Maria who excels at exploiting the adolescent traits of her man. Ghiana wants to keep her unsuspecting husband happy at home, yet have her lover on the side; she uses her astuteness to achieve that goal. Carrying Cristiano's child, Ghiana has her husband thinking that the child is his. She describes him: "È tanto buono, povero ragazzo, ancora obbediente ai suoi genitori, come un bambino" [He's so good, poor boy; he still obeys his parents like a little kid] (547). In both novels, these two women blatantly take advantage of the fact that their men are babies, and then they exploit them using their ability to analyze them psychologically and pounce upon the opportunities presented by their weakness. Bruce Merry provides an interesting point of view.

> Grazia Deledda advances the cause of the disinherited sex cautiously, by showing that contemporary women had a longer memory, better skills at dissimulation and tighter strategies for coping with adversity than their brothers, husbands and fathers. This may be little, but at a time when most male Italian novelists forged female characters who were either eccentric aristocrats or working-class dupes, Deledda's portrayal shows in a systematic counter-proposal that men had in fact, as always, moulded women to suit their fantasies. Women were neither dolls nor dragons, alternately to be stroked or dreaded by their masters. There were real creatures, adept at coping and especially at waiting (35).

Pace Bruce Merry, Deledda's women are not just "adept" at coping, and they do not do a whole lot of "waiting." Many are astute, proactive tacticians. These last two women protagonists strategize consciously and by some could be considered despicable for their chicanery; but on the whole the Deleddan woman is not a nefarious manipulator. The great majority of Deledda's women appear to be disenfranchised individuals in unsatisfying relationships who are trying mightily to carve a place for themselves in a world made for others. Eurialo De Michelis has called *Marianna Sirca* "the sum total of all Deledda's own life experiences up to that point, but brought to the maximum of intensity" (*Deledda e il Decadentismo* 125). He is right. Like the author herself, Deledda's women need to be free. They are intrepid; and in a whole spectrum of ways they too strive for the same independence that the reluctant feminist in Deledda demanded for herself.

Marianna Sirca's obsessive desire for freedom began when her father took her as a child to live with *zio* Prete [her uncle, the priest]; there she was forced to be his personal servant.[37] As a consequence, now she especially prizes her freedom as an independent adult of inherited wealth. Yet, the ghosts from her past haunt her still; she cannot forget that in her youth she was a humiliated dependent. She hates living in Nuoro because she resides in the late *zio* Prete's house. On the contrary, she loves her *casa colonica* [country house] where she feels sovereign and self-reliant. When her father waxes dumbfounded upon learning that she intends to marry their former servant who is now a bandit (and not even a famous one at that) (816), she informs him that it is precisely *because* Simone Sole cannot give her anything that she loves him. Marianna is beholden to no one. When Marianna can no longer control the convoluted situation with Simone Sole and the law, she feels like a chained prisoner (823). Deledda creates a prototypical, liberated woman in Marianna Sirca—one who cherishes and protects her autonomy above all else.

There are many worthy female cousins for Marianna throughout Deledda's novels.[38] But Deledda especially shows her own yearnings for freedom in *Il nostro padrone*, where a painfully envious Sebastiana mentally cries out to her unmarried and unfettered friend:

> Tu sei libera! Sei libera!—ripetè due volte Sebastiana, col suo grido di allodola.—Tu non hai marito, non hai padre, nè madre, nè fratelli (271).

> [You're free! You're free! She repeated twice with her shriek like a skylark.—You don't have a husband, you don't have a father, nor a mother, nor brothers.]

Sebastiana is only eighteen but already feels trapped in a marriage where she is considered nothing more than chattel. It takes no stretch of the imagination to hear the young Grazia Deledda screaming the same words when she realized that her freedom to pursue her writing career was being curtailed for the same reasons that so distress Sebastiana.[39] It must have been especially galling for Deledda, the intelligent, successful and feisty professional woman, to have to obey orders (like her character, Sebastiana), from two prototypical brothers who did not merit a jot of her respect under any circumstances.

Giuliana Morandini points out that, "From her first short stories published under the pseudonym of Ilia di Sant'Ismael, to her articles on domestic life, her obsession with issues about Barbagia [Deledda's native region in Sardinia] is continual: a patriarchal society that negates her as a woman" (22).[40] Morandini is correct: Deledda was "negated" from the first hint as a teenager of her predilection for writing to the indignities perpetrated upon her corpse at the reinterment in Nuoro. Deledda lived to have her day, however. She exacted satisfaction by trying to sort out the problems she perceived in male/female relationships through the therapy of writing. She depicted men as she saw them behave and created women who deal in their own way with the little boy/men with whom they consort. Bruce Merry points out that

> Women in Sardinia in this period were excluded from management, executive action in farming or business and the professions. They were prevented, even when they inherited middle-class status, from travel or education. Hence we can see Deledda making up an alternative meaning for them. For example, she casts women compensatorily into all kinds of love affairs (13).

While Merry is correct about the dismissal and disenfranchisement of Sardinian women, Grazia Deledda does *much more* than just amuse her women with tangled love lives. She also playfully subverts the Sardinian process by exercising exquisite control over her prose. Stealthily she imbeds suggestive allegories in her stories; she drops veiled hints of proscribed behavior; unabashedly she tackles taboo topics. In many instances she even takes on the Church, especially evident in *Marianna Sirca* and *Annalena Bilsini*. And the potent, matriarchal Annalena Bilsini is one of the few Deleddan women who is *not* Sardinian. With this important touch Deledda is telling us that we are dealing with universal truisms, not just parochial issues pertinent only to the hinterlands of Nuoro.

As she was often accused of doing by her contemporary critics, Deledda may have written what appear on the surface to be silly love stories for even sillier women, but a mere scratch beneath the exterior story lines reveals an important subtext that belies the suggestion of a lack of authorial *gravitas*. Quite to the contrary, she presents, instead, very strong women who have to cope with exceptionally weak men—women who must devise strategies to deal with these adolescents in order to achieve spiritual peace and mental harmony (and sometimes to protect themselves financially at the same time). Typically Deledda's strong woman gets what she wants. But what *do* women want? In Deledda's writing, women want their freedom. In a letter to Onorato Roux dated Nuoro 31 October 1894, Deledda writes, "The portrait of my childhood and of my youth up to the day in which I got married and abandoned my native Sardinia, seems to me a biblical portrait, populated by patriarchal figures" (Scano 292). Deledda grew up in patronistic confinement and she made sure to use that experience in her stories. Merry wonders:

> To what extent is her fiction opposed to patriarchy, establishing a mode in which women can appropriate their own world? Did she her-

self intend her female characters to be fused into a single object of desire and abuse? What solutions does she find to the problem of women in isolation or in untenable situations?" (6).

Merry asks important questions. The answers are evident with close reading of her texts. In view of her description of men and of her women's reactions to those men, Merry's queries can be addressed in order: Deledda is unequivocally opposed to patriarchy; women appropriate their own world by combining their wits with their innate, psychological acumen. Deledda probably did intend for her women to be the object of desire and abuse—all the better to depict the adolescent behavior of her men who wielded the power afforded them by accident of birth. She presents in realistic terms a creative *rifacimento* of what she saw in her life. Her adroit solutions reside in her female characters' ability to assess intuitively a given situation without using power; they had none. Rather they use a resourceful and sophisticated psychology.

Deledda's strong women often fall for outlaws, delinquents, bandits, and emarginated men. (Marianna Sirca is the prime example). This is not surprising; for who better than a man on the fringes of society could relate to a woman who, herself, has broken all the rules? The dominating woman *is* the powerless bandit of the gender skirmishes; the male bandit is the powerless figure of Sardinian society; and Sardinia has always been the bandit of unified Italy.[41] Significantly Deledda rarely has her women collude with other females or even seek out kindred spirits among other women; Deleddan women are rarely close friends with other women. Hers are women alone with their struggle for independence. Deledda never waxes overtly political; she never spells out clearly what the interlinear only suggests. Never preachy, she delivers a nuanced message; and her silky narrative is among the most elegant of modern Italian prose.

At the ceremonies for the Nobel Prize for Literature in 1927, in his presentation speech Henrik Schück remarked, "She does not belong to that band of writers who work on a thesis and discuss problems. She has always kept herself far removed from the battles of the day." He continues with his praise of the writer and then quotes from a letter that Deledda once wrote.

I have always been what I am—a soul who becomes impassioned about life's problems and who lucidly perceives men as they are, while still believing that they could be better and that no one else but themselves prevents them from achieving God's reign on earth (Scano 3).

Surely Deledda was speaking in generalities about humankind, but there is ample evidence at the same time that she quite literally perceived *men* as they are, while optimistically admitting to the possibility of improvement in the relationships between men and women.

6

Conclusion

THE PROBABILITIES WERE SLIGHT FOR GRAZIA DELEDDA TO HAVE flourished even as a minor, regional, literary footnote, much less to win the Nobel Prize for literature. Personally and professionally she was insulted and savaged by her family, her home town, her fellow islanders, and her professional peers. Yet she etched her name into the history of literature by dint of her own sheer will to succeed. Against all odds and despite all the critical crosstalk, she left a compelling body of work where, within the context of an intuitive and almost preternatural feminism, prophetically there dwell most of the accepted characteristics of arrested maturation and its attendant manifestations vis-à-vis male/female relations.

Social expectations for emotional maturity are similar across cultural boundaries, at least in the western world.[1] This is evident in almost every internationally accepted, primary research source in clinical psychology where inevitably there appear common criteria for the attainment of adulthood.[2] These include: the ability to deal constructively with reality; to resist instant gratification, deferring immediate cravings in favor of long-lasting fulfillment; to adapt to change positively; to make and persevere with one's goals; to see through well-reasoned plans; to sublimate, directing one's instinctive hostile energy into creative and constructive outlets and to control ensuing anger and possible violence; to discover more contentedness in giving than receiving; to relate to others consistently with shared comfort and helpfulness; to be dependable; to be responsible to others; to honor commitments; to have the capacity to love; and to exhibit the relative absence of symptoms produced by anxiety. Maturity involves keeping one's covenants without quibbling—an absence of excuse-making. Mature adults are normally characterized by their ability to control their anger and to avoid physical clashes. One comes to expect from grown adults a certain amount of patience

151

accompanied by the maturity and ability to hold up under duress, to face problems without emotional collapse or histrionics, to stay the course without bolting when life presents unpleasantness. Maturity involves decision-making skills which also call into play the willingness to stick by those decisions.

Foregrounded in the cultural record, much like maturity, its opposite—arrested maturity—is also uninhibited by societal bias or political borders.[3] In western societies adult-adolescence is considered to be undergirded by narcissism.[4] Not always, but usually, borderline adult behavior appears in sons of relative privilege who felt unloved as adolescents, especially by their emotionally distant fathers.[5] The syndrome is characterized by an ambivalence toward the mother which usually swings wildly from love to hate.[6] The disorder also includes peer-orientation and external definition; an inability to love; prodigal spending and other compulsive manifestations; self-centeredness and exaggerated self-importance; powerlessness to empathize with others; a fear of manhood and responsibility of any kind; procrastination and magical thinking that problems will simply vanish on their own; a lack of self-reliance and self-control; and predictable undependability. Eternal adolescents, typical sufferers of arrested transition are extraordinarily charming and beguiling; they invariably choose a mate who is attracted to a boyishly charismatic man: a nurturing individual who is more than willing to function as the mother figure sought by her immature partner. Typically the strong, maternal woman unintentionally abets the juvenile behavior of her man while at the same time experiencing varying degrees of unhappiness as the relationship progresses.

This is the profile of arrested maturation that emerges from contemporary research; but modern clinical psychologists would do well to read the works of Grazia Deledda where these widely accepted social expectations were already under the writer's microscope over a century ago. Judging from the negative reaction of her fictional women and mature men to Deledda's adult-adolescent heroes' comportment, there is every reason to believe that these modern criteria indeed inform any adult Sardinian's definition of juvenile behavior. Surely cultural conditioning plays a minor role in Deledda's presentation of the syndrome, but that cannot explain away her men's behavior as simply "Sardinian" (or even as a remnant of Nuraghic behavior, for those who accept the mystical interpretation of ancient overtones). For these are universal symptoms. Otherwise how does one deal with the fact that other western cultures describe exactly the same pathology?

On a parochial level there may very well be a "Sardinian" link to the problem; but there is also a stronger and more compelling, ubiquitous connection.[7]

Throughout Deledda's novels truncated maturity functions as a psychological undertow sucking down its sufferers and their loved ones to the depths of fictive drama. Deledda's focus is sharp as she invites us into the realm of this psychological substrate. Arrested maturation is a diachronic phenomenon in Grazia Deledda's works; her afflicted men are not sporadically presented, appearing only occasionally here and there. They do not appear more or less frequently in her earlier works as opposed to her more mature prose. They are *always* there. By dint of the consistency of her characterizations in novel after novel, eventually Deledda maneuvers us into fully expecting men to be juvenile. In one way or another, she uses arrested maturity as a template for almost all of the men in her prose. In the end all of her men begin to blur into one exemplar.

Knowing her background, it is little wonder that Grazia Deledda found solace in her writing and at the same time still populated her stories with varying images from the colorful assortment of men she knew. But what about Deledda's *fictional* men? Perhaps precisely because of both brothers' prodigal behavior, that of their offbeat friends, that of the ordinary men she observed in Nuoro and later her husband, Grazia Deledda became somewhat of an unwilling expert on every adolescent, juvenile trait described today in clinical studies. Indeed Deledda knew the disorder well, even the pessimistic prognosis. She recognized that there is little hope for recovery; arguably few (if any) of her own protagonists mature at the end of the story.[8]

Deledda is consistent and insistent upon *this* as her dominant male model. There are several thematic advantages to such a strategy. In at least one instance (*Canne al vento*), she uses the syndrome as part of an exquisite plan where her elegant depiction of a male character of arrested maturation serves a subtextual purpose—one that the censors would never have allowed to appear in print. Without Giacinto's being a baby boy, there would be no reason for him to be replaced by a real baby boy who then becomes the object of Grixenda's scene of oral gratification. Arrested maturation makes the graphic scene possible. This is one of the few ways Grazia Deledda could get the two protagonists together intimately in order to advance the plot. Thematically necessary scenes of realistic, adult passion would never have been published in Deledda's day. So she found clever ways to skirt the issue. In another case, *Marianna Sirca*, the syndrome is intrinsic to the theme, where Simone's pathetic attempt to return to the womb and play the little boy to Marianna's mother is denied because he has transgressed society's rules. At the end of the novel when the wounded Simone penetrates Marianna's thighs with his head, the only physical result is her becoming drenched with his blood. Deledda subverts the predictable, sexual response of such erotic activity by substituting the symbol of punishment and death (blood) in the place of the tangible effects of stimulation and arousal. This could not happen without the juvenile Simone's head in Marianna's lap for one last time.

Perhaps Grazia Deledda was so exasperated by being a woman in a man's world that she exacted revenge by creating weak male characters and strong women.[9] For surely Deledda's own story is a prime example of what happens when fifty percent of the population is held in emotional slavery. But "revenge" is a strong word and there is little evidence that Deledda had a social axe to grind, not personally nor professionally. Hers was a psychological quest, an examination of interior conflict. A better explanation for the "why" of *this* particular syndrome is that in part she also wants to use the aggregate of psychological symptoms as a springboard to showcase her strongest women. In *Marianna Sirca* Deledda finds a way to transform her female character into an active participant in her own life rather than to relegate her to the traditional subservient role of wife. Deledda flirts both with the classic "man's woman" (one who will marry and cause little trouble), and with a "woman's woman" (a hero rather than a heroine). She turns the tables on stereotypical fin de siècle depictions of women. Marianna never faints onto a conveniently situated chaise longue; she does not graciously sniff the smelling salts held to her nineteenth-century nose. Grazia Deledda's *men* are the passive ones; they are the protagonists who spend a great deal of time in a prone position. (Elias Portolu begins the novel sick in bed; the protagonist of *Colombi e sparvieri* spends just about the entire novel flat on his back, lovesick and languishing.) Nowhere in Deledda's *opera omnia* does the strength of her voice resonate more clearly than in *Marianna Sirca*. Rachel Du Plessis maintains that the only available endings for the nineteenth-century writer's female protagonist are marriage or death.[10] With *Marianna Sirca*, however, Grazia Deledda changes the nineteenth-century endings; Marianna neither marries Simone nor does she die.

Given that Deledda started writing so young in the late nineteenth century, one might anticipate an evolution in her women through the years of her long career. At the beginning of her writing career one could perhaps expect to find the stereotypically passive female, and only later the culmination of assertiveness in women such as Annalena Bilsini and Marianna Sirca— protagonists who engage in open rebellion and who are fully in charge. Yet that is not the case. Deledda knew what her women and men would be like from the beginning of her serious writing career, and very few live up to nineteenth- and early twentieth-century preconceptions of what women ought to be. Nor do the Deleddan male characters evolve. Her male protagonists do not get better or worse over the span of her writing; they consistently exhibit the same borderline personality disorders, dating from the author's youth through her last day of writing.

In literature, in popular media, and in the perception of many individuals, Sardinia is stereotypically the archpatriarchy where women are locked in the house except for accompanied excursions pre-approved by their men.[11] In Deledda's day this notion was accurate. Deledda, however, explodes that cliché while not denying it. Ironically she exposes the inner workings of that male-oriented world. "Ironically" because she shows us the woman who has "the keys"—the woman who runs her house like an empire where not even her husband has such power (under *that* roof at least). Within Deledda's world of ostensible male dominance there is a sub-world where a woman can wield at least some power. Both personally and professionally Deledda shows us how women scratch out an existence under such emotional duress, how they bring to its pinnacle the Italian art of *arrangiarsi* [finding a way]. Grazia Deledda's writing reflects what was happening vis-à-vis the women of her epoch. Deledda deals with a concept that seems to have been burned into woman's collective memory. While she, herself, was not openly political, nevertheless, her work shows an awareness of her contemporaries' feminist ideas. Deledda denied any affiliation with the feminist movement. G. A. Borgese quotes Deledda:

But it's not my fault (since I believe I am neither a feminist nor a worldly person), if we must recognize that women do a bit better than men when things are in a state of decline in modern literature.[12]

She was not one to go public with her private thoughts on the dynamic women's movement of her day, but she certainly incorporated into her prose a feminist map that is still convincing a century later. Deledda opted for the experiential approach in writing. Not a literary theorist, she deals only in literature as mimesis. In answer to a question on the value of feminism, Grazia Deledda answered, "I write novels and short stories: this is my specialty. I find it well and good that women think, study and work" (*Nuova Antologia* 123). She did not elaborate; she did not launch into the theoretical aspects of the question. She was instinctually engaged; she showed her theoretics through her prose. She writes only from her own realistic perspectives.[13]

Do Deledda's women deliberately indulge their males as juveniles as a coping device to make sure they can maintain maternal power over the men? Dowling and Kiley are correct; this is a woman's way of maintaining an acceptable balance so that the man will not stray and leave the her without financial, emotional, and social support. Undoubtedly Deledda had a real understanding of the phenomenon. She had a keen instinct for seeing exactly what was going on; there is reason to believe that the question of control was in part what she had in mind when she created her male/female co-dependencies and put many of her women in charge. To argue otherwise is to obviate the importance of the hundreds of references to this pathology that Deledda makes throughout her prose. Why otherwise would she dwell so consistently, insistently, and incessantly on boys who will not and cannot grow up and on women who probably do not want them to change? Much resides just below the self-evident.

"Fictive" realities become clear when we are presented with a preponderance of examples of the same type of man. Deledda twists, splices, and blurs all of her male characters, eventually to create a "type" of man, an ensemble-character who blends almost perfectly with modern definitions of the problem of arrested maturation. Patterns reveal themselves which on a global level deliver more than just the message of a particular novel, something in addition to just the character description of one man. A cumulative context builds with the complicity of sheer numbers of examples. The result is a "composite man" who looms larger than just the sum of his constituent parts. Eventually something uncomplimentary to men happens in Deledda's prose, but neither are women exempt from their problems.

Grazia Deledda was not just a simple amanuensis, an indiscriminate transcriber of what surrounded her. Instead she used her creativity to fashion original (and gripping) stories, populated by individuals with the traits of people she knew. She took bits here and there to reshape composite characters who resembled everyone yet no one in particular. Perhaps this is part of the reason she was met with such hostility on her own turf: her fellow townspeople saw too much of themselves in her characters. With this elaborate examination of male/female relationships, Deledda is trying to work out her own experiences, to reckon herself as the primary breadwinner of the Madesani family and clearly the stronger partner at a time and in a social milieu where society did not allow for such shocking reversals. Grazia Deledda proved the possibility of having a career, a husband, a home, and a conventional family; and in doing so, she infuriated a great number of individuals from every sector of society. She inserted herself into the traditional frame for "women's writing," but playfully she executed strategies acted out by her female protagonists to subvert the insularity of their limiting cultural prisons. The effect of her prose is stealthy as it undermines what it seems to depict and accept.

The syndrome of arrested maturation pervades our lives today just as it did in Deledda's day. The only difference is that we have given it a name. Arrested maturation is the subtext which runs through every Deleddan novel and numerous short stories in one way or another. As Umberto Eco has remarked, "When the writer says he has worked without giving any thought to the rules of the process, he simply means he was working without realizing he knew the rules" (11).[14] From Deledda's biography we recognize that as an autodidact who spent most of her formative years in culturally forced seclusion, she could have known only what she saw and heard recounted, only what she read in her very limited library.[15] Deledda taught herself practically everything she knew. She was a remarkably intuitive woman even to have recognized that within her own purview there was an emotional affliction waiting to be examined in her narrative. Deledda organized her observations to try to make sense, for herself (and for us), of a seemingly inexplicable phenomenon. Her work is purely empirical, almost totally experiential; she had no training; yet psychologically she got it absolutely right, using all but today's precise, professional terminology. Her message and medium are seamless. Prophetically Grazia Deledda recontextualizes the man/woman relationship—quite an achievement for a solitary woman with all the cards stacked against her save one: the steadfast determination for her voice to be heard.

Appendix: Grazia Deledda's Prose Works

THE FOLLOWING IS A LIST OF GRAZIA DELEDDA'S PROSE WORKS.
She also wrote poetry, several works for the theatre, and numerous essays on various topics. Her private correspondence has been collected in several sources (but the best source for nonprose materials on Grazia Deledda is Dolores Turchi, ed., introduction to Grazia Deledda, *Il paese del vento* [Roma: Newton, 1995]).

This list includes the primary title of each work with the first date of publication of a work's definitive appearance (some works appeared originally in serial form). Many of Deledda's works are often listed in various other sources with differing dates of publication. Every effort has been made to ascertain the correct dates and to be as accurate as possible in this listing; where questions arise, discrepancies are noted.

GRAZIA DELEDDA'S NOVELS

Stella d'oriente. Cagliari: Tipografia "Avvenire di Sardegna,"1891. (Note: This was first published as a newspaper serial in Cagliari, later published as a 130-page novel under the pseudonym of Ilia di Sant'Ismael.)

Fior di Sardegna. Roma: Perino, 1892.

Anime oneste. Milano: Cogliati, 1895.

La via del male. Torino: Speirani, 1896.

Il tesoro. Torino: Speirani, 1897.

La giustizia. Torino: Speirani, 1899.

Il vecchio della montagna. Torino: Roux e Viarengo, 1900.

La regina delle tenebre. Milano: Agnelli, 1901; Roma: Nuova Antologia, 1907.

Dopo il divorzio. Torino: Roux e Viarengo 1902; reprinted by Milano: Treves, 1920 under the title, *Naufraghi in porto*.

Elias Portolu. Torino: Roux e Viarengo, 1903; Milano: Treves, 1907.

Cenere. Roma: Ripamonti e Colombo, 1904.
Nostalgie. Roma: Ripamonti, 1906; first published as a serial in "Nuova Antologia," Roma: 1900.
L'edera. Roma: Colombo, 1906.
L'ombra del passato. Roma: Nuova Antologia, 1907.
Il nostro padrone. Milano: Treves, 1910.
Sino al confine. Milano: Treves, 1910.
Nel deserto. Milano: Treves, 1911.
Colombi e sparvieri. Milano: Treves, 1912.
Canne al vento. Milano: Treves, 1913.
Le colpe altrui. Milano: Treves, 1914.
Marianna Sirca. Milano: Treves, 1915.
L'incendio nell'uliveto. Milano: Treves, 1918.
La madre. Milano: Treves, 1920.
Il segreto dell'uomo solitario. Milano: Treves, 1921.
Il dio dei viventi. Milano: Treves, 1922.
La danza della collana. Milano: Treves, 1924.
La fuga in Egitto. Milano: Treves, 1925.
Annalena Bilsini. Milano: Treves, 1927.
Il vecchio e i fanciulli. Milano: Treves, 1928.
Il paese del vento. Milano: Treves, 1931.
L'argine. Milano: Treves, 1934.
La Chiesa della Solitudine. Milano: Treves, 1936.
Cosima. Milano: Treves, 1937.

GRAZIA DELEDDA'S SHORT STORIES AND COLLECTIONS

Nell'azzurro. Milano–Roma: Trevisini, 1890.
Amore regale. Roma: Perino, 1891.
Amori fatali, la leggenda nera, il ritratto. Roma: Perino, 1892.
La regina delle tenebre. Torino: Origlia, 1892.
Sulle montagne sarde (Storie di banditi). Roma: Perino, 1892.
Racconti sardi. Sassari: Dessì, 1894.
L'ospite. Rocca San Casciano: Cappelli, 1898.
Giaffah. Milano–Palermo: Sandron, 1899.
Le tentazioni. Milano: Cogliati, 1899.
I tre talismani. Milano–Palermo: Sandron, 1899.
La regina delle tenebre. Milano: Agnelli, 1902.
I giuochi della vita. Milano: Treves, 1905.
Amori moderni. Roma: Voghera, 1907.
L'ombra del passato. Roma: "Nuova Antologia," 1907.
Il nonno. Roma: Colombo, 1908.

Chiaroscuro. Milano: Treves, 1912.
Il fanciullo nascosto. Milano: Treves, 1916.
Il ritorno del figlio, La bambina rubata. Milano: Treves, 1919.
Cattive compagnie. Milano: Treves, 1921.
Il flauto nel bosco. Milano: Treves, 1923.
La casa del poeta. Milano: Treves, 1930.
Il dono di natale. Milano: Treves, 1930.
La vigna sul mare. Milano: Treves, 1932.
Sole d'estate. Milano: Treves, 1933.
Il cedro del Libano. Milano: Garzanti, 1939.

Notes

PREFACE

1. For this 35.8-second recording of Grazia Deledda's voice describing the difficulty of being a writer in Sardinia in the late 1800's, access the website: *www.grr.rai.it/archivio/cultura.html*. Unless otherwise indicated, this and all subsequent translations are my own.

2. Luigi Russo magnanimously saw fit to excuse the "modestia delle sue forze femminili" [the modesty of her womanly strengths] in *I narratori* (Milano: Principato, 1958), 93.

3. In his anthology, *The Psychology of Adolescence* (New York: International Universities Press, 1975), Aaron Esman makes clear that what today we call "adolescent behavior" was simply "immature behavior" before the concept of adolescence was established (3–5). It is widely agreed that adolescence as an age unto itself, as a recognized phase in human development, did not exist until late in the nineteenth century. (Previously one was thought of as a child, a small adult, and then an adult; there was no intervening period of maturation.) In his monumental study, *Centuries of Childhood*, trans. Robert Baldick (New York: Knopf, 1962), the French cultural historian, Philippe Arìes points out that the new concept of adolescence, essentially a cultural invention, suscitated great literary interest around the *fin de siécle* (just about the time Deledda was reaching her stride as a writer working in a social vacuum). "People began wondering seriously what youth was thinking. Youth gave the impression of secretly possessing new values capable of reviving an aged and sclerosed society. A like interest had been evidenced in the Romantic period, but not with such specific reference to a single age group, and moreover it had been limited to literature and readers of that literature" (4).

4. See Natalino Sapegno, introduction to *Romanzi e novelle di Grazia Deledda: Cosima* (Milano: Mondadori, 1971), 72.

5. Throughout the body of this study I deliberately do not adopt the contemporary term "Peter Pan syndrome" as described later in this investigation. For Deledda adds much more to the overall picture of the victim of this psychological affliction. As teased out from her prose, her narrative embodiments of the syndrome elaborate a picture of the adult-adolescent of arrested maturation that actually goes well beyond the modern syndrome described professionally by Masterson, Kiley, et al.

6. Neither is the syndrome exclusively the domain of Sardinia or Italy; in her article about the Clinton–Lewinsky sex scandal, Maureen Dowd writes, "Just as movie and television comedy is permeated with the ill-mannered, self-indulgent mentality of adolescent boys, Mr. Clinton has reversed the usual pattern of the Presidency, switching from a paternal model to an adolescent model. He expects us to clean up, ignore or forgive his messes. It is easy to feel sorry

for the likable and boyish President. . . . But the jam Mr. Clinton finds himself in is a direct result of his lack of discipline, his refusal to take responsibility and his willingness to lie, cover up, use loyal aides or smear talkative ex-girlfriends when all other means of escape seem blocked." Maureen Dowd, *New York Times* (3 August 1998): 4.15.

7. Dan Kiley, *The Peter Pan Syndrome* (New York: Avon, 1983) xv.

8. *Pace* Sharon Wood who observes, "However, the centre of [Deledda's] work is neither social criticism nor psychological pathology but an investigation of the conflict between different ethical orders." Sharon Wood, *Italian Women's Writing 1860–1994* (London: Athlone, 1995) 63. Mary McCarthy wrote of Paul de Man, "I can't yet think that he's a really bad person, except as an adolescent is bad, e.g., given to lying, evasion, fantasy, greed, possibly even theft—in short plastic and formless," she could have been describing any of Deledda's male protagonists. She also may not have known that she was in effect also describing what has become to be known as an adolescent of arrested maturation. See David Lehman, "Paul de Man: The Plot Thickens," *New York Times Book Review* (24 May 1992): 19.

9. See the last of Sigmund Freud's "Three Essays on the Theory of Sexuality," *The Standard Edition of the Complete Psychological Works of Sigmund Freud* (London: Hogarth Press, 1905).

10. Nicolino Sarale, *Grazia Deledda: Un profilo spirituale* (Roma: Logos, 1990), 33.

11. ". . . appoggiandomi spesso a fatti che ho sentito narrare nella mia patria e ricordandomi intensamente personaggi conosciuti nella realtà" [. . . often relying on the facts that I have heard in stories from my homeland and remembering vividly the characters I have known from reality.]

CHAPTER 1. INTRODUCTION

1. I am indebted to the excellent essays in Francesco Artizzu's edited volume, *La società in Sardegna nei secoli* (Torino: Edizioni ERI, 1967) for the general information in this section. Especially useful is the work of Giancarlo Sorgia.

2. A ray of hope was offered by a plan to privatize land and abolish feudalism. Known as the Edict of the *Chiudende* of 1820, this act of closure allowed those who actually worked the land to erect stone fences or hedges and claim that land as their own. Effectively, however, this attempt at land reform did not play out as intended. For a fuller discussion of the Edict of the *Chiudende*, see Mario Massaiu, *La Sardegna di Grazia Deledda* (Milano: IPL, 1986), 86.

3. Banditry in Sardinia was second only to Sicily in the number of homicides per 100,000 people: 26.22. This is compared to Lombardy's 2.9 per 100,000 people. Bandits had the run of the island; and they were often aided by the sympathy of a citizenry driven by a deep, centuries old mistrust of the outsiders's concept of justice. See especially Carolyn Balducci, *A Self-Made Woman: Biography of Nobel-Prize-Winner Grazia Deledda* (Boston: Houghton Mifflin, 1975), 69. See also Carlino Sole, "Il periodo Sabaudo fino al 1815," in Francesco Artizzu, ed., *La società in Sardegna nei secoli* (Torino: Edizioni ERI, 1967). Henrik Schück remarked in his "Presentation Speech" at the Nobel Prize Ceremonies in 1927, "The vendetta is still the custom in Sardinia, and a person is respected if he takes blood revenge on the killer of a kinsman. Indeed, it is considered a

crime to betray the avenger. One author writes, 'Even if the reward on his head were three times its size, not a single man in the whole district of Nuoro could be found to betray him. Only one law reigns there: respect for a man's strength and scorn of society's justice.' "

4. In *Cenere* Deledda writes, "Do you think that bandits are bad people? You're wrong; they are men who need to demonstrate their abilities; nothing more. In the old days, men went to war: now there are no more wars, but men still need to fight and they commit robberies, kidnappings and mayhem not to injure anyone, but to show in some way their power, their ability" (115).

5. For additional information on Sardinia's political history, Giancarlo Sorgia is especially useful: "Il periodo spagnolo," in Artizzu, *La Società in Sardegna nei secoli*. In addition, Professor Henrik Schück who introduced Grazia Deledda at the Nobel Prize ceremonies pointed out that for many being a bandit did not stain one's reputation. Quite the opposite! When a bandit was caught and punished, he was not said to be in prison but *in disgrazia* [in trouble, in an unfortunate situation]. When he returned from his sentence, no stigma was attached. He might very well be greeted with the phrase, "May a century pass before another such misfortune befall you!" (97); see Mercede Mundula, *Grazia Deledda* (Roma: Formiggini, 1929), 122–23.

6. For an excellent overview of Deledda's life and work, see Gianni Eugenio Viola, Anna Dolfi, and Franca Rovigatti, *Grazia Deledda: Biografia e Romanzo* (Roma: Istituto della Enciclopedia Italiana, Treccani, 1987).

7. Banditry caused serious problems for the average Sardinian when it became institutionalized as a way of life. Not only did outlaws render life dangerous for the citizens who were merely trying to function within the mundane rules of everyday existence, but banditry also exacerbated their economic situation. See especially Lorenzo Del Piano, "Dal 1815 al 1870," in Artizzu, *La società in Sardegna nei secoli*. See also Salvatore Cambosu, *Il Supramonte di Orgosolo* (Firenze: Vallecchi, 1988); Alberto Ledda, *La civiltà fuorilegge. Natura e storia del banditismo sardo* (Milano: Mursia, 1971); and Giancarlo Sorgia, *Banditismo e criminalità in Sardegna nella seconda metà dell'Ottocento* (Cagliari: Editrice Sarda Fossataro, 1973).

8. The least onerous interest rates were in the large cities, Sassari and Cagliari, but in the interior towns and villages lending rates typically went from 14 percent to 25 percent, but very often rose from 100 percent to 500 percent in towns such as Mandas (Massaiu 98).

9. This may explain in part why being a physician was tantamount to apotheosis in Sardinia. It was every family's dream to send a son to medical school and then have him return to the prestigious position of town doctor. Deledda's novels and short stories include many such cases; and indeed her own brother was in his last year of medical school in Cagliari when he dropped out, much to the despair and public shame of the entire Deledda family.

10. For a more lengthy discussion of medical care in Sardinia during the late 1800s, see Natale Sanna, "Dal 1870 alla Prima Guerra Mondiale," in Artizzu, *La società in Sardegna nei secoli*.

11. Malaria was only eradicated definitively after 1944, when the Allies employed DDT on a widespread basis. See Paul Ginsborg, *A History of Contemporary Italy* (London: Penguin, 1990), 123.

12. Trachoma is still the world's leading cause of preventable blindness. Lawrence K. Altman describes the disease in the *New York Times* (11 November 1998): 1.

13. In 1877, a free educational system was established by the central Italian government for all Italians, but little headway was made in Sardinia to raise literacy rates in the ensuing years. See especially Giannantonio Pompeo, "Le scrittrici della Nuova Italia," in *Scrittrici d'Italia*, Francesco de Nicola and Pier Antonio Zannoni, eds. (Genova: Costa e Nolan, 1995), 7–16.

14. See Delia Nelli's article on contemporary cuisine in Sardinia in "On Neptune's Secret Trail," *La Cucina Italiana* 2.4 (1997): 47.

15. Interestingly one aspect of Sardinian life that was *not* a serious problem was class division. There was not much animosity between the classes, because there was little economic separation between them. *No one* was well-off; landowners did not earn that much more than their employees. Generally the components of the Sardinian heirarchies were not that far apart economically.

16. Massaiu observes just how truly disconnected Deledda was from the intellectual world: "The island had given and continued to give blood and gold to Italy, but essentially remained cut out of the stream of ideas and events of Italian history during and after the fight for unity" (96).

17. See D. H. Lawrence's introduction to the English translation of *La madre* [The Mother] (London, 1928). See also the Italian reprint in the Sardinian newspaper, *Ichnusa* (1–2 March 1951), as cited in Viola, Dolfi, et al.

18. Writing of Deledda's need to deal with the primitive masses of Sardinian passion, D. H. Lawrence observes, "To do that, one must have an isolated mass in the same way that Thomas Hardy isolates Wessex" (*The Mother* [London, 1928]).

19. Grazia Deledda in a letter to the French literary critic, François Haguenin; see Nicoline Sarale, *Grazia Deledda: Un profilio spirituale* (Roma: Logos, 1990), 107.

20. Deledda's first exhilarating glimpse of the sea was when she was fifteen years old, but even then her view was only from a great distance from the top of Mt. Badia across the valley near her inland home. She had not actually been to the shore until her trip to Cagliari in November, 1899—she was twenty-eight years old. Under the pseudonym of Ilia di Sant'Ismael, Grazia Deledda first published a short folkloric piece in a local paper in Nuoro. See the jacket notes of Balducci. See also Martha King, *Cosima* (New York: Italica Press, 1988), viii.

21. Antonio Deledda was seriously interested in poetry to the point of having his own printing press to produce formally the dialect poems which he and his friends exchanged on a regular basis.

22. Concomitantly Deledda published the children's story, "Sulla montagna" [On the Mountain], in the Roman magazine, *Paradiso dei Bambini* [Children's Paradise]. See Alba Amoia, *Twentieth-Century Italian Women Writers* (Carbondale: Southern Illinois University Press, 1996).

23. In his *Bibliografia Deleddiana* (Milano: L'Eroica, 1938), Remo Branca points out that Grazia Deledda published in her lifetime 350 short stories in 18 volumes (by 1938); 30 novellas; 8 fables; 15 sketches; 35 novels (some published as serials in newspapers under the pseudonym of Ilia di Sant'Ismael); 50 articles for magazines and papers; 50 poems written before 1900. Before 1890 she wrote for magazines such as: *L'Ultima Moda* (Rome) from 1888; *Bohème Goliardica* (Cagliari) from 1889; *Vita Sarda* (Cagliari) from 1892; *Rivista delle Signorine* (Florence) from 1900; *Sardegna Artistica* (Sassari) from 1890; *Ateneo Sardo* (Cagliari) from 1898; *La Piccola Rivista* (Cagliari) from 1898; *Donna Sarda* (Cagliari) from 1900; *Vita Italiana* (Rome) from 1895; *Natura ed Arte* (Milan) from 1892; and newspapers such as *La Sardegna* (Sassari) 1889; and *L'Avvenire di Sardegna* (Cagliari) 1891.

24. Commercially her most successful works were *Elias Portolu*, *Cenere* [Ashes], *L'edera* [Ivy], *Canne al vento* [Reeds in the Wind], *Marianna Sirca*, and *La madre* [The Mother]. Translations of her work were not just in the predictable Western European languages, but in all the Slavic languages, in Afrikaans, into Indian dialects (Oriya, for example), and into Japanese and Chinese as well. Complete bibliographical information for quotations from the primary works of Grazia Deledda are in the Appendix, "Deledda's Prose Works."

25. Famously shy and reticent, her acceptance speech was the shortest in history: "I do not know how to make speeches: I would be happy to thank the Swedish Academy for their highest honor, which, in my modest name, it has granted to Italy, and to repeat the blessing of the old shepherds of Sardinia, spoken to friends and family on solemn occasions: Salute! Salute to the King of Sweden! Salute to the King of Italy! Salute to you all, ladies and gentlemen! Viva Sweden, viva Italy!" (Balducci 186).

26. The first was given in 1909, perhaps understandably, to a Swedish woman, Selma Lagerlöf; Giosuè Carducci (1906) was the first Italian to receive the prize for literature.

27. She was part of a Turkish series of stamps issued to honor famous women. Italy, ironically, waited until 1971, the centenary of her birth, before honoring its only female Nobel Prize winner for literature.

28. Deledda had attained a world renown that would have even allowed her to boast of her many invitations to take tea with Queen Margherita of Italy (an ardent reader and supporter), had Deledda not constantly declined from shyness. See Sarale, 95.

29. Even one of Deledda's most vocal critics had to admit that she was Maxim Gorky's favorite contemporary Italian writer. "She was in the good graces of the great Russian writer who several times affirmed that among all the living Italian writers of his time he preferred Deledda; consequently in Italy she became the most widely read author after D'Annunzio: as Treves averred." See Giuseppe Ruju, *Pietro Casu tra Grazia Deledda e Max Leopold Wagner* (Cagliari: Edizioni della Torre, 1981), 90.

30. National and international reviews of Grazia Deledda's work and obituaries from clipping services around the world originally collected by the Madesani-Deledda family are preserved and available for study in the archives of the Istituto Superiore Regionale Etnografico in Nuoro; additional materials are available in Rome at the Archivio Madesani-Deledda instituted by Deledda's late son, Franz, who continued the name Madesani-Deledda and who preserved her private papers which are now with the Madesani-Deledda family. Her books are in the Biblioteca Alessandrina in Rome.

31. In many sources the date of Deledda's birth is erroneously reported as 1876. See Francesco Di Pilla, *La vita e l'opera di Grazia Deledda* (Milano, 1966), 178. Grazia Deledda, perhaps playfully, never corrected those mistakes.

32. Neria De Giovanni comments on the importance of the oral tradition in Grazia Deledda's writing, "Grazia Deledda was like the tip of an enormous iceberg whose submerged part represented the great Sardinian literary tradition in the Sardinian language, transmitted above all orally" (23). See Neria De Giovanni, *L'ora di Lilith: su Grazia Deledda e la letteratura femminile del secondo Novecento* (Roma: Ellemme, 1987).

33. She mentions especially Proto, the servant, who told her many of the stories that he had heard in his day-to-day dealings as footman for the Deledda family. See Grazia Deledda, *Cosima* (Milano: Treves, 1937), 703. In a letter to

Onorato Roux dated Nuoro 31 October 1894, Deledda writes, "Our house was a kind of small, free hotel. From twenty towns in the vicinity of Nuoro there came guests who would stay two to three days, even a week in our home. They were typical folks: the working class, middle class, priests, aristocrats, servants of whom I retain the most vivid of memories," as quoted by Antonio Scano, *Grazia Deledda: Versi e prose giovanili*. Milano: Virgilio, 1972, 293.

34. For an excellent study of depression and manic depression, see Kay Redfield Jamison, *Touched by Fire* (New York: Simon and Schuster, 1993) and *An Unquiet Mind: A Memoir of Moods and Madness* (Random House/Vintage Books: New York, 1995).

35. Blos writes about how these young men have "exalted self-expectations." Being gifted and intelligent, they are under the onerous influence of "parental ambition and narcissistic overevaluation" and they come to expect high achievements from themselves. Their first failures are "crushing blows, usually at the juncture between the late high school and early college years." Blos points out that, "In order to escape from narcissistic impoverishment they rally desperately to continued attempts at 'making good.' " Peter Blos, "When and How Does Adolescence End?", *Adolescent Psychology*, Vol. 5, eds. S. C. Feinstein and P. Giovacchini (New York: Aronson, 1976), 41.

36. Blos is especially informative in his chapters on the topics of "Prolonged Male Adolescence: The Formulation of a Syndrome and its Therapeutic Implications" (37–53) and "When and How Does Adolescence End?" *Adolescent Psychology*, Vol. 5, eds. S. C. Feinstein and P. Giovacchini (New York: Aronson, 1976), 404–22. Blos says "prolonged adolescence" usually occurs in a "middle-class young man, roughly between eighteen and twenty-two, who usually attends college or has, at any rate, some professional aspirations; this fact, more often than not, makes him financially dependent on his family during the years of early adulthood" (38). Blos thinks that this preservation of the status quo "arrests the forward motion" of his maturation process. University years keep "the adolescent process inconclusive" (39). Blos finds that this problem brings with it "ingenious ways to combine childhood gratifications with adult prerogatives" (39).

37. Deledda writes in *Cosima*, "It was Santus with his blue eyes clouded by drunkenness, his tongue tied by the knot of that terrible addiction. In a few days he had spent the family money, his mother's savings, and he returned almost crazed to the sad house, never to depart again. To understand the seriousness of these misfortunes, it is also necessary to consider the spiteful intolerance of the atmosphere where they occurred. Everyone knew everyone else in the small town; they judged one another severely; and those who had the least right to cast the first stone were the most relentless. When people found out about Santus's return in disgrace, there was much gloating and sneering among the family's acquaintances; and the nastiest were the relatives" (740).

38. Grazia had an older sister, Vincenza ("Enza"), who also suffered from depression and experienced occasional epileptic seizures. Vincenza died young in 1896 as the result of a miscarriage. Grazia's three younger sisters were Giovanna, who died at age six of a high fever, Giuseppa ("Beppa" or "Peppa"), and Nicolina ("Nicoletta" or "Allina"). The entire Deledda family consisted of Giovanni Antonio Deledda (1820–1892); Francesca Cambosu (1842–1916); Giovanni Santo "Santus" (1864–1914); Andrea (1866–1922); Vincenza (1868–1896); Giovanna (1874–1880); Giuseppa (1877–1938); Nicolina (1879–1972). Nicolina eventually became an artist and illustrated many of Grazia's

children's stories and worked with her sister on many of her folklore articles. Grazia's best friend in adulthood, Nicolina lived next door to her in Rome sharing a garden border with the Madesani-Deledda family. In her adulthood, Grazia's other sister, Giuseppa, also moved to Rome and lived near her two sisters.

39. Mercede Mundula describes Grazia Deledda as having suffered immensely over Andrea's behavior. "The depth of fear and of pain for Andrea never left the writer. And it was a deep pain that made her think for a long time about the fate of the humanity of the depraved, of those who live outside the law and the rules of society" (*Grazia Deledda* [Roma: Formiggini, 1923], 61). Carolyn Balducci also considers Andrea the model for *Elias Portolu*: imprisoned for a crime he denies ever having committed, brother of an alcoholic, and irresponsible in his attitudes.

40. An extraordinary fourth year of "repetition" was merely a contrivance to allow her to continue her formal education for yet another year. Shedding some light on and providing a context for Grazia Deledda's own education, Natale Sanna points out that "the few women who went to middle school took pedagogical courses; only in the last few years of the century did they begin to enrol in the secondary schools" (245).

41. *Zia* (literally "aunt" in standard Italian), is used as a term of respect in Sardinia, regardless of actual blood relationships. (*zio*, literally "uncle," is the equivalent term of respect for men.)

42. In the short story, "I primi passi" [The First Steps], Deledda describes how this professor was the first to tell her that one of her childhood compositions was good enough to be published. She tells of how she was so proud; and from that professor's encouragement, she started to dream that she could become a writer. Grazia Deledda, *La vigna sul mare* (Milano: Treves, 1932), 792–93.

43. Giuseppe Petronio in *Letteratura Italiana: I Contemporanei*, Vol. I (Milano: Marzorati, 1973), 137–57, quotes Deledda from *Fior di Sardegna* [Flower of Sardinia]: "Oh the pen, the pen of Victor Hugo for just one hour, to describe these internal struggles, these storms in one's brain!" (141). See also Grazia Deledda, "Romanzo intimo," *Racconti Sardi* (Sassari: Dessì, 1894), 69.

44. In *Cosima*, Deledda talks about her girlhood and her favorite shop in Nuoro, the bookstore where at a young age she first became innamored of notebooks, ink, and pens: "all those magical things with which one can translate words into signs and more than words, the thoughts of people" (719). She especially loved notebooks, "and the blackboard of the classroom, with those white signs that the teacher traced, had for her [Cosima/Grazia Deledda] the lure of a window opened onto the dark blue sky of a starry night" (721). Originally entitled *Cosima, quasi Grazia*, in *Cosima* the narrator writes omnisciently about the third-person protagonist, Cosima, as though putting the specimen under a microscope for close inspection. It is universally agreed that this posthumous book was Grazia Deledda's autobiography. A passage from *Cosima* dispels any doubt: "For thousands of pages I have recounted so much of my characters's anguish; I have caused you to have so much sympathy for their pain; now you know: it was my pain and tears, of me Cosima, of me Grazia" (740). Neria De Giovanni also comments on the fact that almost all of Deledda's writing is autobiographical: "As for many women, Deledda's writing about herself became fragmented in many stories, in many novels, in many female heroes in which Grazia planted traces of her own life" (*L'ora di Lilith* 48).

45. Her first royalties payment was for 15 lire, with which she bought a blue

silk scarf from an itinerant vendor. She wrote that whenever she wore it, the scarf reminded her of her self-worth as a writer able to earn money on her own. Years later she wore it on the boat which took her and her new husband from Cagliari to Rome; and, perhaps symbolically, the wind on the deck of the boat caught it and blew the scarf away. See Grazia Deledda, *La vigna sul mare*, 791–92.

46. ". . . out of a physical need, as when other adolescents run through paths of gardens or go to a forbidden place, to a romantic tryst, if they can" (762).

47. "Hers is a story where the protagonist is herself, the world is hers, the blood of the characters, their naïveté, their innocent caprices are hers" (764).

48. She regarded her room and her desk as important friends who abetted her clandestine writing. In her later life, she wrote in "Casa paterna" [Father's House] from *Nell'azzurro* [In the Blue], "I never sit at a desk to write without remembering the writing table where I wrote my first letters, where I sketched many drawings, so many small poems, where finally I wrote my first story. Dear, blessed writing table! When I sat in front of you, I would forget the whole world that surrounded me: you were my confidante, my inspiration, my friend in study and in work, and I loved you like a childhood friend, like a living being" (157–58). See Grazia Deledda, *Nell'azzurro*, as quoted by Antonio Scano in *Grazia Deledda*, 157–58.

49. Despite all the factors militating against her, Deledda was intensely focussed; she was driven to succeed. In a letter to a friend dated Nuoro, 15 May 1892, she wrote, "So I write because I dream of a fame that, I can feel it, I will never attain . . . maybe, so I go along alone and wandering down a path that, here in Sardinia, it is crazy to travel, and I am wasting my youth chasing a golden dream that I know is a mirage, and that I still follow because, I feel, without it I would die of boredom" (Scano 288).

50. In "I primi passi," a reminiscence depicting her early career, Deledda describes that wrenching moment when everything went sour for her on what otherwise would have been a glorious day. "But after the giddiness of success, there followed bitterness and profound discouragement. At home my family did not want me to publish my work, not because they were childish ramblings, but because it just was not right that a girl from a good family, with that attitude of open-minded independence so new to Nuoro, would expose herself to public criticism. And what criticism! I did not care about the personal attacks: I took care of myself first; but one morning, an unforgettable spring morning, while we were getting ready to spend the day in the country, and I was looking forward to enjoying the trip in my own way, among the broom bushes, with the nightingales, the ladybugs, God's lovely butterflies, I receive a large envelope containing a sheet of official, record-office paper in minute handwriting without a signature. It reminded me of one of those irrevocable, awful sentences handed personally by a bailiff to one guilty of terrible crimes. It was in fact a solemn hatchet-job of my published work: and that beautiful day changed for me into a day of death" (*La vigna sul mare* 791–92).

51. Her editor was the "Contessa Elda di Montedoro," pseudonym of Epaminonda Provaglio, editor-in-chief of *Ultima Moda*, who published her first short story. Deledda corresponded with him at length before realizing that he was a man. In a letter to him dated 23 February 1892, she describes how horribly wearisome life was for her in Nuoro. She depicts herself as "a girl who for *entire months* goes without leaving the house, weeks upon weeks without talking to anyone outside the family; locked up in a happy and serene house, yes,

but on whose street no one passes, whose horizon is closed off by depressing mountains; a girl who is not in love, does not suffer, has no thoughts for the future, no dreams, neither good nor bad; no friends, no passtimes, no admirers, nothing, nothing; so tell me, how can she *not* be bored?" (967). See *Grazia Deledda: Opere Scelte*, Vol. I (Milano: Mondadori, 1964), 923–1120.

52. Sapegno describes her as "always distanced as if an absentee, closed in the shell of an inspiration that with the passage of time, she ended up seeming even more apart, remote, archaic" (xii).

53. Sapegno adds that of Naturalism, Idealism, Esthetism, Anti-Naturalism, Modernism, "one does not detect a trace (of them) in Deledda's first novels" (xii)—"not even can one say that she was touched by the events which precipitated the crisis of themes and styles of European literature, as well as that of Italy (from Panzini to Pirandello to the first works of Tozzi)" (xii). Yet Deledda certainly was aware of literary history; her son mentions in several interviews that she was a voracious reader of all literary movements and intensely interested in the arts as well; the various facts of her life point to a very active course of self-directed study as an adult.

54. When asked why there were no Sardinian artists represented at the 1901 Venice Biennale, the mature Grazia Deledda wrote, "Art appreciation did not yet exist in our society; and on the other hand, how could it have been born when the state and the society had much more serious problems which needed rapid solutions?" See Viola et al., which provides a convincing picture of the social milieu in which Deledda labored. The exhibition catalogue quotes Deledda from "Grazia Deledda, I pittori stranieri all'Esposizione di Venezia." *Unione Sarda* (Cagliari), 14 October 1901.

55. See especially Grazia Deledda, *Il paese del vento* (Milano: Treves, 1931), 24. D. H. Lawrence did not find much in her native city to recommend itself either; in *Sea and Sardinia* he wrote about spending a day or two in Nuoro: "There is nothing to see in Nuoro: which, to tell the truth, is always a relief. Sights are an irritating bore. Thank heaven there isn't a bit of Perugino or anything Pisan in the place: that I know of. Happy is the town that has nothing to show" (160). D. H. Lawrence, *Sea and Sardinia* (New York: Doubleday Anchor, 1954).

56. Most of these colorful characters are vividly depicted in the olive-press scenes of her novel, *Cenere* [Ashes], 1904.

57. "Cosima would observe them, she studied them, she learned from them their parlance, superstitions, calamities, and their prayers; and from her observation place she even saw the scene and the characters of the olive press; she heard the stories they told, the songs of the drunkard, the childish laughter of the guy who killed his brother . . . Between one entry and the next that she made into the ledgers, the clients of the olive press told her their dramas: some would beg her to write a letter or an entreaty. In that way she would get the inspiration for a new novel tinged by reality: colored like the black olive paste in the tub of the press that became transformed into oil, into balm, into light" (*Cosima*, 782).

58. Deledda's works talk of heightened emotions often out of control—for example, passion, love and hate. In *Il dio dei viventi* [The God of the Living] the blacksmith says to his enemy, "May you be devoured by worms and may every coin you stole from me, fruit of my labor, may they be spent on medicines, and may your eyes fall out of your head and may your daughter and her sons be ripped limb from limb, gnawed by sickness and by cancer, in front of you, help-

less and unable to assist them" (258). This truly is passion; this is Sardinian hate.

59. Especially interested were the literary critics, Ruggero Bonghi and Angelo De Gubernatis, a linguist who made his scholarly name by collecting and analyzing regional folklore.

60. In 1895, Cogliati, also of Milan, published her first important novel, *Anime oneste* [Honest Souls], for which Ruggero Bonghi wrote a laudatory preface. Deledda had already published the novella, *Stella d'oriente* [Star of the East] in 1890 under the pseudonym of Ilia di Sant'Ismael and *Fior di Sardegna* [Flower of Sardinia] in 1892. Becoming increasingly well known, Deledda began publishing with Speirani of Turin; her novel, *La via del male* [The Path to No Good], appeared in 1896.

61. In the 1909 national elections, for example, unbeknown to her, Grazia Deledda's name appeared on the ballot for the Radical Party's slate for the House of Deputies. History shows that she was the first woman ever to be put forward as a candidate in Italy, but she was so detested in Nuoro that tellingly she won a scant thirty-four votes (vs. over 1000 for her male opponent (De Giovanni 79). Thirty-one of those votes were subsequently declared null and void by the ferociously anti-feminist Election Board of Nuoro, leaving her with an improbable three votes of over 1000 cast! (Viola 70). The election board's feeble excuse for disqualifying 91 percent of her thirty-four votes was that the voters had written extraneous statements on their ballots, such as "Grazia Deledda, Fior di Sardegna" ["Grazia Deledda, Flower of Sardinia" {a play on the title of her first novel}], or "Deledda, Gloria di Nuoro" ["Deledda, Glory of Nuoro"]. Deledda was living in Rome at the time of the election and did not even know she was a candidate from Nuoro for a seat in the House of Deputies. She found out she was on the list after she had already lost the election. From a newspaper article by Giulio Seganti, "Chiacchiere antifemministe con la prima candidata;" the original archival material, without date or masthead, is in the archives of the Museo Deleddiano of the Istituto Superiore Regionale Etnografico di Nuoro.

62. "The next year was even worse, when the publisher Perino came out with her first novel, *Flower of Sardinia*. It was about a girl who made secret dates with young men; the people in her hometown could not understand how she could write about such things without having done them." See Arnaldo Fratelli, "Ricordo di Grazia Deledda," *Il Giornale della Sera* (Roma) (14 August 1946), 10.

63. See Neria De Giovanni, *Grazia Deledda* (Alghero: Nemapress, 1991), 28.

64. Marta Savini reminds us how (in *Cosima*) when one of Grazia's stories would be published, for example, in an illustrated women's magazine, her two old-maid aunts would rush to the Deledda house and "spread the terror of their criticism." And Oreste Del Buono talks about how vilified Grazia Deledda was in Sardinia. Her first short story, "Sangue sardo," caused such a local scandal when it was published in 1888, that her mother was by then positive she would *never* be able to marry off her remaining nubile daughters. "[The aunts] who did not know how to read and who burned pages with drawings of sinners and fallen women, would descend upon the cursed house, spreading the terror of their criticism and of their even worse predictions. Even Andrea was shaken and his dreams about Cosima's future became clouded by indistinct fears. 'Don't ever write love stories again at your age,' she was warned" (9). See Marta Savini, ed., *Grazia Deledda: Un profilo spirituale* (Roma: Newton Compton, 1993). See also Oreste Del Buono, "Nana e brutta eppure Grazia Deledda," *La Stampa* (Tuttolibri) (29 April 1995), 5.

65. See Deledda, *Opere scelte* 1015.

66. Palmiro Madesani (1865–1946) was originally from Mantova; he held the position of Segretario d'Intendenza [Secretary of Superintendency] in Rome at the Ministry of Finance; after Deledda's writing career was established, by family necessity he also became her fulltime agent and business manager.

67. For additional information see Dolores Turchi, ed., introduction to *Il paese del vento* (Roma: Newton Compton, 1995).

68. The Madesani's temporarily lived on Via Cadorna, then Via Salustiana #4, and then permanently on Via Porto Maurizio, now named Via Imperia. There for the rest of her life, Deledda enjoyed a magnificent view from her garden of the grand cypresses surrounding Rome's monumental cemetery of Verano from one corner and of the Alban Hills from another. Occasionally Madesani would be on work assignments which enabled the family to live at length in Venice and in Turin. In 1910 they lived in Paris after which they rented a home on the French Riviera. Augusts were reserved for trips to Nuoro. In 1911, Grazia Deledda's mother moved to Rome to be with her daughters in the last years of her life. Grazia Deledda never returned to Sardinia after 1911.

69. Sardus, named for "Sardus Pater," the founder of Sardinia (Balducci 166), died at age thirty-seven. Franz had a career in chemistry; he did advanced graduate work in Rome at eventually taught at the University of Rome.

70. Spagnoletti writes, "And it must be admitted that she had a haphazard literary formation, that of an autodidact. Cheap lyricism, superficial carelessness, rough imitations of the most dissimilar contemporary authors: Dumas, Bourget, De Amicis, seem to weigh heavily on her first works almost like a condemnation. . . . But the romantic eruptions of the precocious writer from Nuoro with only a fourth grade education [sic] and with an avid love of reading the books inherited from her priest uncle, were not destined to last long. All by herself and very quickly, she realized the emptiness and disorganized quality of these experiments, and slowly she rid herself of them never to look back." *Romanzieri italiani del nostro secolo* (Milano: Eri, 1967), 13.

71. Deledda once got a negative review of her work in the journal *Arte e Vita* [Art and Life] 3 (1 January 1922), 45; the article was by Pietro Casu; in response she promptly wrote an irate rebuttal to the editor, Luciano Gennari, "Now to you, dear Gennari, since it is the first time I have seen my books mentioned in your magazine, I am sending you the second last one published . . . and I beg you to read it and judge it according to your conscience as a Christian and according to the fundamental principles of *Art and Life* and tell me if Christ would have thrown out of the Temple Paulo and his mother [protagonists of her badly reviewed novel *La madre*], along with the other priests-nevertheless-men and the women and children and all the poor of spirit and the good thieves to whom I am proud of having brought to life with my work. (Signed Grazia Deledda)".

72. It is said that Luigi Pirandello was so enraged by her success that he wrote *Suo Marito* [Her Husband] just to satirize Grazia Deledda and Palmiro Madesani. Pirandello's *Suo Marito*, written around 1909 and published in 1911, tells the story of a woman writer who comes to Rome from the provinces and supported by her loving husband, suceeds as a writer. A situation of which Ferroni says Pirandello "explicitly alludes to the situation of Grazia Deledda." Giulio Ferroni, *Storia della letteratura italiana (Il Novecento)* (Milano: Einaudi, 1991), 143. Referring to Pirandello's play, Balducci adds, "the woman is depicted as making social blunders and being somewhat ignorant and unattractive while the slick husband is described in far worse terms, with the suggestion that

he was carrying on with another woman. The book was a terrible blow to Grazia. What was worse, its contents seemed to suggest the collusion of another party, someone who knew intimate details of her life. [Possibly] Ugo Ojetti with whom Grazia had corresponded" (171).

73. In 1916, a film was made of *Cenere* starring Eleonora Duse, directed by Febo Mari; this event marked the beginning of Deledda's lifelong friendship with Duse.

74. For the entire description of this episode, see Sarale 95.

75. From all accounts she was *extremely* shy. Her two surviving sisters, Nicolina and Giuseppa, were her best friends in Rome. They both lived nearby; Nicolina was her next door neighbor, even sharing a garden. They saw each other daily. "she was without fear only in front of the written page." Lucio D'Ambra, *Corriere della Sera* (27 August 1936).

76. Evidently Deledda was also a quietly charitable woman, but she was never forthcoming about her many acts of kindness and generosity. For example, Sibilla Aleramo also lived in Rome on Via Margutta 42, and at a certain point found herself financially strapped. Deledda anonymously sent Aleramo the honorarium from one of her short stories, "Fortunia," recently published in the *Tribuna* so that Aleramo would not have to worry about money, for a while at least. Deledda never told her friend that she was the benefactor (Sarale 102). After she had won the Nobel Prize, Mussolini asked her if there was anything he could do for her. She asked for nothing for herself, but she did request the release from political prison for an anti-Fascist friend. He was freed the next day. She never told him she was responsible (Balducci 182). Deledda was always concerned with the plight of the lower classes and the oppressed. In her prose as well, she treats the poor, the disenfranchised, and the servant classes with great care and sensitivity.

77. Despite the way she was ostracized, Deledda was loyal to Sardinia. When asked by a publisher to write something special about the stereotypical banditry and delinquency of her native land, she remarked that she would never sully her homeland by concentrating on its negative aspects. Her graciousness and magnanimity toward Sardinia were beyond what one would expect under the circumstances. They were also perhaps exactly what was needed to cope with an untenable situation. "I will never write such things, and I will never besmirch the name of my homeland, as so many other Sardinian authors have done, even if they payed me all the gold in the world." See Antonio Scano, *Viaggio letterario in Sardegna* (Foligno-Roma: Campitelli, 1932), 289.

78. She had been nominated and was a finalist for the previous six years; Mussolini preferred Ada Negri, however; and it is widely reported that Grazia Deledda's unsuccessful nominations had been quietly vetoed by the Duce himself.

79. When asked about her recollections of Grazia Deledda, Dr. Adriana Ghergo recounted this vivid memory to me in a personal conversation years later in Rome.

80. The body arrived in Sardinia on 20 June from Rome. It was first taken to lie in state in the Sanctuary of the *Madonna del Rimedio* in the city of Orosei, which Deledda had described so vividly in *Canne al vento*. The next day the body arrived by rail in Nuoro; and, despite the way they treated her in life, her remains were preceeded by the mayors from scores of Sardinian cities carrying their colorful municipal standards. Her casket was carried by young men dressed in local, folkloric costumes. The cortège consisted of family members,

city officials and the people of Nuoro. They walked to the city's cathedral for a
funeral Mass; then they carried Grazia Deledda's coffin up to the Deledda home
and paused for a moment to honor the place where the deceased began her career. The cortège proceeded to the *Chiesa della Solitudine* for the interment.
For the newspaper article, "Quel sarcofago ancora vuoto," upon which this description is based, access the website: www.unionesarda.it/unione/1997/05-11-
97/05-11-97nuo01a02.html.

81. Other Italian newspapers chose to parry the topic of her notoriety, instead to create of her death an opportunity for fascist propaganda. On 18 August 1936, a certain R.F. in *Il Mattino* wrote, "With the death of Grazia Deledda
now more than ever, Italy, which is the only nation that can remake Europe
"European," needs for its writers, composers, painters, sculptors, and poets to
create and to make a name for themselves with the judicial, military, social, col-
onizing and artistic rebirth of the universality of Rome. And let them be an essential part of this." To ignore completely Grazia Deledda in her own obituary
is perhaps the most backhanded of ways to mark the passing of one who refused
to write for the regime when explicitly invited to do so by Mussolini.

82. Yet there were still the inevitable differences in treatment between men
and women. Maria Giacobbe points out that the Swedish newspapers treated
Deledda differently from the male Nobel Prize winners. Whereas the men were
written up for their scientific research, she was praised for being a good housewife and a good gardener, especially of artichokes. Referred to by the Swedish
equivalent of "little lady," she was praised in print for her prudence and modesty. "Grazia Deledda Praised," (but the verb, *priset*, in Swedish has its roots
in *pris*, i.e., prize or prized) for her good qualities as a housewife and "for her
top-quality vegetables" resounded the headline over three columns of news-
print, while the subheading, in much smaller print, says: "Fibiger and Wilson"
(who were the Nobel recipients for medicine and physics) "speak of their research" (3). See Maria Giacobbe, "Grazia Deledda a Stoccolma," Website: www.
geocities.com/athens/agora/9587/giacob.htm

83. "But while the brave young woman progressed toward conquering that
seductive reality so yearned for in her dreams, her fellow islanders's lack of understanding and the open hostility of a few of them . . . filled her with bitterness" (Scano 18–19).

84. Deledda was not alone; in her biography of Natalia Ginzburg, Maja Pflug
writes, "When she was writing rather than studying, she always felt guilty. But
when she wasn't writing, she felt doubly guilty and would say to herself, 'I have
to write' " (36). See Maja Pflug, *Natalia Ginzburg: Arditamente Timida* (Milano: La Tartaruga, 1997). There are many other examples of women who were
made to feel shame for their epistolary activities, the most classic representa-
tions of which include Sibilla Aleramo's *Una donna* and Alba de Céspedes's
Quaderno proibito. See also Ellen Nerenberg, *Italian Women Writers*, ed. Rinaldina Russell (Westport, CT: Greenwood Press, 1995), 104–10.

85. See Grazia Deledda, *La vigna sul mare* (792) [*The Vineyard on the Sea*].

86. Stanis Manca was the drama critic for a Roman newspaper, *La Tribuna*;
a Sardinian nobleman (his father was the Duke of Asinara), Manca especially
appealed to the young Grazia Deledda with whom he carried on a long correspondence, much of which is reproduced by Sarale.

87. Indeed in the first three decades of the twentieth century, just about
everyone knew of her work. In his chapter on Nuoro, D. H. Lawrence writes,
"So, we stop at the Dazio, the town's customs hut . . . After which we slip into

the cold high-street of Nuoro. I am thinking that this is the home of Grazia Deledda, the novelist" (*Sea and Sardinia* 148). Lawrence was a fond admirer of Deledda's work; this is evident from the fact that he agreed to write the introduction to *La madre*.

88. Carolyn Balducci describes a scene where the hearse repatriating Deledda's remains from the Sardinian airport at Olbia broke down on the highway. A police escort was quickly substituted for the hearse, prompting a sympathetic Sardinian to shout at the cortège, "The police couldn't stop her during her life, so they had to arrest her after she was dead" (194).

89. See "Quel sarcofago ancora vuoto" at the website: www.unione sarda.it/ unione/1997/05-11-97/05-11-97nuo01a02.html.

90. There were notable exceptions, however. Attilio Momigliano had very positive things to say, especially in his introduction to her *Romanzi e novelle di Grazia Deledda* (Milano: Mondadori, 1941). See also Attilio Momigliano, *Storia della letteratura italiana* (Messina, 1935); Momigliano considered Deledda one of the best writers of the twentieth century.

91. Antonio Scano described the atmosphere in which she labored as "A not very encouraging ambience, on the contrary, completely hostile" (*Grazia Deledda* 8). Scano was among the few who sympathized with Deledda's critical fate.

92. "The imprudent judges of Stockholm who had issued that surprising verdict" (Sarale 98). Benedetto Croce in *La letteratura della Nuova Italia* (Bari: Laterza, 1945) (see 315, et passim) was usually not positive about Deledda's writing; he found disturbing the lack of any lyricism in her work; he objected to her style of stringing one fact after another without eliciting the reader's emotion. He liked, however, her descriptions of nature; yet he complained about her prose being monotonous: "One fact after another." See, however, Dino Provenzal's introduction to *Canne al vento* in *L'opera di Grazia Deledda* (Milano, 1927); Provenzal disagrees with Croce and suggests that Croce read Deledda's later novels to notice dramatic improvements.

93. Deledda's polite refusal to write the preface was the beginning of a bitter and very real animosity between the two Sardinian writers; for some reason Casu became insulted by her letter. "I already have so many enemies in Sardinia that I feel an ill wind in my face every time I go there. I love our land all the same and for this reason I don't want to increase the number of my enemies. So please forgive me; I have to say "no" more for love than for any other reason. A preface from me, even if I could write it, believe me, would bring you more negative than positive results. I accept with gratitude your dedicating a work to me, and as soon as I am able, I will do everything I can to help you. But for now I need absolute rest. Pray for me, Grazia Deledda" (Giuseppe Ruju, *Pietro Casu tra Grazia Deledda e Max Leopold Wagner* [Cagliari: Della Torre, 1981], 81–83).

94. Casu accused Deledda of "fanning the fires of sensuality," and of "aggrandizing certain condemnable affairs of the heart" and "other ill-conceived passions." He was especially upset that she was "not horrified by them," and that she did not "add one word of commentary." He condemned her for exalting and praising the "thieves, hobblers, bandits, robbers, fallen women, witches, sorceresses, usurers, corruptors, adulterers, and killers" of her own invention. He called her characters an "obscene phantasmagoria dressed practically as heroes." Casu denounced Deledda for being "biased and against the Catholic religion and spirit." He was especially upset with her fictional priests who "do and say things that dishonor the doctrine of which they mundanely and shamelessly

misinterpret." He calls them "disgraceful and miserable people like all the other Deleddan characters—slobs in body and soul, ignorant and perverse, in a word, repugnant." He laments that "they advise people to do evil, they drag people to depravity, they are the cause of offence: the blind and the leaders of the blind, they destroy rather than edify: they are conscious or unconscious accomplices of all manner of barbarousness and of all filth; they are absolutely not priests of Christ but of Belial. Poor is the land that has the misfortune to have such monsters as representatives of God." Pietro Casu, *Arte e Vita* (December 1921). See also *Rivista dei Giovani* (Torino) (15 September 1936), 528–29.

95. "Almost all the Sardinian characters created by Deledda (read "created" because they are a product of her imagination) are intellectually and morally reprehensible . . . Is it really the case that all these Sardinians are so nasty, so bitter and so unpleasant? . . . Hers is clearly not a work of art nor a work of truth. It is instead a demolition job, calumny, corruption, and treason toward a generous and strong people." Luciano Lucatelli, *La Civiltà Cattolica* (25 October 1912), 338–40. See also Ruju 87.

96. The highly influential Pietro Casu was as biased as a literary critic could possibly be. He even found Deledda's love scenes objectionable. Any objective reader would agree, however, that love scenes in her work are all but nonexistent. The careful student of Deledda would be hard pressed even to remember one of them. The most conservative censor would deem benign the few amorous scenes that do exist. Casu backhandedly delivers a compliment to Deledda for not being too risqué; yet, on the other hand, he reprimands her for her lack of delicacy. "Granted she does not appear disgusting and lascivious in her love scenes, as do so many other veristic novelists, nevertheless she often abandons herself to overly vivid and cruel descriptions, and she lacks that delicacy that one expects from a woman in writing about certain things that would be better left unsaid or that would be better depicted differently" (Ruju 92).

97. Ruju tries to attenuate Casu's harsh words; he does not find Deledda quite so demonic as Casu did. His exculpatory words attempt to add balance to Casu's vitriol. "In any case we cannot say that she wanted to present in Agnese a hardened sinner and in Paulo a troubled lecher. And it was not her intention to dress Maddalena and Elias in the clothing of adulteress and sacrilegious man. Her characters are just weak people who get lost in the dizzying game of temptation. She describes them not as a function of the positions they occupy but in the fragility of their human lives. The author herself has compassion for the people she invents. In fact she tries to soften them and to justify them because they are children of a land that made them so, actors on a stage that requires those expressions" (98).

98. See Francesco Dore. "Religiosità e Moralità nell'Opera di Grazia Deledda," *L'Orthobene* (Nuoro), (6 Sept. 1936), 36.

99. Ruju points out that because of Casu's first article about her, there broke out a rivalry between the two. "At first veiled, consisting of just words and brief notes. Then open, heated, offensive, with letters of protest and bitter criticism" (83).

100. Quoted in Natalino Sapegno, *Romanzi e novelle: Cosima* (Milano: Mondadori, 1971), 772.

101. See Alfredo Galletti, *Storia letteraria d'Italia: Il Novecento* (Milano: Vallardi, 1967), 404–6.

102. See Renato Serra, *Le lettere* (Roma: Bontempelli, 1914), 112–13.

103. See Arnaldo Bocelli, "Grazia Deledda," *La Stampa* (Torino) (28 September 1971), 3.

104. "The defect of objectivity, the constructive fragility, the weakness or really the inconsistency of psychological analysis, the absolute insignificance of the characters, the total lack of interest that they inspire . . ." Quoted in Sapegno, introduction to *Romanzi e novelle*, xiii.

105. "Italian criticism is unjust with Grazia Deledda . . ." Pietro Pancrazi, *Scrittori d'Oggi*, 1–3 (Bari: Laterza, 1946), 68, quoted in Massaiu.

106. See Marino Moretti, preface to *Lettere di Grazia Deledda a Marino Moretti* (Rebellato: Padova, 1959).

107. "Writing about herself is too compromising for a woman; she must first put on the armor against prejudice and misunderstandings. One of these defense weapons, maybe the best, is success. Once success is attained, she can risk talking and writing about herself openly. Modestly hidden among the creases of her fictional characters, the traces of her own biographical experience scattered throughout her preceding works get blended, and without additional intermediaries, she writes about herself, of her hometown, Nuoro, of her overly stern mother and too lenient father, of death, of the pain of the first urges to write, of her first sexual instincts, of her first royalties sent by the publisher, of her dreams of escaping and of glory; of Rome, desired and craved as revenge and of her flight from a society that does not accept difference, above all *women* who are different." (De Giovanni, *L'ora di Lilith: su Grazia Deledda e la letteratura femminile del secondo Novecento* [Roma: Ellemme, 1927], 48). Deledda still remains a somewhat misunderstood figure even among women. In a footnote to a contemporary study, Paola Blelloch relegates Deledda to the ranks of those women who "dedicated most of the space in their books to romantic topics (Carolina Invernizio, Lialà, etc.)" (26). See Paola Blelloch, *Quel mondo di guanti e delle stoffe: profili di scrittrici italiane del '900* (Verona: Essedue, 1987).

108. "Almost all of her stylistic inadequacies, all the presumed mediocrity that national criticism has often noticed in Deledda's works, are nothing but the particulars of women's esthetics, in its manifestation (even if archaic and timid, above all because of her insecurities with literary forebears) and in the resultant necessity to adhere to external, masculine models which did not correspond to Grazia Deledda's feminine *weltanschauung*" (De Giovanni, *Lilith* 53).

109. In her introduction to "Women's Time," in Julia Kristeva, *The Kristeva Reader* (New York: Columbia University Press, 1986), editor Toril Moi writes, "According to Kristeva, female subjectivity would seem to be linked both to cyclical time (repitition) and to monumental time (eternity), at least in so far as both are ways of conceptualizing time from the perspective of motherhood and reproduction. The time of history, however, can be characterized as linear time: time as project, teleology, departure, progression and arrival. This linear time is also that of language considered as the enunciation of a sequence of words. In "Women's Time," Kristeva's explicit aim is to emphasize the multiplicity of female expressions and preoccupations so as not to homogenize 'woman,' while at the same time insisting on the necessary recognition of sexual difference as psychoanalysis sees it" (187).

110. See Carol Gilligan, *In a Different Voice* (Cambridge: Harvard University Press, 1982).

111. ". . . [those] who want at all cost to insert Grazia Deledda into one of the contemporary literary currents: verism, regionalism, decadentism, esthetism. Even Benedetto Croce understood neither her art nor her value. Grazia Deledda did nothing but to take from herself, steeped in her land and her people, in the suffering and the religiosity of her kin" (Sarale 106–07).

112. "Criticism is by now in agreement in recognizing as the salient characteristic of the Sardinian writer her incapacity to completely adhere to any of the literary–cultural movements of her time." See Ada Testaferri, ed. *Donna: Women in Italian Culture* (Ottawa, Canada: Dovehouse, 1981), 120.

113. "She is outside of all the limitations of literary schools, [she has] a kind of autonomous art, without forebears, true only to her land and her people" (Scano 17).

114. For example, Eurialo De Michelis and Emilio Cecchi devote most of their attention to the topic of whether Deledda was a Decadent writer. De Michelis agrees with Cecchi, who states in his introduction to *Romanzi e novelle di Grazia Deledda* that Deledda is not a Decadent. See Eurialo De Michelis, *Grazia Deledda e il decadentismo* (Firenze: La Nuova Italia, 1938). "Her life as a housewife, her rudimentary education, the homebody sobriety of her choices, her absolute detachment from fads and literary circles, all prove it." See Emilio Cecchi, *Romanzi e novelle*, Vol. 2 (Milano: Mondadori, 1945), 7. Even a seemingly benign debate on the topic of literary -isms brought out the worst in otherwise credible critics. Olga Lombardi sees Deledda as having been influenced by D'Annunzio's stylized pastoral fables, to wit "Le figlie di Iorio." Lombardi argues that Deledda was nurtured literarily by ultra-romantic readings; this is evident, to Lombardi at least, from Deledda's emphasis on melodramatic orchestration of literary events. Lombardi also believes that Deledda learned to depict luxurious sensuality directly from D'Annunzio (5). Titta Rosa does not think that Deledda is a Decadent at all; he invites the reader to compare any page of her early work (*Anime oneste*, for example) to D'Annunzio's *Piacere* [Pleasure] to be convinced of the enormous differences between the two writers. See Giovanni Titta Rosa, *La Fiera Letteraria* (20 December 1925). See Olga Lombardi, introduction to *Il vecchio della montagna* in *Invito alla lettura di Grazia Deledda* (Milano: Mursia, 1979), 30.

115. I disagree with Natalino Sapegno who in his preface to *Romanzi e novelle* maintains that "Deledda's characters are almost never imbued with an energetic and coherent internal life or with a personality all their own." He sees them as "characters sketched out with quick impressionistic details." He avers that, "even when they attain a psychological reality, it is revealed in flashes, in an episodic way." Sapegno deems Deledda's psychology as one that is "extremely spotty, elementary and not at all persuasive." For him, her "plots seem arbitrary and not very natural, unmotivated and contradictory" (xix). Sapegno calls Deledda's a "summary psychology" (xxii). Throughout this study I hope to demonstrate, on the contrary, that Deledda's characters indeed have a well-fashioned internal life, and in many salient cases, a richly developed psychological personality.

116. See especially Mario Miccinesi, *Deledda*, Il Castoro 105 (Firenze: La Nuova Italia, 1975), and Mario Aste, *Grazia Deledda: Ethnic Novelist* (Potomac: Scripta Humanistica, 1990).

117. Giovanna Abete agrees that Grazia Deledda is pure intuition and deals with "human nature" as she knows it best; that is, she deals with what she sees. "In my judgment Grazia Deledda's merit resides in the connection between her old-fashioned character and human nature; she calls upon human nature in all of her writing. It seems to me human nature coincides with her whole philosophy, a philosophy whose development stopped at the level of intuition, which even though it never reached the levels of logic, nevertheless deserves to be taken into consideration by the critics as the dominant reason for her personal-

ity and her art" (107). Giovanna Abete, *Grazia Deledda e i suoi critici* (Roma: Abete, 1993).

118. See Elisabetta Rasy, *Le donne e la letteratura* (Roma: Editori Riuniti, 1984), 41.

119. "More rigorous is her psychology . . . This almost scientific rigor of Deledda's psychology reveals itself with very few outward signs, but they are deeply imbedded in a vital prose, as perhaps no other novelist knows how to accomplish in Italy today" (Fratelli, *L'Idea Nazionale* 21 November 1925).

CHAPTER 2. THE SYNDROME OF ARRESTED MATURATION

1. See Francesca Duranti, *Lieto Fine* (Milano: Rizzoli, 1984), 199; the narrator, Aldo, speaks about himself.

2. See Patricia Spacks, "The Difference it Makes," *A Feminist Perspective in the Academy*, eds. Elizabeth Langland and Walter Grove (Chicago: University of Chicago Press, 1981), 7–24: "to approach the text with a concern for the nature of the female experience in it—the fictional experience of characters, the deducible or imaginable experience of an author" (14).

3. See Sarale and Di Pilla for lengthy examples and discussions of Deledda's private correspondence. Even in her professional correspondence, Deledda referred to men as babies. In a letter dated Nuoro, 28 March 1892, to Epaminonda Provaglio regarding a certain Giorgio Venturini, a would-be writer from Trieste, she remarks, "I dealt with him as a child, because, really, in reading his letter I felt a mixture of pity and laughter, of irony and seriousness, as with a child's story of misfortune."

4. Miccinesi is correct about the autobiographical links to Deledda's works when he remarks that *Sino al confine* (1910), contains much Deleddan autobiographical information. He cites Luca as a hopeless alcoholic, which recalls Deledda's own brothers. He discusses Gavina's parents as reminiscent of Deledda's own parents. Miccinesi also sees Gavina' house as being similar to Deledda's (58). Miccinesi provides just one example, but others are too numerous to mention. See especially, however, *Anime oneste* and *L'edera* for many familial references, undeniable descriptions of the Deledda family home, and allusions to certain autobiographical episodes which later are detailed in *Cosima*.

5. Writing about *Cosima*, Sharon Wood observes, "Under the light guise of fiction the 'c'est moi' is clear" (58).

6. See *Grazia Deledda: Opere Scelte*, Vol. 1 (Milano: Mondadori, 1964), 980.

7. Giuseppe Ruju believes, on the contrary, that Deledda has no ideology, that she just writes for the joy of telling a story. "The great Sardinian does not write because she feels within herself an idea that must emerge to be communicated to others and to convert them to her own position. No. None of this interests her. Grazia is just a woman who knows how to write and who wants to write the stories, the facts and the legends of a land which she likes and which the readers like. She only writes to tell stories. But she does not have any ideology" (98).

8. The primary characteristics of this syndrome, as well as a great deal of the description of its victims as summarized here, are based on the published research of and from several interviews I conducted with the late psychologist, Dan Kiley. See Dan Kiley, *The Peter Pan Syndrome* (New York: Dodd, Mead, 1983). I owe a personal debt of gratitude to Dan Kiley for his help with this

précis and for his invaluable assistance in compiling a bibliography in this area. As well, the works of James F. Masterson are especially valuable. See also Akhtar, Thomson, Dowling, Elkind, Ellis, Erikson, Emmons, Gunderson, and Bodkin. Also useful are Janus, Johnson, Kernberg, Kohut, Lasch, Levine, Levinson, and Pyszczynski.

9. Kiley cautions in *The Wendy Dilemma* (New York: Arbor House, 1984), that the syndrome "is a complicated behavioral pattern, the causes of which are multifactored and interactive" (90).

10. Interestingly enough, however, the syndrome rarely appears in women of the same socio-economic profile and family background. Researchers have yet to determine why. For further discussion of this syndrome vis-à-vis women, see Kathryn Dalsimer, *Female Adolescence: Psychoanalytic Reflection on Works of Literature* (Yale University Press, 1986); Kiley's *The Wendy Dilemma*, and Dowling's *The Cinderella Complex* (New York: Summit, 1981). To my knowledge in Deledda's works, there is only one reference to a woman being immature. In *La vigna sul mare*, Alys is a dreamer who does not approach life in an adult way. After childbirth, "le pareva di essere lei, il bambino: era stata lei, a nascere" (676). [*She* felt like the baby: it was *she* who was born.]

11. See Nancy Leffert and Anne Petersen, "Patterns of Development During Adolescence," *Psychosocial Disturbances in Young People*, ed. Michael Rutter (Cambridge University Press, 1995), 67–104.

12. Spagnoletti writes that Deledda's "secret is that of all true novelists—to bring reality to the level of fantasy," (15).

13. "Tu non sei un uomo . . . tu sei un bamboccio di formaggio fresco; basta che una donnicciuola ti soffi addosso, puf . . . , perciò tu sei atterrato, morto, disfatto" [You're not a man; you're a blob of unripened cheese; all you need is an air-headed woman to breathe on you—poof—and you're flattened, dead, undone.] (47).

14. Goat's milk cheese is the gold standard of Sardinian cheeses; cheese made with cow's milk is considered weak; it has no flavor, no force. "Uomo sei tu? Un fuscello sei, una statuetta di cacio di vacca! Non vedi che non puoi stare in gambe, e che il tuo viso è verde come una rana?" [You're a man?! You're a twig of straw, a hunk of cow's milk cheese. Can't you see that you can't even stand up and that your face is green like a frog's?] (83).

15. Dalsimer points out that "with the onset of puberty, it becomes essential that the parents be relinquished as the primary objects of love. This constitutes one of the most painful, but also one of the most significant, psychological tasks of adolescence" (6). Unfortunately for Elias, and for all of his fictive brothers, the task of relinquishing the parents, especially the father, is a formidable one indeed.

16. Marilyn Migiel observes, "*Cenere* takes as its protagonist a young man who is an illegitimate child. Twice abandoned by his parents—first by his father who leaves him with his mother (with whom he spends the first part of his infancy), then by his mother, who leaves him with his father (toward whom he feels no real tie)—Anania Atonzu Derios spends most of the novel preoccupied with and searching for his mother, whom he fears has begun to lead a degrading life. Obviously, the psychological situation Deledda creates in Anania need not be the result of a parent figure that is physically distant; such cases of alienation can be found even when the parent is "present," because the crucial factor is that the child-protagonist become aware that his relationship with his origins is not unproblematic." See Marilyn Migiel, "The Devil and the Phoenix: A Reading of Grazia Deledda's *Cenere*," *Stanford Italian Review* (1985): 55–73.

17. Freudian psychology, however, proves less useful in a study of this type. Diane Johnson corroborates the notion that Freud concerns himself mostly with "individual private experience" rather than universal, more clinical problems. "Another prominent Jungian, Robert Johnson, uses familiar literary figures (Don Quixote, Hamlet, and Goethe's Faust) rather as Freud used Oedipus, to explicate stages in the development of a mature masculine personality: childhood, adolescence, where he says most men stay, and the fully integrated man represented by Faust. . . . None of these authors, like Gilmore, makes much mention of Freud, perhaps because Freudianism, with its emphasis on individual and private experience, is not concerned with the way 'private fantasies find collective expression in such parts of the masculine definition as an ethic of 'facing' or a morality of generosity,' as Gilmore puts the question" (15). See Diane Johnson, "Something for the Boys," *The New York Review of Books* (16 January 1992): 13–17.

18. See Erik Erikson, *Identity: Youth and Crisis* (New York: Norton, 1968), 70.

19. Deledda's heroes often rely upon a mentor to see them through the difficult times. Carol Gilligan is useful as she draws upon the work of Levinson, especially his conception of the idea of "the dream." See Carol Gilligan, *In a Different Voice*, quoting Daniel J. Levinson, *The Seasons of a Man's Life* (New York: Alfred A. Knopf, 1978), 152–53.

20. "Se egli sta per farsi uomo di Dio, in verità che comincia bene!" (129). [If he's about to become a man of God, this is some great beginning!]

21. Deledda's literary allusions to D'Annunzio, the ultimate narcissist, are mirrored in her creation of self-centered male characters. Perhaps it was "the age" of self-indulgence; on the other hand, how then does one explain away such juvenile characters as Michele of Moravia's *Gli indifferenti* and his many, many "literary brothers" created years, decades later?

22. And in *La via del male*, Pietro also feels neglected as he thinks to himself, "Nessuno gli voleva bene; nessuno gliene aveva mai voluto. Non aveva una sorella, un parente giovane con la quale volersi bene e confortarsi a vicenda" [Nobody loved him, nobody ever loved him. He did not have a sister or a young relative with whom to love and comfort each other.] (228–29).

23. For a more complete discussion see Stone and Church, "Physical Development in Adolescence," *The Psychology of Adolescence*, ed. Aaron Esman (New York: International Universities Press, 1975), 64.

24. When young men lack the security and love of their parents (which contributes in these cases to a failure to establish an identity of their own), they are most prone to be easily led by others of their own age group. They crave the approval of their friends to replace of the lack of positive, constructive attention from their parents. Typically their immature character traits preclude making true friends; worse, they do not recognize the false nature of what they consider their treasured "friendships." Dalsimer has some interesting insights into this topic. "With the loosening of the ties to the parents, there is a repeated search for new relationships. At first, this search characteristically turns to one's own sex: in early adolescence, friendship assumes unprecedented importance. The friend is often idealized; for part of what the adolescent seeks is to replace what has been lost as the parents are diminished in his or her estimation. Now, it is in the relationship with the friend that the young adolescent feels enhanced, participating in the qualities possessed by (or attributed to) the other" (8).

25. "Rivide il sorriso lieve della grande bocca ferina di Bantine; esitò a pro-

mettere" [He re-envisioned the wry smile of his friend Bantine's large, feral mouth; he hesitated to make the promise [to Marianna].] (799).

26. For additional elaboration, see Gerard Fountain, "Adolescent Development," *Journal of the American Psychoanalytic Association* 9 (1961): 414–33.

27. "Disperando completamente di sè stesso, vedendosi più debole di quel che era, si domandò con meraviglia perchè, dopo quanto aveva fatto di cattivo e spregevole nella sua vita" [Despairing completely, seeing himself weaker than he really was, he wondered with surprise why, after all the bad and despicable things he had done in his life.] (264).

28. Deledda adds several collateral symptoms that have yet to be added formally to modern definitions of the syndrome. For example, while Kiley observes that excessive alcohol consumption is usually a reliable indicator of arrested maturation, Deledda adds to the paradigm other addictive behaviors as well, such as compulsive gambling. Her fictive gambler, who experiences euphoria over winning, is not really ecstatic over winning, but over having transgressed his woman's prohibition of gambling; he will lie about his gambling, deny responsibility, and then in one way or another make it the woman's fault.

29. For a fuller discussion, see "Why Someone Would Risk It All," *US News and World Report* (9 February 1998): 40.

30. Massaiu is correct in his interpretation of the Elias/Maddalena dilemma (after her husband/his brother, Pietro, dies and leaves her widowed with Elias' child). "Elias wants to be a priest to escape the temptations of the world, to expiate his sins, to not fall victim again to his own passion. Maddalena has other views on the matter. She reminds him with clarity, with strength, of his responsibilities as a father. In her opinion, Elias wants to suppress his conscience with an egotistical act, through a renunciation which means, not salvation, but the denial of his obligations as a father to an innocent baby. For this reason the mother's voice becomes sorrowful, warm, firm and emotional. It is like the very voice of a conscience healed from a long torpor, from a virulent case of tuberculosis" (159).

31. Lorenzo Giusso also sees Elias as irresponsible, as a product of literary Naturalism—a toy in the hands of fate; he sees his problems as being external to himself: "A kind of total irresponsibility, oppresses Elias Portolu, imposed by the climate, the boundless loneliness of the grazing grounds, by patriarchal respect for illicit love and atavistic fear of sin; that same total irresponsibility which Taine defines as the virtue and the vice of inevitable facts, such as the growth of potatoes and beets. . . . In this definition of Elias Portolu we discern the peremptory laws of Naturalism—man conceived as a plaything in the hands of destiny, love depicted as a hidden snare or a slide down which men will inevitably slip, while all around them are rites, songs, dances, age-old folkloric usages which become confused with the immobility of the grazing areas and of the *nuraghe* which are also inscribed with the inviolable laws of Nature" (3). Lorenzo Giusso, "Le creature femminili di Grazia Deledda," *L'Unione Sarda* (31 October 1937): 3.

32. Maureen Dowd has a different term for the little boy who demands that his messes be cleaned up by someone else. "Bill Clinton is like a little boy, hiding behind the skirts of his powerful women, hoping they can shield him from the effects of his fatal attraction to big hair and big trouble. In psychology they have a term for the narcissist who never emotionally matures, who throws tantrums and expects everyone else to clean up his messes: the Highchair King." Maureen Dowd, "Hiding Behind Skirts," *New York Times* (26 August 1998): A23.

33. Similarly when zio Martinu counsels Elias Portolu to tell the truth to his brother and claim Maddalena for himself before it is too late (before Pietro marries her), Elias decides instead to escape from all moral responsibility. He opts to abdicate his emotional responsibility to his future lover, Maddalena, and run away to become a priest instead (77).

34. ". . . fra le mani e parve un bambino che volesse nascondersi" [in his hands and seemed to be a little boy who wanted to hide] (245). In *L'Ombra del passato* [The Shadow of the Past] one of the male characters at times feels as though he has returned to his boyhood (369), and at other times "come per un ritorno ai suoi istinti infantili, sentiva ancora una volta una smania di fuggire" [he felt once again an urge to run away, as if he were returning to his childish instincts] (369).

35. "Quale fatalità aveva il diritto di giuocarsi così degli uomini?" [What kind of fate had the right to toy with men like this?] (106).

36. "Eh, le feste son belle e i Santi son buoni, ma il vino, la gente, lo spasso, accendono il sangue, e se uno non è savio molto, ma molto, può commettere grandi errori ed essere indotto in tentazione" [Oh, parties are great and the saints are good, but wine, people, fun heat up your blood, and if you aren't really, really wise, you can make big mistakes and be led into temptation.] (55).

37. Elias is not alone! In *On the Road*, Jack Kerouac characterizes the essence of masculine irresponsibility. One of the main characters, Dean Moriarty says, "All my jail-problems are pretty straight now. As far as I know I shall never be in jail again. The rest is not my fault" (120). The narrator remarks, "The truth of the matter is we don't understand our women; we blame on them and it's all our fault" (122). In a later episode the women have just reproached Dean Moriarty for being irresponsible and juvenile. "Then, too, there was a strange sense of maternal satisfaction in the air, for the girls were really looking at Dean the way a mother looks at the dearest and most errant child, and he with his sad thumb and all his revelations knew it well, and that was why he was able, in tick-tocking silence, to walk out of the apartment without a word . . . " (195). Jack Kerouac, *On the Road* (New York: Penguin, 1976).

38. Giovanna Abete judges Elias's imprisonment a gross injustice, although there is nothing in the novel to indicate that Elias did or did not commit the crime for which he was punished (24).

39. It is not just Deledda who has hit upon this notion; her male characters are very similar to Nanni in Verga's "La Lupa" (145). See Giovanni Verga, *Tutte le novelle* (Milano: Mondadori, 1970).

40. For an excellent analysis of the social taboo of incest in Sardinia see Mario Aste, *Grazia Deledda: Ethnic Novelist* (Maryland: Scripta Umanistica, 1990).

41. Mundula says of Elias, "Elias is one of the many Deleddan characters who are weak and blame fate and destiny for their lack responsibility to choose and to act according to their conscience, that is, according to real morals" (18). Mundula recognizes that Deledda deems it "necessary for man to take on responsibility, and interrogating his bare and unbiased conscience, on his own, to begin his own redemption based on the dictates of his conscience" (186).

42. Elias screams, "Così vanno le cose del mondo, zio Martinu! Ed è la sorte, è il demonio che ci perseguita" [So go the events of the world, Uncle Martinu! It's fate; it's the devil who hounds us.] (124). Martinu responds, "Il demonio! Il demonio! Tu ce l'hai col demonio! Sono stufo di sentirti parlare così. Chi è il demonio? Il demonio siamo noi!" [The devil! The devil! You are obsessed with

the devil! I'm sick of hearing you talk like this. Who is the devil? The devil is us!] (124).

43. "E la donna gli aveva proposto di fuggire dal paese, di vivere o morire uniti. Nell'ebbrezza egli aveva accettato la proposta" [And the woman had suggested that they run away from the town, to live or die united. In his inebriation with her, he had accepted the plan.] (32).

44. "Sentì voglia di gridare, di rinfacciare e rimproverare alla madre di a-verlo portato via dal paese per avviarlo in una strada che non era la sua" [He felt the desire to scream out, to throw back in her face and to reproach his mother for having taken him away from their home town and put him on a vocational path that wasn't for him.] (37).

45. "È il demonio che mi ha preso col suo laccio" [It is the devil who ensnared me] (88). This time it is not his lover, not his mother, but the devil (most probably the same one who has been assailing Elias Portolu).

46. "Son diventato ciò che tu mi hai fatto diventare" [I have become what you have turned me into] (89).

47. "Mi hai perduto . . . tu m'hai perduto!" [You led me astray; you've turned me into a lost soul!] (92).

48. "E tentò di maledire la donna che li aveva divisi, che li avea uccisi entrambi" [And he tried to curse the woman who had come between them, who had killed them both] (125).

49. A similar scene occurs in *Marianna Sirca*. In Simone's stead, his spokesperson and best friend, Costantino, manages with clever words to deflect attention from the broken promise to the situation's being all Marianna's fault. "Marianna, cosa avevi fatto tu di un uomo. Lo avevi ridotto come un fanciullo. Egli pronunziava il tuo nome anche dormendo: e ancora lo pronunzia, ancora è come un fanciullo" [Marianna, what have you made of a man. You have reduced him to being like a kid. He would pronounce your name even while sleeping: and he still does; he is still like a little boy.] (838).

50. ". . . libri romantici che avevano formato la gioia e il tormento della sua adolescenza" [romantic books that had comprised the joy and the torment of his adolescence] (445).

51. In his introduction to *Cenere*, Vittorio Spinazzola points out that Anania has refused to *farsi adulto* [to become an adult], therefore his "personality succumbs to a morbid, destructive tendency" (xi). See Vittorio Spinazzola, *Romanzi sardi* (Milano: Mondadori, 1981).

52. After a talk with the faithful servant, Efix (*Canne al vento*), Giacinto seems to want to change. Given his previous life of scandalous dissipation, this sudden desire must be classified as truly miraculous, having been brought about by a saintly character the likes of Efix. Only divine intervention could have effectuated this sea change in the notorious Giacinto. One has reason to be skeptical, however; for, Giacinto only *says* he will reform. In the event, we never really see that happen.

53. "Aveva voglia di fargli qualche smorfia e di cavare la lingua, come da bambino a quelli che lo indispettivano" [He wanted to make faces and stick his tongue out at him as when he did as a child to those who trifled with him] (709).

54. "A volte gli sembrava di essere ancora ragazzetto, quando stanco delle preghiere che sua madre gli faceva recitare, fuggiva nella brughiera e per fare qualcosa andava a buttare giù le pietre dei paracarri" [At times he felt as if he were still a little boy when, tired of the prayers that his mother made him say, he would escape to the moors and just to do something he would knock down the stones of the wayside posts] (166).

55. See Isaac Newton Kugelmass, *Adolescent Immaturity* (Springfield, IL: Charles C. Thomas, 1973).

56. Mario Aste agrees with Miccinesi that Paulu in *L'edera* is an accurate representation of Grazia Deledda's male characters. "By not making choices Paulu allows the forces allied with death to overcome him to the point of exhaustion and final destruction. He is weak, and he cannot and will not become a man. He will be able to become so only by following the example of Annesa; he will refuse to accept responsibility on his own, allowing the Snake to take over, as the means of overcoming his weakness and apathy" (84).

57. Mario Aste sees "the old man of the mountain" as an almost stock character in Deledda's prose; he points out that this may be a remnant of Sardinia's Nuraghic past. "An alternative world known only to the initiated emerges from the real one. This world becomes a universe populated by bandits, black magic, fables, unfulfilled desires, folklore, and mystery. Deledda's language seems in conformity with itself to the world of ancient rituals and atavistic local superstitions which forever force the will of her characters into submission by the magical powers of charms, incantations, formulae and ritualistic ceremonies" (61).

58. "Ah, se non avessi peccato nè frequentato i mali compagni, non sarei stato in quel luogo (prison), avrei conosciuto Maddalena prima di Pietro, e adesso non sarei così infelice. Mi hanno domato, è vero, ma mi hanno reso debole come una femminuccia" [Ah, if I hadn't sinned nor kept bad company, I would not have been in that place [prison], I would have met Maddalena before Pietro did and now I wouldn't be so unhappy. They straightened me out, it's true; but they made me weak like a little woman] (185).

59. Deledda provides an interesting touch at the end of the novel that causes a link to be made with his father's and zio Martinu's metaphor of eagles and thrushes. Elias's son's nickname is *l'uccellino* [little bird], an inherited reflection of Elias's own weakness. Metaphorically Elias was never one of his father's powerful eagles; Elias Portolu's son inherits his weakness, cleverly underscored with an appropriate avian nickname. Significantly the son is a sickly child who dies at the end of the novel.

60. "Perchè tu mi hai fatto così debole, o Signore?" [Oh, God, why did you make me so weak?] (148). Earlier Elias had said, "Io sono un uomo, non mi posso vincere, perchè tu mi hai fatto così debole, o Signore? Ho sempre sofferto nella mia vita" [I'm a man; I can't overcome myself, oh God, why did you make me so weak? I've always suffered in my life] (68).

61. "Ma cosa posso far io? Non mi sono fatto io così; se mi fossi fatto io, mi sarei fatto col cuore di pietra. Ma, chi sa, col tempo mi passerà questa pazzia" [But what can I do about it? I didn't make myself like this; if I had invented myself, I would have given myself a stone heart. But who knows, maybe with time this craziness will pass] (68).

62. For a brief, contextual discussion of primary and secondary narcissism, see Samuel Shem, M.D., *The House of God* (New York: Dell, 1995), 264.

63. In *Cenere* Anania, too, finally finds a partial solution to his problems. Migiel remarks, "That Anania must be surrounded by death in order to realize the absurdity of his power struggle (which is also a linguistic power struggle) presents us with a disturbing ethical dilemma. But here the novel ends and no narrative voice questions further; perhaps we even believe in the (present or future) transformation of the protagonist. Yet the question hounds the reader, and we cannot but ask whether the devil has been permanently banished by the flames of the phoenix or whether he will appear yet again" (73).

64. The male protagonist of *Colombi e sparvieri* describes his own illness and recognizes his fragility at the same time: "ero così sensibile . . . così . . . così . . . come una foglia d'erba che ad ogni soffio si curva" [I was so sensitive so so like a leaf of grass that bends with every breeze.] (153). In *Il tesoro* Cosimo, an ineffectual, irresponsible figure, contemplates suicide, but rather than kill himself, he unscrupulously claims a three thousand *lire* bounty to pay off his debts. Even he then realizes that he is a coward: "Disperando completamente di sè stesso, vedendosi più debole di quel che era . . . " [Despairing completely about himself, seeing himself even weaker than he actually was . . .] (264). Even the inside cover notes of the 1965 edition of *Elias Portolu* point out that "Al centro del romanzo è il tema della nevrosi e debolezza maschile che, insieme all'altro, dell'intrepidezza e dell'intuitiva forza femminile, percorre tante pagine della scrittrice" [At the heart of the novel is the theme of male neurosis and weakness, which runs through so many of the writer's works, together with the other theme of female bravery and intuitive strength].

CHAPTER 3. REFLECTION AND SELF-REFLECTION

1. Deledda was most influenced by what she saw at home. Bruce Merry observes, "Objectively speaking, we may say that the brothers who provide her first social role model are uneducated and churlish. Andrea, for example, siphons off most of the family's money into his own pocket. Cosima [biographical name for Deledda herself] sees this state of affairs but she forgives them because they are, after all, men behaving like boys" (7). See Bruce Merry, *Women in Italian Literature* (Capricornia, Australia: James Cook University of North Queensland, 1990).

2. Along the same lines, even the young town doctor courts a girl *come un ragazzo* [like a young boy] (669). In *La fuga in Egitto* [*The Flight into Egypt*], Gesuino is attracted to Ornella; "in Gesuino operava un torbido subbuglio sensuale, quasi d'adolescente" [in Gesuino there obtained a torbid, sensual turmoil, almost like an adolescent's] (174). In *L'argine* [*The Embankment*] when Franco sees Agar he thinks, "mi riduce ad uno stato spasmodico di adolescente in fermento di vita" [she reduces me to the spasmodic state of an adolescent in the tumult of life] (185). In *L'ombra del passato* the protagonist lounges in bed "sognando come un adolescente" [dreaming like an adolescent] (357).

3. The terms "babies," "infants," "kids," "little boys" in Italian can be (and are, in Deledda's cases), rendered with the one word *bambini*. These English terms are most often interchangeable in Deledda's prose; and unless there is clear evidence in individual instances of the term *bambino*'s referring exclusively to one of those choices (i.e., specifically, for example, to mean "infant" vs. "little boy,"), I use them interchangeably throughout this study.

4. "Operava da uomo od operava da bambino? Era una sciocchezza, era un eroismo, il suo?" [Am I acting like a man or acting like a baby? Is mine foolishness or heroism?] (224).

5. "Ero grande e pensavo ancora cose da bambino" [I was grown up and I still thought like a little boy] (748). In the short story, "Un grido nella notte" ["A Scream in the Night"], the narrator tells how happy he was when his wife was alive, "come neppure da bambino" [happier than I was as a boy] (572). In *L'ombra del passato*, Adone finds out he is really very wealthy; he cannot believe it. "Sono un bambino; sono un vecchio" [I'm a baby; I'm an old man] (311). In

Sino al confine Luca knows he is a juvenile, but he accuses the family of having judged him "come un bambino" [like a baby] (75). In *Nel deserto* the protagonist sees himself as a baby too; "mi sembra talvolta d'essere un bambino" [sometimes I feel like a baby] In *Nostalgie* [*Yearnings for the Past*], (192). Antonio confesses to Regina that "quella sera mi accorsi che io ero ancora un gran fanciullone" [that evening I realized that I was still just a big kid] (185). And in *Annalena Bilsini* when Annalena tells Baldo she thinks he may be in love with Lia, he answers that in these matters he is "ancora un bambino" [still a baby] (647).

6. Despite his resolutions of manliness, Anania cannot face his mentor and protector, Carbone (his girlfriend's father), having learned the self-damning news that Anania's long-lost mother is a prostitute. Fear renders him incapable of asking in person for Carbone's daughter's hand in marriage; he is also terrified to talk to Carbone about his mother's scandalous background (what he correctly considers the kiss of death to any plans he might have to marry Carbone's daughter). Instead, in his weakness, he writes to Margherita and begs her not to leave him; he fails altogether to communicate with her father, Carbone.

7. Transferring psychologically from the mother to a mother figure is a common event in Deledda's writing. See *Colombi e sparvieri* (162); some of Deledda's men need motherly women to complete their image of themselves. See *L'ombra del passato* (350).

8. Alba de Céspedes, *Il Quaderno Proibito* (Milano: Mondadori, 1971).

9. Stefano Fedeli wrote and presented a play in Sardinia in 1991; based on Grazia Deledda's *Elias Portolu*, the author calls it a "a liberal theatrical reduction of the novel of the same name by Grazia Deledda." Interestingly Fedeli's Elias shows no signs of arrested maturation whatsoever. See Stefano Fedeli, "Elias Portolu" (Sassari, Italy: Chiarella, 1991).

10. "È un grande fanciullo che ha bisogno di essere guidato e tenuto con mano ferma" [He's a big baby who needs to be guided and held with a firm hand] (140). In *Il dio dei viventi* Bellia's mother considers her son "sempre un fanciullo per lei" [always a little boy for her] (56). And when a woman from *Annalena Bilsini* awakens one of her sons, she reminds her of "un uccellino di nido" [an unfledged baby bird] (544). In *La madre* when Paulo's mother thinks of him, "vedeva ancora le ciglia di lui sbattersi come quelle di un bambino pronto a piangere e il suo cuore di madre si scioglieva finalmente di pietà" [she could still see his eyelashes batting like those of a baby about to cry, and her mother's heart finally melted from compassion] (90).

11. In another instance Priamo goes to Michela to talk about Gavina; Michela reports back to Gavina. "Egli piange come un bambino e dice che stando vicino a me gli sembra d'esserti vicino . . . posso cacciarlo via?" [He cries like a baby and says that being around me he seems to be nearer to you [Gavina] . . . can I kick him out?] (100).

12. See *L'incendio nell'uliveto* (575); *Il segreto dell'uomo solitario* (547 and 610); and *Il paese del vento* (66).

13. The sick Jorgj in Columba's view is "come un bambino morto. Sembrava un bimbo, un bimbo morto, un piccolo Jorgj debole, un bambino morente" [like a dead baby. He was like a baby, like a dead baby, a small, weak Jorgj, a dying baby] (168).

14. ". . . muovendo di nuovo la testa col suo gesto fanciullesco" [moving his head in that boyish way of his] (794).

15. A *cinghialetto* [suckling wild boar] roasted on a spit is the signature culinary specialty of Sardinia and a traditional gift to take to one's hosts.

16. When Maria finds that he really did kill Francesco, her first husband, she thinks back to their innocence and remembers him "mite come un bambino" [gentle as a baby] (399). See also *Nel deserto* (277) and *Il dio dei viventi* (206).

17. In the short story, "L'ultima" ["The Last One"], a woman describes her aging husband as "innocente come una creatura di sette anni" [innocent as a seven year old boy] (718). In *La danza della collana* the old maid aunt is on a bus; she sees a man she thinks she knows; his eyes for her are "d'una bontà infantile" [of childlike goodness] (112).

18. See *Nel deserto* (192); *Le colpe altrui* (98); *Il dio dei viventi* (100); *L'argine* (63); and *Il vecchio e i fanciulli* (631).

19. Perhaps the biggest imaginative stretch in Deledda's sometimes overly metaphoric prose is the train porter in *Nel deserto* who looks like "un bambinone col grembiale" [a great big baby in his service apron] (264).

20. "Che ella mi riporti una seconda volta con sè, come da bambino" [I wish she would take me away with her again, like when I was a little boy] (119–20).

21. Deledda's narrators have a mild fascination for men with baby teeth. There are at least five instances, beginning with *Dopo il divorzio* where when we first see Costantino, he has boyish teeth. In *Annalena Bilsini* Annalena's new admirer in her view has teeth like a baby's: "come quelli dei bambini" [like those of babies] (596). In *La Chiesa della Solitudine* Aroldo has a "bellissima bocca, con le labbra lucide infantili e i denti che parevano ancora quelli di latte" [a beautiful mouth, with glossy babylike lips and teeth that seemed still to be baby teeth] (11). In *Nostalgie* Regina is very attracted to Antonio's "bei denti da bambino" [beautiful baby teeth] (251). The mention of little boys and their baby teeth, in the last instance, allows the conversation to produce a clever twist on Giacinto's being an immature adult. In *Canne al vento* Don Predu complains about Giacinto's being a liar. "dice le bugie, così perchè gli sembran verità, come i bambini" [He tells lies like that because to him they seem to be the truth, like babies]. Efix observes, "Come un bambino davvero." [Really like a baby]. Don Predu answers, "Un bambino che ha tutti i denti però!" [a baby who has all his teeth however!] (117). This exchange between Efix and Don Predu over Giacinto's teeth allows Deledda to contrast the two ways of dealing with his behavior. Efix is more indulgent, while the irritable Don Predu has grown cynical about Giacinto.

22. This scene is reminiscent of one where a male figure in *Sino al confine* is also likened to a baby: "paffuto e roseo come un bambino" [chubby and pink like a baby] (85).

23. Rackstraw Downes, ed., *Fairfield Porter: Art in Its Own Terms: Selected Criticism, 1935–1975*. (New York: Taplinger, 1979).

CHAPTER 4. THE WOMAN HE LOVES

1. Peter Blos, *The Adolescent Passage* (New York: International Universities Press, 1979), 40.

2. In his follow-up study to *The Peter Pan Syndrome*, Kiley describes psychologically the woman who constitutes the "enabling" half of this codependency. See *The Wendy Dilemma*.

3. As Kiley believes, psychologically the prognosis is not optimistic, for only rarely can the sufferer conquer his problem, even with the most sophisti-

cated of clinical analysis. Few cases obtain help through therapy; for the sufferers are hampered, sometimes even doomed, by their own inability to grow up. Ironically that very incapacity to mature precludes their seeing the problem for what it is. It takes maturity to seek help in overcoming immaturity. Indeed, many refuse even to consider their behavior problematic. Not so for the women who love these men; they are frustrated by their men's seemingly inexplicable behavior. The male victims want to get out of their rut. Yet if their mates attempt to help, the women become targets of their emotional abuse. The men plead for attention; but when they are given what they seem to crave, they mock the very act of others' concern. Usually their marriages end in divorce; and their suicide rate is relatively high, especially in middle age. Kiley considers the affliction "devastating to the emotional well-being of the individual and his family" See Kiley, *Peter* 35, for a full discussion of this aspect of the syndrome.

4. Grixenda of *Canne al vento* inspires Miccinesi to remark that she is "A typical Deleddan female character, the woman in love whose passion is capable of any sacrifice, of enduring all suffering, but who above all is psychologically bent toward faithfulness, a faithfulness which, as in th case of Anessa of 'Ivy,' allows no possibility of giving up or abandon. There is also in Grixenda a single-minded passion, i.e., the predisposition to love only one man, and (for as hard as it is to win him, for all the effort and pain that it takes to bend him to her feelings) to not give in under any circumstances" (*Deledda* [Firenze: La Nuova Italia, 1975], 69).

5. In "Something for the Boys," Diane Johnson observes, "Like Bly, Sam Keen, in *Fire in the Belly*, blames men themselves, or society, more than women or feminism, for male unhappiness, and says the remedy lies within men, not with women. Like Bly, he argues that men are too bound to women and cannot be "manly" until they separate from their mothers (difficult in these days of the absent father), go on a journey, find a vocation, and generally become "mature," in a series of steps" (*New York Review of Books*, 16 January 1992, 15).

6. To complement the above psychological sketch, Kiley has also constructed a chronology of the sufferer of arrested maturation; see *Peter*, 5–6.

7. Quoting Giacinto Spagnoletti in Luigi Russo, *I narratori* (Milano: Principato, 1958).

8. Showalter has asked, "What kinds of knowledge do critics need in order to apply medical and clinical concepts to literary texts?" (25). "The annals of medicine and the case histories of psychoanalysis offer literary critics extraordinary insights into consciousness and story-telling" (33). See Elaine Showalter, "On Hysterical Narrative," *Narrative* 1.1 (January 1993): 24–35.

9. See Peter Blos, "When and How does Adolescence End?" *Adolescent Psychology*.

10. In *The Adolescent Passage*, Blos points out that these adolescents "were regarded by both parents, or more emphatically, the mother, as destined to do great things in life . . . Children who rely on their parents' fantasies about them expect life to unfold according to their mother's or father's promises and expectations. Prolonged adolescence averts the crisis of a crushing realization that the world outside the family fails to recognize the imaginary role which the child has played for almost two decades. . . . When these adolescents attempt the rupture of their childhood dependencies, they soon realize that this move is accompanied by a narcissistic impoverishment for which they are not prepared and which they cannot tolerate. They thus continue to live in the self-image which their mothers, fathers, sisters or brothers created for them" (44–45). See Peter Blos, *The Adolescent Passage*.

11. Cecchi explains away Paulo's obsessions with his mother and with Agnese as his "having been made a slave to a woman" (8). Others refer to the male dilemma as demonic possession. For those who do not accept that facile reasoning, there may be another explanation: maybe Paulo needs to grow up.

12. Agnese is not the only strong woman to deliver *ultimata*; writing on *Cenere*, Migiel observes that, "after reading Margherita's ultimatum to him, Anania gives a self-serving analysis of the necessity of breaking away from her, noting how false Margherita is, how ignorant she is, how egotistical she is . . ." (69).

13. Sharon Wood believes that "Paolo's dilemma, between desire and conscience, is also the choice to be made between mother and lover, dependence and adulthood, Christianity and paganism" (72).

14. Numerous other examples show men tied to their mothers and their mother figures, unable to break free. The women are always the stronger of the partnership, the ones in control; the men are always the subservient half of the partnership. In *La giustizia*, Stefano gets angry *fanciullescamente* [boyishly]; when Maria calms him down, he feels in her voice "quasi una materna carezza, e si calmò" [almost a mother's caress and he calmed down] (51). Later recovering from swamp fever, Stefano thinks how it would be nice to have a woman nurse him back to health and "put him to sleep" (10). Stefano craves a mother's hand to heal him. He is like the protagonist of *La danza della collana*, who is walking alone and lonely along a city street and fixes upon a woman who reminds him of his mother. " 'Mamma, mamma' mormorò come un bambino smarrito" ['Mama, mama,' he murmured, like a lost little boy] (94).

15. In *Le colpe altrui* Deledda stages the spectacle of an entire chorus of women tending to one befuddled man who needs his mother. Mikali is in despair over his brother's death; he is inconsolable; he takes to his sickbed. His former girlfriend, Battista, wants to nurture him in his pain. So she brings him a comforting bowl of fava beans lovingly simmered in milk. "Intervennero le altre donne e lo pregarono come un bambino. 'Mangia, Mikali, mangia, gioiello d'oro!' " [The other women intervened and they begged him like a baby: 'Eat, Mikali, eat, golden jewel'] (144). Later Mikali too sees himself as a baby; he starts to cry. "Era l'affanno nostalgico del bambino percosso e scacciato dalla madre e che ha bisogno di ritornare a lei per consolarsi" [It was the nostalgic anxiety of the little boy shaken and sent away by his mother, the boy who needs to return to her for consolation] (291).

16. Migiel also notes in *Cenere* the "obviously erotic overtones" (57) of such a sleeping arrangement.

17. Mario Miccinesi makes an interesting observation, prompting one to wonder why it is not "irrational" when men appropriate women in the same ways as described below. He sees Deledda's female characters as women who look upon love as possession. In Miccinesi's opinion, her women want only to appropriate their men. "Very often the woman is reduced to the state of one whose behavior is guided only by a blind and absolute instinct. In this one recognizes what we have defined as "animality" in their behavior. Almost always when the women find themselves in this state of irrationality, their thought becomes obtuse, unclear and reality takes on a totally false appearance" (83).

18. Later Simone protests to Marianna that all he wants is to be free and to "essere il tuo servo; scaverei la terra ai tuoi piedi perchè non ti fosse dura" [to be your servant; I would dig the dirt at your feet so that it wouldn't be hard for

you [to walk on]] (797). He tells her that he even prays; "questo tu hai fatto di me: così Dio mi aiuti, mi hai fatto ritornare come un bambino" [this you have done to me: God help me, you have turned me into a little boy again] (797). He then puts his head on her breast and lets it slide into her lap.

19. Massaiu makes a valid point about *La madre*, and how Paulo's mother sacrificed her life for his career and his well-being. The picture of renunciation and altruism, she is always there for him. "And Maria Maddalena [his mother] dedicates herself to her Paulo with a renewed love, with a fresher spirit of abnegation. She goes to his little room to tidy it up and in the humble dining room, she sets the table with enough bread and cookies to feed the twelve apostles, despite her presentiment that he won't eat anything. But she is happy to busy herself for him" (208). Massaiu continues, "The mother's ambition and her instinct to protect her son and to lead him away from temptation are present from the first words of the book" (201). Massaiu adds, "Maternal love—the invincible desire to hearken her son to a life of renewal of lost purity—are so elevated and irrepressible in this heroic working woman that by now nothing counts for her except for the salvation of her son" (215).

20. In *L'ora di Lilith* Neria De Giovanni points out that Grazia Deledda in her own life liked her men a bit effeminate. (In fact on more than one occasion Deledda refers to her own husband as "just a boy" (see Balducci 1). De Giovanni cites a passage which refers to Deledda's first love interest, a young adolescent named Fortunio: "Note the specific attention paid to his eyes, which are 'feminine,' his hair is long, also feminine, it doesn't offer the feeling of virile strength, but let's say a more feminine one of a languorous caress. Even other male protagonists in Deledda's novels are presented with feminine touches, especially in the eyes; more resolute are the women, more 'virile;' while their men are often characterized by their lack of will, by weakness and feminine physical traits" (34).

21. At a certain juncture in *Le colpe altrui*, Andrea begins to cry; "E scoppiò a piangere; ed erano gemiti striduli, e un singhiozzare femineo, un piovere di lagrime fino al pavimento" [And he burst into tears; and his were shrill wails, and a feminine sobbing, a rain of tears down to the floor] (105). In *L'incendio nell'uliveto* Stefano is described as "come una femmina . . . tu ne farai quel che vorrai" [like a woman you can do with him whatever you please] (618). In *L'edera* Deledda effeminizes Paulu: "E la sua voce fresca e sottile come quella di una donna risonava nel silenzio del sentiero" [And his fresh and subtle voice, like that of a woman, resonated in the silence of the footpath] (87).

22. Sharon Wood agrees that Elias Portolu's state of 'moral weakness' is "pointed to by his effeminate, pallid appearance" (64).

23. ". . . quel ragazzo bello e debole come una donna, nell'ora della bufera si rifugiasse in lui come l'agnello sotto il sovero" [. . . that boy, beautiful and weak as a woman, when in a storm comes running to him like a lamb runs under a cork-oak] (23–24). In at least two instances when Elias's father delivers a strong animal simile to describe what his son is *not*, zio Martinu then describes Elias specifically as the opposite of a forceful beast (eagles vs. thrushes; lions vs. lambs).

24. Blos writes, "The basic identification with the mother reaches a crisis for the growing boy when puberty confronts him with the problem of his sexual identity. This dilemma was aptly expressed by an older male adolescent who said, "There is one thing one should know and be sure of and that is whether one is a man or a woman" (*Adolescent Passage* 46).

25. Although Migiel sees more to it in *Cenere*: "Anania's femininity is brought to the attention of the reader when Anania is called upon to play the part of a woman in a school play. Anania refuses the offer, but the occasion allows for comments about how Anania "rassomiglia a una donna" [looks like a woman] (87). Anania's sexual ambiguity (i.e., his being stronger sexually or frailer than he "should be") should be read in connection with his preoccupation about his right to be on the side of the strong or the weak. His sexual ambiguity is very quickly subsumed into the concern for class or economic ambiguity. Notably, what is of prime importance to Anania is not the threat to his masculinity posed by appearing in the guise of a woman, but the threat posed by appearing in a play presented by rich students for the benefit of the poor, and therefore by affirming his tie with the rich" (57).

26. Similarly, Priamo of *Sino al confine* is presented as a dandy. "Troppo lusso, troppo lusso, quel ragazzo! È vestito di seta e con nastri come una donna" [Too elegant, too foppish, that boy! He's dressed in silk and bows like a woman] (99).

27. On the topic of men dressing as women, Michèle Perret observes, "In fact, the reason for transvestitism is not the same for men and women: it has been said that men wear women's clothing to have more easy access to the woman they want, whereas women dress like men, at times to flee from a man, and in all cases to benefit from masculine privileges: the right to inherit, to travel unaccompanied . . . Therefore although the period of transvestitism for the man is one of intense sexual activity, for the woman more often it is a period of asexuality" (329). Michèle Perret, "Travesties et Transsexuelles: Yde, Silence, Grisandole, Blanchandine," *Romance Notes* 25.3 (1985): 328–40.

28. In the face of numerous examples of effeminacy and implied homosexuality among men, the single, veiled reference to lesbianism concerns Marianna Sirca's faithful servant, Fidela (who results in the end to be not so faithful after all). Fidela confesses at the beginning of the novel that she really would have preferred to be a man. She harbors a hate "contro tutti gli uomini terribili e le cose spaventose che egli rappresentava: odio e proposito fermo di combattere contro di lui come contro il male stesso in persona" [against all terrible men and the frightening things that they represent: a hate and a firm intention to fight against him as against evil incarnate itself] (809). Fidela is so horrified to find that her beloved Marianna is having a love affair with a man that Fidela even suggests having Marianna exorcised! In the event, jealously Fidela betrays her rival, Simone, to the law, thus precipitating the novel's violent conclusion.

29. Blos notes that "When the normal adolescent conflict of bisexuality presses for a final settlement, prolonged adolescence circumvents it by a perseveration in the bisexual position. In fact, this position becomes libidinized and any abandonment of it is resisted rather than sought. The gratifications thus obtainable play into the need for limitless possibilities in life, and simultaneously, assuage castration anxiety by perpetuating the ambiguity of sexual identity. This ambiguity is significantly reflected in the adolescent's vocational or educational floundering, his ineffectualness and eventual failure" (*Adolescent Passage* 46).

30. "Lentamente, una evoluzione spirituale succede entro di me e la mia percezione diventa più acuta e sottile. Vi sarete accorto che scrivo molto meglio di prima, certamente scrivo ancora male, ma vedrete col tempo!" [Slowly, a spiritual evolution is taking place within me and my perceptions are becoming sharper and subtler. You will notice that I am writing a lot better than before;

certainly I still write badly, but you'll see with the passage of time!] (1). Giovanna Cerina observes that Deledda "not only controls her choices but pays attention to new cultural trends, that she dedicates herself to a poetic and above all narrative apprenticeship with new thematic and formalistic beginnings, paying attention to excesses of language use, syntactic and grammatical slips, gradually working out a narrative and stylistic standard suitable for the peculiarities of life in Barbagia. See Giovanna Cerina, preface to Vol. 1, *Grazia Deledda: Novelle*, available at: www.sardinia.net/bibliothecaSarda/007dele/1/1_prefaz.htm.

31. See Margaret Waller, "Le commencement de la fin? Le deuil de l'homme au seuil du XIXe siècle," *Rhétoriques fin de siècle*, eds. Mary Shaw and François Cornilliat (Christian Bourgeois, 1992). While writing about the French turn-of-the-century hero, Margaret Waller describes quite accurately the Deleddan hero as well, "The hero of the 'sickness of the century' shows a passivity, a sensitivity, a vulnerability that one finds in the contemporary image of the ideal woman. 'Feminine' by nature or 'feminized' by circumstances, the hero of the 'sickness of the century' is prone to introspection, irresolute to the point of paralysis. This facet of his 'femininity' is presented as a character flaw, a weakness that locks him into a position of emotional slavery more typical of female characters than male, and which attaches him inextricably to a woman" (163).

32. In fact, much of her non-prose writing is about Sardinian folklore; and she wrote extensive essays for newspapers, magazines and folklore studies—articles about life in Sardinia, native costumes, religious festivals, etc. Giuliana Morandini points out that Deledda aims to create a literature that is "completely and exclusively Sardinian" (22).

CHAPTER 5. MANIFESTATIONS OF THE SYNDROME: RELATIONSHIPS

1. See Ruju's reprint of Casu's article in *Arte e Vita*.

2. In the short story, "La scommunica" ["The Excommunication"], the female protagonist learns after all that she can indeed live in peace; "Bastava non andar in giro per il mondo e non aver fiducia negli uomini" [All you have to do is don't travel around and don't have faith in men] (644). Most probably Deledda was writing about humankind in general; on the other hand, perhaps she had something else in mind.

3. ". . . un uomo come tutti gli altri, nemico come tutti gli altri" [a man like all the others, an enemy like all the others.] (819).

4. "Ebbene, che vuoi? . . . Tu non mi hai dato mai aiuto, mai amore, mai nulla di tuo: e adesso vieni a tentare di togliermi quello che è mio?" [So now what do you want? . . . You have never helped me, you have never loved me, nor given me anything of yourself: and now you come and try to take away what is mine?] (820).

5. Neria De Giovanni points out that "Grazia Deledda instead gives to her female characters a dramatic capacity to choose. And often it is the woman who decides the fate of her man. She overburdens herself in anguish and remorse for him" (67).

6. He even tells her that he has taken up the unmanly activity of praying; "questo tu hai fatto di me: così Dio mi aiuti, mi hai fatto ritornare come un

bambino" [This you have made of me: so help me God, you have turned me into a little boy again] (797).

7. In one touch Deledda tells us more about the Sardinian attitude toward banditry than could entire, comprehensive sociological studies. With a rare stroke of humor, the author paints a scene where Marianna Sirca's father is both astonished and horrified that she wants to marry the bandit, Simone Sole. In complete dismay he admonishes her that at least she could have fallen for a *famous* bandit, the likes of Giovanni Corraine!

8. "Sono qui, riprendimi, fa di me quello che vuoi, Marianna, perdonami. Dimmi almeno che mi perdoni" [I'm here; take me back; do with me what you will; Marianna, forgive me. Tell me at least that you forgive me] (857). Sharon Wood attributes the Marianna-Simone exchange as a "desire for self-admiration. Marianna wishes to show that she is a free and independent woman, a *padrona*, by marrying whomsoever she chooses, even a bandit. . . . Mocked by those he admires for giving in to a woman, for letting himself be talked into losing his most valued possession, his liberty, he sends his servant Costantino to inform Marianna of his change of heart. Marianna's response of scorn and contempt is a challenge to Simone's courageous virility" (69). For Simone Marianna is property. Wood quotes Deledda in translation, "Marianna, who used to order him about, who wouldn't even look at him, Marianna loved him and had promised to wait for him. Taking hold of her was to take hold of all the things which she represented" (70).

9. Deledda reserves dog master imagery mostly for *Marianna Sirca*, but in *La fuga in Egitto* another instance appears where not only are the women also the dominators in this novel, but the men seem to like it that way. Adelmo thinks, "mi stenderò ai tuoi piedi come un cane fedele" [I will lie at your feet like a faithful dog] (251). In *L'ombra del passato* Adone follows Caterina "come un cagnolino" [like a puppy] (209). In *Il paese del vento* the female protagonist narrates how she escorts a blind man to a banquet; she takes his hand to make sure he sits with her; he feels an especial affinity toward her and tells her that he will be "like her faithful dog." "Sono qui, con lei, signora, come un cane fedele. Le appartengo per tutta la vita" (123). [I am here with you, madam, like a faithful dog. I belong to you for the rest of your life.] In *La Chiesa della Solitudine* Aroldo's vision of himself is also decidedly canine. He is grateful merely to be in Maria Concezione's house; he thinks he would be content if only she would just keep him "like a faithful dog." "Lasciatemi qui; non fiaterò; tenetemi come un cane fedele" [Leave me here; I won't even breathe; keep me like a faithful dog] (64). Aroldo does not care if Maria Concezione treats him shabbily; "Ella può calpestarmi" [she can stomp on me] (52) as the Madonna does to the serpent. Aroldo learns that she has cancer; he vows that if she calls for him, he will be at her feet "like a dog" (250).

10. In this case Simone is younger than Marianna; it is also significant that in their youth Simone used to be a servant of the Sirca household. For at one point, Marianna thinks "sebbene il polso le ardesse ancora per la stretta di lui, ella si sentiva sempre la padrona; era certa che con un solo suo sguardo lo avrebbe sempre atterrato" [even though her pulse quickened when he squeezed her hand, she still felt like the boss; she was sure that with only one glance she would have floored him] (742).

11. Mario Aste remarks that "This desire for human love is stronger in the woman than in the priest; in it she sees her personal fulfillment, through the acceptance of instinctual natural forces. Her passion, simple but destructive,

can be overcome only by another blind instinctive force: the love of a mother for her son" (56).

12. Consider, for example, Sebastiana of *Il nostro padrone* [*Our Master*] who thinks about Bruno "bent before her like a thin plant stem ready to snap" (259). In *Colombi e sparvieri*, as soon as Marianna, his vision of beauty, enters the room, Jorgj, the languishing hero, imbues her with improbable powers: "Allora parve a Jorgj che la stamberga si allargasse, diventasse spaziosa e fragrante come un paesaggio primaverile. Una pace luminosa, un trepido sogno di bellezza e di luce si stesero attorno al suo letto, attorno alla casupola e via via per tutto il mondo" [Then it seemed to Jorgj that the room grew larger, became more spacious and fragrant as the countryside in springtime. A luminous peace, a trembling dream of beauty and light spread around his bed, around the small house and slowly over the whole world] (151–52). In his head she becomes all this without even trying; indeed, she is unaware of her madonna-like effect upon him.

13. Elias is not alone in his obsession with Maddalena. The critic, Antonio Baldini, was also inamoured of this fictive siren. As though speaking directly to Deledda, Baldini rhapsodized: "As for me, whom solitude has rendered rather covetous, every time you made Maddalena appear for me, my heart started to pound" (109–13). See Antonio Baldini, "Grazia Bravamano," *Salti di gomitolo* (Firenze, 1920).

14. *L'incendio nell'uliveto* is a novel where an arch-matriarch controls those around her, this time in the incarnation of Agostina Marini. But even she is outshone by rich, old *zia* Paschedda who jealously guards the keys to all the provisions and treasures of the house (even from her own husband). She is a household dominatrix; she treats the men of the family like children: "Li teneva come bambini" [She kept them like baby boys.] (592). And in *Il segreto dell'uomo solitario*, Sarina dominates completely the male servant under her command; "pareva lo dominasse e lo facesse agire come una domatrice di belve" [like a tamer of wild animals she seemed to dominate him and to make him behave] (490). Later when her much older husband tries to escape from his sickbed, she hovers over him too, "parlandogli con parole infantili come si fa coi bambini per tenerli buoni" [speaking to him with baby talk as one does with children to make them behave] (492).

15. In *The Wendy Dilemma*, Kiley has some insights on precisely that issue, to wit: some women accept responsibility for half of the partnership and "expect the same in return, refusing to indulge his immature ways" (13). Trouble ensues when the expectation of reciprocity is not fulfilled. The Deleddan woman only experiences a problem if she stays with him, and he does not honor his half of the partnership, refusing to grow up.

16. Bruce Merry discusses women in collusion with one another: "This kind of margin may be conceded to embattled female characters by the astute woman novelist. It hints that women develop a sharper sensitivity about currents running between figures inside the extended patriarchal family and that they appropriate to themselves the power of revealing or concealing a secret. This facility is not a banal extension of the clichè about 'female intuition'. Rather, it acknowledges that engaged domestic experience may allow women to concentrate more effectively on the network of the private" (21).

17. Tellingly the English translation of Deledda's *Canne al vento* is *Reeds in the Wind*.

18. See Harriet Lerner, *The Dance of Anger* (New York: Harper and Row, 1985).

19. Writing about Annessa of *L'edera*, Miccinesi remarks, "Yet once again a female character resigns herself to pain and atonement: rebellion seems like a remote possibility in the Deleddan world" (55). He goes on to describe how the Deleddan woman is completely dedicated to her man, how she is capable of total self-sacrifice. Miccinesi characterizes this male/female symbiosis as "a different way of conceiving of life, of facing evil or pain" (52). In some cases, perhaps this is true; however, the woman's is not a "different," conscious choice, but the results of an age-old syndrome which make the principal actors dysfunctional human beings, usually incapable of being helped. The opposite obtains in cases such as *Marianna Sirca* and *Annalena Bilsini*.

20. See Rosemary Dinnage, "The Wounded Male," *Times Literary Supplement* (13 December 1991): 7. In her review of Liam Hudson and Bernadine Jacot, *The Way Men Think* (Yale University Press, 1991), Dinnage writes that the contention of the book she is reviewing is that the adult male is "wounded," that children of both genders are born of a woman and nurtured by the same, that to grow into a man, the boy must rebuff femaleness "and the primitive comfort it has given him, and launch out on his own. This painful process creates the wound. It accounts for misogyny of all kinds, for fear of entrapment by the threatening female of the species, for insensitivity towards the personal and humane, for aggressivity and a need to be in control. It makes men liable to treat people as things and things as people. 'Inside most males but not inside most females there must be a species of existential gulf.' Misogyny 'lingers in a hinterland where notions of separation and engulfment, erotic excitement and dismay mingle.' The girl child, however, whatever vicissitudes she may have to undergo, can address life from a psychologically coherent foundation. . . . Nevertheless, the wound—the necessary, painful breaking of the original bond—remains in their opinion omnipresent among men."

21. In Costantino's perceptive (albeit self-serving) opinion, Simone's love for Marianna is "fatta più di odio che d'amore" [consists more of hate than love] (847).

22. Paola Blelloch sees Deledda's female characters as distinct from her male characters in that they are double victims, first because they are women in an archaic society and second because they are subject to the behavior of violent and vindictive men. She sees the women as having to sacrifice much more than the men, as in *Canne al vento*, for example (42–43).

23. But when a man (Simone Sole in *Marianna Sirca*), describes his own head, it is *sweet* on the inside: "come il frutto del castagno che fuori è tutto spine e dentro è dolce come il pane" [like the fruit of the chestnut tree which on the outside is thorny and on the inside is sweet as bread] (753).

24. This link conveniently opens up the question of who becomes a priest, part of Deledda's constant examination of clerics, so well documented by the unhappy critics, Casu and Ruju.

25. See Grazia Deledda, "Sangue sardo" (Roma: Newton, 1995), 31. This short story was first published in the women's magazine, *Ultima Moda* 309–10, 1892.

26. George Will, "Rank Films a Cultural Symptom," *Lawrence Journal-World* (19 June 2000): 7B.

27. For an excellent article on the literature of rape from a woman's point of view, see Jacqueline Reich, "Rewriting Rape," *Italian Culture* XVI, 2 (1998): 217–33.

28. "E si sentì destare dentro come una bestia feroce che gli dormiva in

fondo alle viscere e d'un tratto svegliandosi lo squassava tutto e lo faceva bal-zare: un urlo di fame e di dolore gli risuonava dentro, gli riempiva di fragore le orecchie e di sangue gli occhi. Si buttò giù convulso, premendo a terra il petto e le viscere per schiacciare la bestia e respingerla a fondo nel suo covo" [And he felt awakening within himself a wild beast who slept deep inside his belly and suddenly awakening it jolted him completely and made him jump: a howl of hunger and pain resonated within him, the din filled his ears and blood filled his eyes. Agitated he threw himself to the ground, pressing his chest and his belly to the earth to squash the beast and shove it back to the depths of its lair] (757).

29. For two more famous instances of horseback riding allegories, see Giovanni Boccaccio, *Decameron* VI, 1 and IX, 10.

30. For an excellent discussion of children's guilt and hostility toward the mother see Phyllis Grosskurth, "The New Psychology of Women," *New York Review of Books* (24 October 1991): 25–32.

31. See C. Dionisotti and C. Grayson, eds., *Early Italian Texts* (Oxford: Blackwell, 1965) for a fascinating study of one of the earliest Italian texts (late eighth to early ninth century). Written in early Italian/late medieval Latin, it is an *indovinello* [enigma] common to western European oral tradition at that time. "Se pareva boves, alba pratalia araba, et albo versorio teneba, et negro semen seminaba." Like Osea of *Annalena Bilsini*, the medieval farmer prepared his oxen; he plowed the white field; he held the white plow and he sowed the black seed. The difference from the Deleddan model is that on one level in the medieval case the passage has been interpreted thusly: "The fingers of the hand when writing, the paper, the pen, and the ink are represented respectively by the oxen driven by the farmer, the field he is ploughing and the plow he guides" (1–3).

32. See Julia Kristeva, *The Kristeva Reader* (170). Kristeva points out that the Blessed Virgin Mary is the perfect object of men's desires because she is so removed from paternal sternness. This idea is an interesting explanation for Deledda's men with stern fathers who turn to madonna figures and then behave as the juvenile vis-à-vis their mother substitutes.

33. "Mi farò amare da lui assai, assai" [I'll make him love me very, very much] (135).

34. "Ed Elias non poteva distaccare la figura di lei da quella del bambino" [Elias couldn't detach her image from the baby's] (145).

35. Giancarlo Buzzi, *Grazia Deledda* (Torino: Fratelli Bocca, 1953), 146.

36. Bruce Merry observes, "We can borrow the table devised by Marcuse in his Freudian study *Eros and Civilization* (1955) and categorize Deledda's women as obedient to the dictates of the 'reality principle,' while the male characters seek their own satisfaction" (21).

37. Marianna Sirca only learns later that her servitude was arranged by her widowed father in implicit exchange for *zio* Prete's inheritance.

38. In *Sino al confine*, for example, Gavina wants to be free "Io voglio vivere sola, indipendente" [I want to live alone, independent] (93). In *Nel deserto*, flouting convention, a minor female character decides she does not need a man at all. She opens a *pensione* instead, and finds it sufficient upon which to live, along with her good memories which are all she needs.

39. In their landmark study, *The Madwoman in the Attic*, Gilbert and Gubar expound on the nineteenth-century woman writer as a madwoman (77–78). While none of Grazia Deledda's women qualifies as an example of the type Gilbert and Gubar describe, it might be that Deledda was experiencing the feel-

ings of self-division of Gilbert and Gubar. She was a product of a patronistic system, but clearly was a rebel against its strictures. See Sandra Gilbert and Susan Gubar, *The Madwoman in the Attic: The Woman Writer and the Nineteenth-Century Literary Imagination*. (New Haven: Yale University Press, 1984).

40. Giuliana Morandini has written: "A third generation, those born between 1840–1860, in the most intense moment of creative fervor, knows the crisis of the 1880's and 90's and the positivistic embitterment that this crisis brings what with its repressive and limiting stereotypes prevailing over women. Thus backsliding occurs; there is a return to the evasive writing of the beginning of the 1800's; with a blossoming of sentimentality, they dedicated themselves widely to writing children's literature. It was women writers born between 1880–1890, beyond shyness and polemics, who succeeded in lucidly investigating feminine existence, recognizing in it dramatic and unheard-of detail. They write without any longer feeling themselves to be in an inferior position and are uplifted at least in part by gender conditioning" (9). Born in 1871, Deledda was clearly a woman before her time, if one accepts Morandini's categorizations. While Deledda did indeed write many children's short stories, the vast majority of her work is not sentimental at all; very definitely it is not for children. See Giuliana Morandini, *La voce che è in lei: Antologia della narrativa femminile italiana tra '800 e '900* (Milano: Bompiani, 1980).

41. It is possible to read Deledda's conception "of the clash between the individual and the social order as the literary correlative of the relations between an island which is only in theory part of a post-Unification reality" (Wood 60). Grazia Deledda's women are a personal embodiment of that collision, and on a man/woman paradigm, he is a baby and she is a nurturer (man is Sardinia and woman is the "continent"). Wood continues, "It is the clash between the old and the new, the individual and the moral order, the margin and the centre, the male and the female, which constitutes the core of her work, and the consequences of the trangression of rigid codes which form its drama" (63).

CHAPTER 6: CONCLUSION

1. In his introduction to Elio Vittorini's *Sardegna come un'infanzia* (Milano: Mondadori, 1974), Silvio Guarnieri introduces the (unsubstantiated) notion that there might be something about Sardinia itself that brings out the adolescent. "Vittorini goes back and claims for his own a juvenile, boyish, adolescent condition; and here is the value of the echoes of childhood or adolescence which does not stop with or does not just condense itself in the title of the book, but which permeates the entire book" (11).

2. See Akhtar, Masterson, Elkind, Knaus, Emmons, Gunderson, and Bodkin on the syndrome as a universal concept.

3. See especially Monica Bogliardi, "Mammoni d'Italia," *Panorama* (28 March 1996): 164–67.

4. Even a century ago at least one British book reviewer (of *Cenere*) had little use for narcissistic men: "Also, we do not, as a rule, care to hear much about young men who are obsessed with a morbid fear through their growing years, who blaze into love as children, and flare out upon an instant, after years of intense adoration of the beloved object." See "Concerning New Novels," *Sketch* (1 July 1908).

5. Dalsimer has established that normally during adolescence the childhood ties to parents are in the process of being relinquished, "but new bonds have not yet been consolidated." There ensues "a period of transition in which an enlarged self-preoccupation must substitute—temporarily and partially—for relations with others." Normally "the propensity of young persons to magnify themselves ordinarily subsides in time, as the withdrawal into the self yeilds to the establishment of new ties outside the family" (7–8). The key words concerning Deledda are "temporarily" and "partially." Her men never relinquish Dalsimer's "enlarged self-preoccupation."

6. Dalsimer cites an interesting passage from a classic paper by Anna Freud, "I take it that it is normal for an adolescent to behave for a considerable length of time in an inconsistent and unpredictable manner; to fight his impulses and to accept them; to ward them off successfully and to be overrun by them; to love his parents and to hate them; to revolt against them and to be dependent on them; . . . to be more idealistic, artistic, generous and unselfish than he will ever be again, but also the opposite: self-centered, egoistic, calculating. Such fluctuations between extreme opposites would be deemed highly abnormal at any other time of life. At this time they may signify no more than that an adult structure of personality takes a long time to emerge, that the ego of the individual in question does not cease to experiment and is in no hurry to close down on possibilities" (Anna Freud, *The Psychoanalytic Study of the Child* [New York: International Universities Press, 1958], 275–76). For Deledda's men the "adult structure of personality," never emerges; the boy never matures.

7. Anna Dolfi quotes Deledda from a letter to Pirro Bessi written on 20 May 1907. "L'uomo è, in fondo, eguale dappertutto" [Down deep, man is the same everywhere] (72). See *Lettere e note autobiografiche della Deledda*, ed. A. Momigliano (Firenze: La Nuova Italia, 1954). Deledda was most probably referring to mankind in general in this citation; nevertheless, there is room for interpretation in her words.

8. In Deledda's entire *opera omnia* there is only one instance where there are clear indications that the man is maturing. In *La Chiesa della Solitudine*, Aroldo vows that he will not leave the dying Concezione in her hour of need, whereupon Concezione realizes that he is finally growing up. The irony is that the maturing process does not happen until the last five pages of Deledda's last novel; a double irony is that Aroldo matures just as Concezione dies, thus depriving her of enjoying the results of his learning process. "Concezione felt that the boy of yesterday had become a man like a little soldier who had gone to war" (252).

9. Writing for therapy is not new; the curative powers of authorship for a woman are well documented in literary criticism. There is an interesting example in Deledda's work as well. In *La vigna sul mare* the female protagonist is depressed and feeling useless, so she decides to write a novel, something "per uno e per tutti, che parla di chi scrive e di chi legge" [something for everyone, something about the writer and the reader] (686). See Grazia Deledda, "Chiaroscuro" (1912) in *Romanzi e novelle*, Vol. 1, (Milano: Mondadori, 1941). Silvio Negro quotes the author, "The truth is that in the housewife, who published a book a year, in reality there was hidden a grand spirit. "If I had been born a man," we read in another of her letters, "I would have been a hermit; I would have lived in an hermitage in the immense arms of nature from where I would have returned only rarely amongst men to study them and to feel sorry for them. As a woman I have to adapt and be flexible, to live among those who, loving me and protecting me, complete my existence" (3).

10. See Rachel Blau Du Plessis, *Writing Beyond the Ending* (Bloomington: Indiana University Press, 1985), 3–4.

11. See especially the Taviani brothers' autobiographical film, *Padre, Padrone*.

12. See "Grazia Deledda," *La vita il libro* (Torino) (1911): 95–102.

13. Dalsimer writes, "a work of literature . . . must resonate with enduring features of psychological reality . . . this resonance contributes to the power of the work over the imagination of the reader" (3). Gitlin writes, "There is frequently a biblical quality to Deledda's prose, at least in translation. It is hard not to feel, when reading her, that whatever the particularities of late nineteenth century Sardinians, her readers are getting close to some pure ore of human emotion." Todd Gitlin, "Rediscovering the Simple Lyricism and Moral Complexity of Sardinian Writer Grazia Deledda," *Chicago Tribune* (20 September 1998): Books, 3.

14. See Umberto Eco, *Postscript to the Name of the Rose* (New York: Harcourt, 1984).

15. Natalino Sapegno stresses that Deledda had "in general almost no contact with the literary and cultural experiences of her contemporaries" (xi).

Works Cited

Abete, Giovanna. *Grazia Deledda e i suoi critici*. Roma: Abete, 1993.

Akhtar, Salman, and Anderson Thomson. "Overview: Narcissistic Personality Disorder." *American Journal of Psychiatry* (January 1982): 10.

Aleramo, Sibilla. *Una donna*. Feltrinelli: Milano, 1983.

Altman, Lawrence K. "Big Push to Prevent Blinding Disease with Single-Dose Antibiotic." *New York Times* 11 November 1998: 1.

Alziator, Francesco. *Storia della letteratura di Sardegna*. Cagliari, 1954.

Amoia, Alba. *Twentieth Century Italian Women Writers: The Feminine Experience*. Carbondale: Southern Illinois University Press, 1996.

Apollonio, Mario. "Grazia Deledda." In *Letteratura dei contemporanei*. Brescia, 1956.

Arìes, Philippe. *Centuries of Childhood*. Translated by Robert Baldick. New York: Knopf, 1962.

Arpesani, Ninina. *Interviste e Critiche Femminili*. Rome: 25 May 1907.

Artizzu, Francesco, ed. *La Società in Sardegna nei secoli: lineamenti storici*. Torino: Edizioni Radiotelevisione Italiana, 1967.

Aste, Mario. *Grazia Deledda: Ethnic Novelist*. Potomac, Md: Scripta Humanistica, 1990.

Baldini, Antonio, ed. "Grazia Bravamano." In *Salti di gomitolo*. Florence, 1920.

Balducci, Carolyn. *A Self-Made Woman: Biography of Nobel-Prize-Winner Grazia Deledda*. Boston: Houghton Mifflin, 1975.

Bellonci, Goffredo. Preface to *Grazia Deledda, Premi Nobel 1926*. Milano: Mondadori, 1981.

Blelloch, Paola. *Quel mondo di guanti e delle stoffe: profili di scrittrici italiane del '900*. Verona: Essedue, 1987.

Blos, Peter. *The Adolescent Passage*. New York: International Universities Press, 1979.

———. "When and How does Adolescence End?" In *Adolescent Psychology*, Vol. 5, edited by S. C. Feinstein and P. Giovacchini New York: Aronson, 1976.

Boccaccio, Giovanni. *Decameron*. New York: Penguin, 1980.

Bocelli, Arnaldo. "Grazia Deledda." *La Stampa (Torino) 28 September 1971: 3*.

———. *Letteratura del Novecento*. Roma: Sciascia, 1975.

———. Essay. In *Nuova Antologia*. 36–39, Roma, 1 September 1936.

Bogliardi, Monica. "Mammoni d'Italia." *Panorama* (28 March 1996):164–67.

Borgese, Giuseppe Antonio. *La vita e il libro*. Torino: Bocca, 1911.

Borlenghi, Aldo. *Narratori dell'Ottocento e del primo Novecento*. Milano: Ricciardi, 1963.

Branca, Remo. *Bibliografia deleddiana*. Milano: L'Eroica, 1938.

———. *Il segreto di Grazia Deledda*. Cagliari: Fossataro, Editrice Sarda, 1971.

———. *Atti del Convegno nazionale di studi deleddiani*. Cagliari: Fossataro, 1974.

Brancati, Vitaliano. *Sogno di un valzer*. Milano: Bompiani, 1982.

Briziarelli, Susan. "Woman as Outlaw: Grazia Deledda and the Politics of Gender." *Modern Language Notes* 1 (1995): 20–31.

Bruno, Francesco. *Grazia Deledda*. Salerno: Di Giacomo, 1935.

Buono, Enza. *Grazia Deledda*. Bari: Saggio Critico, 1951.

Buzzi, Giancarlo. *Grazia Deledda*. Torino: Fratelli Bocca, 1953.

Caesar, Anne. *"Savage Sardinia." Times Literary Supplement* 6 November 1992: 21.

Cairns, C. *Italian Literature: The Dominant Themes*. Devon, England: Newton Abbot, 1977.

Cambosu, Salvatore. *Il Supramonte di Orgosolo*. Firenze: Vallecchi, 1988.

Capuana, Luigi. *Gli 'ismi' contemporanei*. Milano: Fabbri, 1973.

Casu, Pietro. *Arte e Vita* December 1921.

———. "Il Caso Deledda," *Rivista dei Giovani (Torino)* 15 September 1936: 528–29.

Cecchetti, Giovanni. *Giovanni Verga*. Boston: Twayne, 1978.

Cecchi, Emilio. *Romanzi e novelle*. Vol. 1. Milano: Mondadori, 1941.

———. *Romanzi e novelle*. Vol. 2. Milano: Mondadori, 1945.

———. "Grazia Deledda." In *Storia della letteratura italiana*, ed. by Carlo Marzorati. Il Novecento. Vol. 9. Milano: Mondadori, 1941, 539–42.

Cerina, Giovanna. *Deledda e altri narratori*. Cagliari: CUEC Editori, 1992.

———. "Grazia Deledda e 'Vita Sarda.' Tre anni di apprendimento." *Rileggere Grazia Deledda*, edited by Antonio Prost. Cagliari: 1986.

———. Preface to Volume 1. *Grazia Deledda: Novelle*. Available at Sardinia.net/bibliothecaSarda/007dele/1/1prefaz.htm.

Chiara, Talia. *Grazia Deledda*. Milano: Marucelli, 1938.

Chroust, Giovanna. *Grazia Deledda e la Sardegna*. Roma–Milano: Augustea, 1932.

Ciusa Romagna M. *Onoranze a Grazia Deledda*. Nuoro–Cagliari, 1959.

Collu, Ugo. *Grazia Deledda nella cultura contemporanea*. Vols. 1–2. Nuoro: Consorzio per la pubblica lettura "Salvatore Satta," 1992.

Corona, Daniela. *Donne e scrittura: atti del seminario internazionale* (Palermo, 9–11 June 1988). Palermo: Luna, 1990.

Costa-Zalessow, Natalia. *Scrittrici italiane dal XIII al XX secolo: testo e critica*. Ravenna: Longo, 1982.

Croce, Benedetto, ed. "Grazia Deledda." In *Letteratura della Nuova Italia*. Bari: Laterza, 1950.

Cutrufelli, Maria Rosa. *Scritture, scrittrici*. Milano: Longanesi, 1988.

Dalsimer, Katherine. *Female Adolescence: Psychoanalytic Reflection on Works of Literature*. New Haven: Yale University Press, 1986.

D'Ambra, Lucio. Obituary of Grazia Deledda. *Corriere della Sera* 27 August 1936:3.

de Céspedes, Alba. *Il Quaderno Proibito*. Milano: Mondadori, 1971.

De Chiara, Bice. *Psicologismo deleddiano in Elias Portolu e Canne al vento*. Napoli: Loffredo, 1974.

De Giovanni, Neria. *L'ora di Lilith: su Grazia Deledda e la letteratura femminile del secondo Novecento*. Roma: Ellemme, 1987.

———. *Grazia Deledda*. Alghero: Nemapress, 1991.

———. *Come leggere "Canne al vento" di Grazia Deledda*. Milano: Mursia, 1993.

———. ed. *Carta di Donna: Narratrici italiane del '900*. Torino: SEI, 1996.

De Gubernatis, Angelo. *Piccolo dizionario dei contemporanei*. Roma: Stamperia Editrice, 1893.

De Michelis, Eurialo. Introduction to *Opere scelte di Grazia Deledda*. Milano: Mondadori, 1964.

———. *Grazia Deledda e il Decadentismo*. Firenze: La Nuova Italia, 1938.

———, ed. "Riassunto sulla Deledda." In *Novecento e dintorni*. Milano: Mursia, 1976.

De Nicola, Francesco and Pier Antonio Zannoni. *Scrittrici d'Italia: del Convegno nazionale di studi* (Rapallo, 14 May 1994). Genova: Costa and Nolan, 1995.

Del Buono, Oreste. "Nana e brutta eppure Grazia Deledda." *La Stampa* 29 April 1995: Tuttolibri, 5.

———. "Rileggere Grazia Deledda." *Notizie letterarie* (Milano) April 1964: 4.

Del Piano, Lorenzo. "Dal 1815 al 1870." In *La Società in Sardegna nei secoli: lineamenti storici*, edited by Francesco Artizzu. Torino: Edizioni Radiotelevisione Italiana, 1967.

Dessì, Giuseppe. *Scoperta della Sardegna*. Milano: Il Polifilo, 1966.

———. "Grazia Deledda cent'anni dopo." *Nuova Antologia* 1 November 1971: 78–85.

Dinnage, Rosemary. "The Wounded Male." *Times Literary Supplement* (13 December 1991): 7.

Dionisotti, C., and C. Grayson, eds. *Early Italian Texts*. Oxford: Blackwell, 1965.

Di Pilla, Francesco. "Grazia Deledda." *I premio Nobel per la letteratura italiana 1926*. Milano: Fabbri, 1964.

———. *La vita e l'opera di Grazia Deledda*. Milano, 1966.

Dolfi, Anna. *Grazia Deledda*. Milano: Mursia, 1979.

———, "Sei letture deleddiane." In *Del romanzesco e del romanzo*. Roma: Bulzoni, 1982.

Dore, Francesco. "Religiosità e Moralità nell'Opera di Grazia Deledda." *L'Ortobene (Nuoro)*, 6 September 1936:8.

Dowd, Maureen. "Hiding Behind Skirts." *New York Times* 26 August 1998: A23.

———. "The Abyss of Desire." *New York Times* 13 January 1999: A25.

Dowling, Colette. *The Cinderella Complex*. New York: Summit, 1981.

Dreyfus, Edward. *Adolescence*. Columbus, OH: Charles Merrill, 1976.

Du Plessis, Rachel Blau. *Writing Beyond the Ending*. Bloomington: Indiana University Press, 1985.

Duranti, Francesca. *Piazza mia bella piazza*. Milano: La Tartaruga, 1978.

——. *Lieto Fine*. Milano: Rizzoli, 1984.

——. *Progetto Burlamacchi*. Milano: Rizzoli, 1994.

Eco, Umberto. *Postscript to the Name of the Rose*. New York: Harcourt, 1984.

Elkind, David. *The Hurried Child*. Reading, MA: Addison-Wesley, 1981.

Ellis, Albert, and William J. Knaus. *Overcoming Procrastination*. New York: Signet, 1979.

Emmons, Robert. "Narcissism: Theory and Measurement." *Journal of Personality and Social Psychology* 52 (1987): 11–17.

Erikson, Erik. *Identity: Youth and Crisis*. New York: Norton, 1968.

Esman, Aaron, ed. *The Psychology of Adolescence*. New York: International Universities Press, 1975.

Falchi, L. *L'opera di Grazia Deledda*. Milano: La Prora, 1937.

Fedeli, Stefano. "Elias Portolu." Sassari: Chiarella, 1991.

Feinstein, S. C., and P. Giovacchini, eds. *Adolescent Psychology*. Vol. 5. New York: Aronson, 1976.

Ferroni, Giulio. *Storia della Letteratura Italiana Il Novecento*. Milano: Einaudi, 1991.

Flora, Francesco. "Grazia Deledda." *Rassegna d'Italia* January 1948:6.

——. "Grazia Deledda." *Storia della letteratura italiana*. Milano: Mondadori, 1940: 159–87.

——. "Grazia Deledda." In *Saggi di poetica moderna*. Messina: D'Anna, 1949, 177–84.

Floris, Antonio. *La prima Deledda*. Cagliari: Castello, 1989.

Fountain, Gerard. "Adolescent Development." *Journal of the American Psychoanalytic Association* 9 (1961): 417–33.

Frabotta, Biancamaria. *Letteratura al femminile: itinerari di lettura a proposito di donne, storia, poesia, romanzo*. Bari: De Donato, 1980.

Fratelli, Arnaldo. "Ricordo di Grazia Deledda." *Il Giornale della Sera (Roma)*, 14 August 1946: 10.

——. *L'Idea Nazionale* 21 November 1925:3.

Freud, Anna. *The Writings of Anna Freud*. Vol. 2. New York: International Universities Press, 1936.

——. *The Psychoanalytic Study of the Child*. New York: International Universities Press, 1958.

Freud, Sigmund. *The Standard Edition of the Complete Psychological Works of Sigmund Freud*. New York: Hogarth Press, 1905.

Galletti, Alfredo. *Storia letteraria d'Italia: Il Novecento*. Milano: Vallardi, 1967.

Gallino, T. G. *La ferita e il re: Gli archetipi femminili della cultura maschile*. Milan: Cortina, 1986.

Giacobbe, Maria. *Grazia Deledda. Introduzione alla Sardegna*. Milano: Bompiani, 1974.

——. "Grazia Deledda a Stoccolma." Available at www.geocities.com/athens/agora/9587/giacob.htm.

Gilbert, Sandra, and Susan Gubar. *No Man's Land: The Place of the Woman Writer in the Twentieth Century*. New Haven: Yale University Press, 1987.

————. *The Madwoman in the Attic: The Woman Writer and the Nineteenth-Century Literary Imagination*. New Haven: Yale University Press, 1984.

Gilligan, Carol. *In a Different Voice*. Cambridge: Harvard University Press, 1982.

Ginsborg, Paul. *A History of Contemporary Italy*. London: Penguin, 1990.

Ginzburg, Natalia. *Le piccole virtù*. Torino: Einaudi, 1966.

Gitlin, Todd. "Literary Resurrection. Rediscovering the Simple Lyricism and Moral Complexity of Sardinian Writer Grazia Deledda." *Chicago Tribune* 20 September 1998: Books, 3.

Giusso, Lorenzo. "Le creature femminili di Grazia Deledda." *L'Unione Sarda* 31 October 1937: 3.

Graber, Julia A., Jeanne Brooks-Gunn, and Anne Petersen, eds. *Transitions through Adolescence*. Mahwah, New Jersey: Lawrence Erlbaum Associates, 1996.

Grosskurth, Phyllis. "The New Psychology of Women." *New York Review of Books* 24 October 1991: 25–32.

"Growing Old vs. Growing Up." *Lawrence Journal-World* 1 February 1999: A2.

Gunderson, Erik, A. Ronningstam, and B. Bodkin. "The Diagnostic Interview for Narcissistic Patients." *Archives of General Psychiatry* 47 (1990): 676–80.

Jamison, Kay Redfield. *Touched by Fire: Manic Depressive Illness*. New York: Simon and Schuster, 1993.

————. *An Unquiet Mind: A Memoir of Moods and Madness*. New York: Vintage, 1995.

Janus, Sam. *The Death of Innocence*. New York: Morrow, 1981.

Johnson, Diane. "Something for the Boys." *The New York Review of Books*. 16 January 1992: 13–17.

Johnson, Robert. *Transfiguration: Understanding the Three Levels of Masculine Consciousness*. San Francisco: Harper, 1989.

Keillor, Garrison. "About Guys." *New York Times* 27 November 1992: 2.11.

Kernberg, Otto. *Aggression in Personality Disorders and Perversions*. New Haven: Yale University Press, 1992.

————. *Object Relations Theory and Clinical Psychoanalysis*. New York: Jason Aronson, 1976.

————. *Severe Personality Disorders: Psychotherapeutic Strategies*. New Haven: Yale University Press, 1984.

Kerouac, Jack. *On the Road*. New York: Penguin, 1976.

Kiley, Dan. *The Peter Pan Syndrome*. New York: Dodd, Mead, 1983.

————. *The Wendy Dilemma*. New York: Arbor House, 1984.

Kohut, Heinz. *Advances in Self-Psychology*. New York: International Universities Press, 1980.

————. *The Analysis of the Self: A Systematic Approach to the Psychoanalytic Treatment of Narcissistic Personality Disorders*. New York: International Universities Press, 1971.

————. *The Psychology of the Self*. Madison, WI: International Universities Press, 1978.

————. *The Restoration of the Self*. Madison, WI: International Universities Press, 1977.

———. *The Search for the Self*. Madison, WI: International Universities Press, 1978.

———. *Self Psychology and the Humanities*. Madison, WI: International Universities Press, 1985.

Kristeva, Julia. *The Kristeva Reader*. Edited by Toril Moi. New York: Columbia University Press, 1986.

Kugelmass, Isaac Newton. *Adolescent Immaturity*. Springfield, IL: Charles C. Thomas, 1973.

Lasch, Christopher. *The Culture of Narcissism*. New York: Warner, 1980.

Lawrence, D. H. *Sea and Sardinia*. New York: Doubleday Anchor, 1954.

———. Introduction. *The Mother*. London, 1928. Reprinted in *Phoenix. The Complete Works of D. H. Lawrence*. Vol. 4. London: 1968:263–66.

Ledda, Alberto. *La civiltà fuorilegge. Natura e storia del banditismo sardo*. Milano: Mursia, 1971.

Leffert, Nancy, and Anne Petersen. "Patterns of Development During Adolescence." In *Psychosocial Disturbances in Young People*, edited by Michael Rutter. Cambridge: Cambridge University Press, 1995.

Lerner, Harriet. *The Dance of Anger*. New York: Harper and Row, 1985.

Levine, Judith. *My Enemy, My Love: Man-Hating and Ambivalence in Women's Lives*. New York: Doubleday, 1992.

Levinson, Daniel J. *The Seasons of a Man's Life*. New York: Alfred A. Knopf, 1978.

Lilliu, Giovanni. *La società in Sardegna nei secoli*. Torino: Edizioni Radiotelevisione Italiana-Edizioni RAI, 1967.

Lombardi, Olga. *Invito alla lettura di Grazia Deledda*. Milano: Mursia, 1979.

———. *Enciclopedia della donna*. Vol. II. Roma: Editori Riuniti, 1965.

Lucatelli, Luciano. *La Civiltà Cattolica* 25 October 1912.

MacKinnon, Catharine A. *Feminism Unmodified: Discourses on Life and Law*. Cambridge: Harvard University Press, 1987.

Marci, Giuseppe. "Grazia Deledda. Scrittrice della letteratura sarda." In *Rileggere Grazia Deledda*, edited by Antonio Prost. Cagliari: Della Torre, 1986.

Mariotti, Carlo. *"Elias Portolu*: Romanzo di Grazia Deledda." *Unione Sarda (Cagliari), 1903:3*.

Marcuse, H. *Eros and Civilization*. London: Sphere Books, 1969.

Massaiu, Mario. *La Sardegna di Grazia Deledda*. Milano: Istituto Propaganda Libraria, 1986.

———. *Sardegnamara, una donna, un canto*. Milano: Istituto Propaganda Libraria, 1989.

Masterson, James F. *Countertransference and Psychotherapeutic Technique*. New York: Brunner and Mazel, 1983.

———. *The Narcissistic and Borderline Disorders*. New York: Brunner and Mazel, 1981.

———. *The Emerging Self: A Developmental, Self, and Object Relations Approach to the Treatment of the Closet Narcissistic Disorder of the Self*. New York: Brunner and Mazel, 1993.

———. *From Borderline Adolescent to Functioning Adult*. New York: Brunner and Mazel, 1980.

————, ed. *New Perspectives on Psychotherapy of the Borderline Adult*. New York: Brunner and Mazel, 1978.

————. *Comparing Psychoanalytic Therapies*. New York: Brunner and Mazel, 1991.

————. *Search for the Real Self: Portrait of a Narcissist*. New York: Free Press, 1991.

Il Mattino, "Grazia Deledda." Napoli, 18 August 1936.

Merry, Bruce. *Women in Italian Literature*. Capricornia: James Cook University Press of North Queensland, 1990.

Miccinesi, Mario. *Deledda*. Il Castoro. 105. Firenze: La Nuova Italia, 1975.

Migiel, Marilyn. "The Devil and the Phoenix: A Reading of Grazia Deledda's *Cenere*." *Stanford Italian Review* (1985):55–73.

Miller, Laura. "Henry James: Losing it at the Movies." *New York Times Book Review* 19 January 1997: 31.

Miller, Nancy K. *The Poetics of Gender*. New York: Columbia University Press, 1986.

Minerva, Obituary of Grazia Deledda. Paris, 30 August 1936.

Momigliano, Attilio. *Storia della Letteratura Italiana*. Messina: Principato, 1935.

————. "Intorno a Grazia Deledda." *Corriere della Sera* 15 June 1945:3.

————. *Romanzi e novelle di Grazia Deledda*. Milano: Mondadori, 1941.

Moravia, Alberto. *Gli indifferenti*. Milano: Bompiani, 1964.

————. *La noia*. Milano: Bompiani, 1960.

Morandini, Giuliana. *La voce che è in lei: Antologia della narrativa femminile italiana tra '800 e '900*. Milano: Bompiani, 1980.

Moretti, Marino. Preface to *Lettere di Grazia Deledda a Marino Moretti*. Padova: Rebellato, 1959.

Mundula, Mercede. *Grazia Deledda*. Roma: Formiggini, 1929.

Negro, Silvio. "Torna a Nuoro Grazia Deledda, Donna di Casa e Premio Nobel." *Corriere della Sera* 20 June 1959: 3.

Nelli, Delia. "On Neptune's Secret Trail." *La Cucina Italiana* 2.4 (1997): 47.

Nerenberg, Ellen. *Italian Women Writers*. Edited by Rinaldina Russell. Westport, CT: Greenwood Press, 1995.

Neubauer, John. *The Fin-de-Siècle Culture of Adolescence*. New Haven: Yale University Press, 1992.

Nozzoli, Anna. *Tabù e coscienza: La condizione femminile nella letteratura italiana del Novecento*. Firenze: La Nuova Italia, 1978.

Nuova Antologia "Un'inchiesta sul femminismo." 154 July–August (1911): 121–28.

Onorati, Aldo. *Il crepuscolo del Novecento*. Modica: Edizioni Setim, 1976.

Pancrazi, Pietro. *Scrittori d'Oggi*. Vols. 1–2, Bari: Laterza, 1946.

Parsani, Maria Assunta. *Femminile a confronto: tre realtà della narrativa italiana contemporanea*. Roma: Lacaita, 1984.

Paulucci, Branca. *L'Avvenire d'Italia (Roma)*, 30 August 1936:3.

Pellegrino, Angelo. "Grazia Deledda." In *Dizionario Biografico degli Italiani*. Roma: Treccani, 1980.

Pellizzi, Camillo. *Le lettere italiane del nostro secolo*. Milano: Longanesi, 1929.

Perret, Michèle. "Travesties et Transsexuelles: Yde, Silence, Grisandole, Blanchandine." *Romance Notes* 25.3 (1985): 328–40.

Peterson, Thomas. *Alberto Moravia*. New York: Twayne, 1996.

Petronio, Giuseppe. *Letteratura Italiana: I Contemporanei*. Vol. 1. Milano: Marzorati, 1973.

———. "Rileggendo Grazia Deledda." *Rileggere Grazia Deledda*. Edited by Antonio Prost. Cagliari: Il Maestrale, 1986.

Pflug, Maja. *Natalia Ginzburg: Arditamente Timida*. Milano: La Tartaruga, 1997.

Pilia, E. *La letteratura narrativa in Sardegna*. Cagliari: Nuraghe, 1926.

Piromalli, Antonio. *Grazia Deledda*. Firenze: La Nuova Italia, 1968.

———. *Letteratura Italiana, Novecento*. Vol. 3. Milano: Marzorati, 1980.

Pompeo, Giannantonio. "Le scrittrici della Nuova Italia." In *Scrittrici d'Italia*, edited by Francesco di Nicola and Pier Antonio Zannoni. Genova: Costa e Nolan, 1995.

Porter, Fairfield. *Fairfield Porter: Art in Its Own Terms: Selected Criticism, 1935–1975*, edited by Rackstraw Downes. New York: Taplinger, 1979.

Prost, Antonio. *Rileggere Grazia Deledda*. Cagliari: Il Maestrale, 1986.

Provenzal, Dino. *Canne al vento e pagine di altri romanzi*. Milan: Mondadori, 1966.

———. Introduction to *Canne al vento* by Grazia Deledda. Milano: Mondadori, 1956.

Puccini, Sandra. "Condizione della donna e questione femminile 1892–1922." In *La questione femminile in Italia dal '900 ad oggi*, edited by G. Ascoli. Milan: Angeli, 1977.

Pyszczynski, Thomas F., and Allan Greenberg. "Self Regulatory Perseveration." *American Psychologist* January (1987): 121–30.

"Quel sarcofago ancora vuoto." Available at: www.unionesarda.it/unione/1997/05–11–97/05–11–97NOU01a02.html.

Ramat S. "Due saggi su Grazia Deledda." In *Protonovecento*. Milano: Il Saggiatore, 1978.

Rasy, Elisabetta. *Le donne e la letteratura*. Roma: Editori Riuniti, 1984.

Ravegnani, Giuseppe. *Uomini Visti*. Milano: Mondadori, 1955.

Raya, Gino. *Il romanzo*. Milano: Vallardi, 1950.

Reich, Jacqueline. "Rewriting Rape." *Italian Culture* XVI, 2 (1998): 217–33.

Romagna, Mario Ciusa, ed. *Onoranze a Grazia Deledda*. Nuoro, 1959.

Rombi, Bruno. "Il romanzo impiegato d'imposte e il premio Deledda." *Misure Critiche* January–June 20 (1990): 74–75.

Roncarati, Licia. "L'arte di Grazia Deledda." *Rassegna d'Italia* January 1948: 108–12.

Ruju, Giuseppe. *Pietro Casu tra Grazia Deledda e Max Leopold Wagner*. Cagliari: Della Torre, 1981.

Russo, Luigi. *I Narratori*. Milano: Principato, 1958.

Rutter, Michael, ed. *Psychological Disturbances in Young People*. Cambridge: Cambridge University Press, 1995.

Sacchetti, Lina. *Arte e Umanità di Grazia Deledda*. Cervia: Centro Documentazione, 1981.

Salis, Mario. *Sardegna, personaggi e problemi*. Nuoro: Della Torre, 1980.

Sanguinetti-Katz, Giuliana. "La scoperta dell'identità femminile nel romanzo *Cosima* di Grazia Deledda." *RSItal* June 12.1 (1994): 55–73.

Sanna, Natale. "Dal 1870 alla Prima Guerra Mondiale." *La Società in Sardegna nei secoli: lineamenti storici*, edited by Francesco Artizzu. Torino: Edizioni Radiotelevisione Italiana, 1967.

Sapegno, Natalino. Introduction to *Romanzi e novelle di Grazia Deledda*. Milano: Mondadori, 1971.

———. *Pagine di storia letteraria*. Palermo: Manfredi, 1960.

Sarale, Nicolino. *Grazia Deledda: Un profilo spirituale*. Roma: Logos, 1990.

Savini, Marta, ed. *Grazia Deledda: I grandi romanzi*. Roma: Newton Compton, 1993.

Scano, Antonio. *Grazia Deledda: Versi e Prose Giovanili*. Milano: Virgilio, 1972.

———. *Viaggio letterario in Sardegna*. Foligno–Roma: Campitelli, 1932.

Schück, Henrik. "Presentation Speech." Nobel Prize for Literature; Nobel Prize Foundation. Available at: nobel.se/laureates/literature-1926-press.html.

Serao, Matilde. "Telegrafi dello stato (Sezione Femminile)." In *Il romanzo della fanciulla*. Napoli: Liguori, 1985, 7–48.

Serra, Renato. *Le lettere*. Roma: Bontempelli, 1914.

Shem, Samuel, M.D. *The House of God*. New York: Dell, 1995.

Showalter, Elaine. "On Hysterical Narrative." *Narrative* 1.1 January (1993): 24–35.

Sketch. "Concerning New Novels." 1 July 1908.

Sole, Carlino. "Il periodo Sabaudo fino al 1815." In *La Società in Sardegna nei secoli: lineamenti storici*, edited by Francesco Artizzu. Torino: Edizioni Radiotelevisione Italiana, 1967.

Sole, Leonardo. "Dalla struttura del romanzo alla riscrittura drammatica: una traccia per un difficile itinerario." In *Rileggere Grazia Deledda*, edited by Antonio Prost. Cagliari: Il Maestrale, 1986.

———. "Adattamento e riscrittura." In *Rileggere Grazia Deledda*, edited by Antonio Prost. Cagliari: Il Maestrale 1986.

Solomon, Marion F. *Narcissism and Intimacy*. New York: Norton, 1989.

Somalia Fascista. Mogadiscio, 28 December 1937.

Sorgia, Giancarlo. "Il periodo spagnolo." In *La Società in Sardegna nei secoli: lineamenti storici*, edited by Francesco Artizzu. Torino: Edizioni Radiotelevisione Italiana, 1967.

———. *Banditismo e criminalità in Sardegna nella seconda metà dell'Ottocento*. Cagliari: Editrice Sarda Fossataro, 1973.

Sovente, M. *La donna nella letteratura oggi*. Fossano: Esperienze, 1979.

Spacks, Patricia. "The Difference it Makes." In *A Feminist Perspective in the Academy*, edited by Elizabeth Langland and Walter Grove. Chicago: University of Chicago Press, 1981.

Spagnoletti, Giacinto. Introduction. *Deledda, I grandi romanzi*. Roma: Newton Compton, 1993.

———. "Scritti in onore di Grazia Deledda." *Il Convegno* July 1959.

———. *Romanzieri italiani del nostro secolo*. Milano: Edizioni Radiotelevisione Italiana, 1967.

Spinazzola, Vittorio. *Romanzi sardi*. Milano: Mondadori, 1981.

———. "La Deledda tra arcaismo e modernismo." In *Rileggere Grazia Deledda*, edited by Antonio Prost. Cagliari: Il Maestrale, 1986.

Squarotti, G. Barberi. "La tecnica e la struttura del romanzo deleddiano." In *Romanzi Sardi*. Milano: Mondadori, 1981.

Stanton, Domna C., ed. *Discourses on Sexuality: From Aristotle to Aids*. Ann Arbor: University of Michigan Press, 1992.

Stone, L. Joseph, and Joseph Church. "Physical Development in Adolescence." In *The Psychology of Adolescence*, edited by Aaron Esman. New York: International Universities Press, 1975.

Tanda, Nicola. "Grazia Deledda." *Letteratura italiana contemporanea*. Roma: Lucarini, 1980.

———. *Dal mito dell'isola all'isola del mito Deledda e dintorni*. Roma: Bulzoni, 1992.

Testaferri, Ada, ed. *Donna: Women in Italian Culture*. Ottawa, Canada: Dovehouse, 1981.

Theroux, Paul. "The Ferry to Ichnusa." In *The Pillars of Hercules*. New York: Putnam, 1995.

Titta Rosa, Giovanni. "Intorno a Grazia Deledda," *Fiera Letteraria* 20 December 1925:6.

Tomkins, Calvin. "Love for Sale." *New Yorker* 11 August 1997: 67.

Tonelli, Luigi. *Alla Ricerca della Personalità*. Milano: Modernissima, 1923.

Tozzi, Federico. *La realtà di ieri e di oggi*. Milano: Alpes, 1928.

———. "Grazia Deledda." *Sapientia (Rome)*, January 1916: 7–8.

Turchi, Dolores, ed. *Sangue sardo* by Grazia Deledda. Roma: Newton, 1995.

———. ed. Introduction to *Il paese del vento* by Grazia Deledda. Roma: Newton, 1995.

US News and World Report "Why Someone Would Risk It All." 9 February 1998: 40.

Valle, N. *Grazia Deledda*. Cagliari: Fossataro, 1971.

Vallone, A. "La 'condizione femminile' nel romanzo italiano d'oggi." *Otto/Novecento* 4.1 (Jan–Feb 1980): 143–74.

Verga, Giovanni. *Tutte le novelle*. Milano: Mondadori, 1970.

Vinall, Shirley. "Francesca Duranti: Reflections and Inventions." In *The New Italian Novel*, edited by Z. Baransky and L. Pertile. Edinburgh, Scotland: Edinburgh University Press, 1993.

Viola, Gianni Eugenio, Anna Dolfi, and Franca Rovigatti. *Grazia Deledda: Biografia e Romanzo*. Roma: Istituto della Enciclopedia Italiana, Treccani, 1987.

Viti, Gorizio. *Il Romanzo Italiano del Novecento*. Messina: D'Anna, 1979.

Vittorini, Elio. *Sardegna come un'infanzia*. Milano: Mondadori, 1974.

Will, George. "Rank Films a Cultural Symptom." *Lawrence Journal-World* (19 June 2000): 7B.

Wood, Sharon. *Italian Women's Writing 1860–1994*. London: Athlone, 1995.

Wright, Simona. "Elementi narrativi nell'opera deleddiana con particolare attenzione all'*Incendio nell'uliveto*." *Northeast Modern Language Association-Italian Studies* 18(1994): 83–103.

Zoja, Nella. *Grazia Deledda*. Milano: Garzanti, 1939.

Index

211